M000282482

PRAISE FOR *IRENA'S GIFT*

"In *Irena's Gift*, Karen Kirsten proves yet again that family stories and densities of human affection, when they ran up against that calamity we call the Holocaust, are as individual as fingerprints. News withheld, and what is passed on in doubt and affections, is always dramatic if it can be creatively depicted, and Karen Kirsten more than fulfils that task of narration and enchantment here."
—Thomas Keneally, *New York Times* bestselling author and Booker Prize winner for *Schindler's List*

"*Irena's Gift* interrogates the messy complexity of family, both its tenderness and nurture but also its corrosive anger and rejection. It's a disturbing investigation into the power of secrets to harm and to haunt."
—Geraldine Brooks, *New York Times* bestselling author and Pulitzer Prize winner

"As Karen Kirsten sets out to solve the mystery of her mother's past, she takes us on a very personal journey of discovery. Skillfully, she unearths a thrilling story of war and survival against all odds. A keen researcher and sleuth, Karen uncovers a truth both astonishing and heartbreaking. *Irena's Gift* is a beautiful, insightful, heartfelt and nuanced book. Masterfully crafted, it is both history and a memoir, but also so much more. Essential reading for anyone interested in World War II, trauma or family histories, this is one of the best second-generation Holocaust books ever published. I loved it and couldn't put it down."
—Ariana Neumann, *New York Times* bestselling author of *When Time Stopped*

"Deeply moving and beautifully written, *Irena's Gift* is a powerful unravelling of mysteries and memory. The journey of reconstruction and reconnection brilliantly evokes a lost era full of pain and love, as well as laying out the intricacies of intergenerational trauma. In addition to its value as Holocaust history, *Irena's Gift* deserves to become a classic of the memoir genre."
—Lucy Adlington, *New York Times* bestselling author of *The Dressmakers of Auschwitz*

"An extraordinary story of how secrets and lies can tear a family apart."
—Maya Lee, author of *The Nazis Knew My Name*

"This is a story of extraordinary women, survival and sacrifice. A must read."
—**Tara Moss, human rights and disability advocate, and author of** *The War Widow* **and** *The Ghosts of Paris*

"With extremism and fascism again threatening democracies, *Irena's Gift* is a must-read for our times. Stunningly researched, it explores themes of identity, secrets, grief and forgiveness. The author addresses the importance of naming our history and wrestles with the complexity of human nature—why a Nazi officer saved her mother."
—**Michelle Bowdler, author of** *Is Rape a Crime?*, **longlisted for the 2020 National Book Award and a TIME 100 Must-Read Books of 2020 selection**

"An epic story and an epic search for the truth that is beautifully written and meticulously weaved together, in a page-turning read I couldn't put down. . . . Compulsive enough to read in a single sitting, this is ultimately a story of love, healing, hope and humanity that will tug at your heartstrings."
—**Sue Smethurst, author of** *The Freedom Circus*

"Karen Kirsten goes on a quest to piece together her family's secrets and finds much more than a tale of survival from history's nightmare. She tells a story of disillusionment and faith. She reminds us that sometimes heroes can be repulsive, and sometimes lies keep families together. *Irena's Gift* is beautifully written, deeply researched and deeply felt."
—**Kevin Birmingham,** *New York Times* **bestselling author of** *The Sinner and the Saint*

AN EPIC
WORLD WAR II
MEMOIR OF SISTERS,
SECRETS AND SURVIVAL

IRENA'S GIFT

Karen Kirsten

CITADEL PRESS
Kensington Publishing Corp.
www.kensingtonbooks.com

CITADEL PRESS BOOKS are published by

Kensington Publishing Corp.
900 Third Avenue
New York, NY 10022

Copyright © 2023 by Karen Kirsten

Originally published by Penguin Random House Australia.

All rights reserved. No part of this book may be reproduced in any form or by any means without the prior written consent of the publisher, excepting brief quotes used in reviews.

All Kensington titles, imprints, and distributed lines are available at special quantity discounts for bulk purchases for sales promotions, premiums, fund-raising, educational, or institutional use. Special book excerpts or customized printings can also be created to fit specific needs. For details, write or phone the office of the Kensington sales manager: Kensington Publishing Corp., 900 Third Avenue, New York, NY 10022, attn Sales Department; phone 1-800-221-2647.

CITADEL PRESS and the Citadel logo are Reg. U.S. Pat. & TM Off.

Epigraph from *You Learn by Living* by Eleanor Roosevelt. Copyright © 1960 by Eleanor Roosevelt. Copyright renewed 1988 by Franklin A. Roosevelt. Used by permission of HarperCollins Publishers.

10 9 8 7 6 5 4 3 2 1

First Citadel hardcover printing: August 2024

Printed in the United States of America

ISBN: 978-0-8065-4365-9

ISBN: 978-0-8065-4367-3 (e-book)

Library of Congress Control Number: 2024934884

For my nieces: Brooke, Jade and Emma.

And for Joasia, your memory will always be a blessing.

You gain strength, courage and confidence by every experience in which you really stop to look fear in the face . . . You must do the thing you think you cannot do.

Eleanor Roosevelt

Author's Note

While I am not a historian, I have attempted to corroborate my family's recorded memories and those they recounted to me with historians, with deeply researched historical accounts, extensive research in archives, documentation, artifacts and diaries. In addition, letters, recorded testimonies, photographs and film footage helped me reconstruct historical scenes. Undoubtedly, there are mistakes. They are mine.

Because we all remember events differently, this story changes as I tell it, depending on whose point of view I am examining. When trying to inhabit a history and experiences not my own, I investigated gaps in my mother's and grandparents' accounts and any disparate information to determine if and how their stories connected. It was like poking an earring into my earlobe, trying to find the hole.

Besides where I have flagged details and dialogue for the reader as pictured or imagined, dialogue is as recorded by me or others, the USC Shoah Foundation or from published works. Occasionally, I have simplified dialect for clarity and combined descriptions.

PART ONE

PART ONE

I

Magpies warbled in the gum trees as we walked up the path to Nana Alicja's ground-floor flat in the upper-crust Melbourne suburb of Toorak. I pushed the buzzer, then heard Nana's poodle barking and sniffing beneath the door, the *donk, schlep, schlep* of Nana shuffling down the hallway with her walking stick. As the door slowly opened, I sensed my mother beside me bracing herself.

'What you have there?' My grandmother raised her head of perfectly coiffed, auburn-dyed hair as far as her bowed shoulders would allow. She smiled at me warmly, but barely acknowledged Mum.

I levered open a box containing cakes we had selected from Nana's favourite patisserie: a hazelnut meringue gateau for Nana, mille-feuille filled with crème patissière for Mum and me, and strawberry tarts for us all. Nana inhaled the rich vanilla scent. 'Mmmm!' she said, grinning. She brushed off my mother, who was trying in vain to peck her on the cheek, and made her way back down the oil-painting-lined hallway to the galley kitchen that smelled of beef fat and carrot. Nana's part-time Polish caregiver had made a stew.

I followed Nana and arranged the cakes on a platter while watching Mum in the lounge room trying to calm the dog. As Nana reached into a cupboard for her gold-rimmed china, light streamed in from the courtyard and caught the blue-green numbers tattooed on her forearm: 2 4 5 3 3 5, though they'd softened over time, morphing into her skin folds and sunspots.

I was four or five when I first asked about the numbers. I was sitting with my younger sister, watching Nana Alicja chop beetroot and onions for a soup. Nana's knife hit the cutting board: *rap, rap, rap*. She tilted her head high to prevent the onion fumes stinging her eyes.

'It's our phone number,' Nana said. 'So I won't forget it.'

'Who put it there?'

Papa Mietek poked his nose over his newspaper.

'Oh, just some man.' Nana scraped the onions into a pot. She put down the knife and passed us a tin filled with European chocolate biscuits.

I often suspected Nana Alicja wasn't telling the truth. On her birthday we'd stand around her Edwardian mahogany dining-room table delicately forking her freshly baked strawberry and meringue cake from her best china. I'd ask how old she was. 'About fifty,' she'd reply nonchalantly. Every year.

Papa Mietek would pour champagne into flutes and pass them around to the adults, then to my sister and me, with just enough for a toast. 'Sto lat! Sto lat! Niech żyje, żyje nam!' — *One hundred years! May she live one hundred years!* we'd sing in Polish.

We were never sure of Nana's age, or what she looked like when she was young; there were few photos of her. It didn't occur to me back then to read anything into the absence, and, besides, Nana treated me like a princess. She'd bake me cakes, shop with me at Polish and Hungarian food stores like The Chocolate Box in Camberwell, dress up to take me to the ballet and Chopin concerts, and collect seashells with me on the beach with her poodles. I didn't want to question her stories. I was too busy basking in her love.

Now Nana's poodle was licking my leg in her kitchen.

'I like zis hair.' Nana nodded at my new bob. She always took an interest in my appearance and made approving comments of the sort she rarely made of my mother. 'Put cakes in lounge room,' Nana commanded.

I joined Mum and placed the platter, cups and silver cake forks on the coffee table, then poured Nana a strong cup of French press as she slowly lowered herself into a recliner. Mum moved the platter to make room for Nana's cup. My body tensed – I knew what was coming.

'Don't touch zat!' Nana barked as my mother retracted her hand.

Nana often lost her temper at Mum for no reason, criticising her and snapping. My father had nicknamed Nana 'The Dragon'. I would stay silent during these outbursts. Perhaps I held my tongue because Nana's behaviour scared me, or because I knew by then that she had suffered unspeakable horrors in Auschwitz. Maybe, too, I felt flattered she spoiled me. Perhaps it was easier for me to justify because I was never on the receiving end of her fury.

To this day, I still don't understand why Mum bothered to visit Nana Alicja every week only to be humiliated. Now I feel ashamed I didn't speak up for her. Once, after witnessing Nana's spitting insults, my sister-in-law asked Mum why she put up with the treatment.

'Because she is my mother,' Mum said pragmatically.

But the problem – as we knew by then – was this was only partially true.

2

The thing about secrets is they are like a loose thread in a jumper; if you pull hard enough, the whole garment falls apart. My mother tells me that growing up, she'd long suspected she didn't belong to her parents. Alicja's hair was auburn and Mietek's light brown, but Mum's was jet-black. Her chocolate-coloured eyes were not hazel, like theirs; her stubby nose contrasted with Alicja's slim one. Alicja and Mietek were tall and lanky, whereas Mum was a curvaceous five-foot-two. 'Short, dark and wide,' she would say.

It went beyond appearance, though. My mother never felt loved by her parents. At times, she believed they hated her. Sometimes they'd hit her if she persisted with her circuitous questions about the war or the black-and-white photos from Poland on Alicja's dresser. Yet they seemed to tolerate questions from her younger brother, Tony. Once, she says, the bruises from Mietek's wallopings were so severe she stole money from Alicja's purse to purchase bandages so as not to attract awkward questions at school. On her way home at the end of the day, she hid the bandages in her bag so Alicja and Mietek wouldn't notice she'd covered her arms.

Then there were the strange nightmares Mum had as a child: men in uniform shooting guns, dark rooms where one needed to stay quiet. Alicja and Mietek dismissed these and showed no interest in her dreams or memories: they wanted her to simply keep quiet and behave. Mum begged Alicja and Mietek to explain the scary men, but they tried to convince her to admit she'd imagined them, just like the world she'd often conjure at night in bed before trying to sleep, where her 'special' friends would hug her and listen to her secrets. 'They said my imaginary life was lies,' Mum tells me now.

As a teenager, Alicja and Mietek also screened her dates. They mandated Jewish boys from well-to-do immigrant families which Mum found strange, as the parents of her Aussie friends didn't voice such concerns. It felt overbearing and protective; a form of control, not love.[1] They seemed to care little about her hopes for the future, yet it was deeply important to them that, instead of the Aussie Goyish men she kissed or the biker gang she hung out with, she should date only Jewish men.

My mother believed she'd failed to live up to her refugee parents' lofty ambitions. Mietek had wanted her to pursue law or engineering, insisting she learn Latin, French and maths.

After my mother failed maths, she decided she wanted to teach children art and history. When she announced at eighteen she was enrolling at Gippsland Teachers' College – which did not require a bachelor's degree, but did require, as she'd intended, that she live on campus a few hours' drive away – her parents threw their hands in the air, yelled and called her ungrateful. 'You'd think I'd started a war,' Mum says.

By contrast, Mum's brother, Tony – an upbeat and relaxed child – received warmth and adulation. When Tony graduated from medical school, they presented him with a car, a flashy white MG convertible. When Mum graduated from teachers' college, they gave her a pen.

A year after college, my mother left home for good to marry my Australian-born father, whose Swiss immigrant parents were neither well-to-do nor Jewish. Alicja's best friend had introduced them. 'She thought he was Jewish because of his big nose!' Mum later told me, chuckling.

My handsome father was a sales executive who'd worked in Europe for a global chemical company. Alicja's friend thought Alicja and Mietek might approve of my father's rising trajectory.

After my parents married, it was my father who showed my mother how to cook basic meals. Alicja baked babkas and stewed goulashes, yet she'd taught Mum nothing about taking care of a household, about sexual matters or raising children. Maybe Alicja's memories of her own mother were too painful to recall. Maybe the war had eradicated her ability to bond. Regardless, everything my mother knew about parenting she learned herself. When her first-born baby wailed, my mother mostly didn't pick me up. Later, she armed herself with Dr Spock's *The*

Common Sense Book of Baby and Child Care and fed her babies when they cried, instead of adhering to a strict schedule. She wanted her four children to feel secure. She wanted to create a household full of warmth and love, one that was nurturing. Her own dysfunctional home haunted her. She'd never leave me home alone with a crying sibling, as Alicja had done, while she and Mietek jitterbugged across nightclub dance floors. This was how most weekends went: Mum listening to her baby brother wailing through her bedroom wall.

When it was her turn to be a mother, Mum attended meetings at the Nursing Mothers' Association. A gregarious, practical woman, she made quick friends with fellow young mums. They taught her how to soothe a colicky baby, treat nappy rash, bake moist cakes – and how to welcome her husband home after a hard day at the office with fresh eyeliner, lipstick and a baby-spit-free miniskirt.

I was nine and a half and at school the day my mother heard a car turn off the dirt road where we lived, in Warranwood, about thirty minutes' drive from Nana Alicja's. Mum always complained about the dust from that road. Whenever a car passed by, a sandy cloud rose over our clay-tile-roofed homestead. It was worse in summer, when it rarely rained and the paddocks behind the house were brown and bare and our cows wandered further to find food. On hot days like that February summer morning, my mother would close windows and draw curtains to keep the house cool, yet the dust still crept in. She would wipe away the layer that powdered the furniture and her neatly arranged knick-knacks.

That particular day, she glanced out the kitchen window and saw the postman. He handed her a thick, heavy envelope pasted with Canadian stamps. She placed the letter on the kitchen bench. She fixed herself a cup of tea. She poured coffee for my father, who was home preparing for a business trip.

Because my mother never started the day without make-up, fragrance, a necklace and matching earrings, she carried the coffee to my father in his study smelling of Chanel No. 5, an apron tied round her waist. She then returned to her cup in the kitchen, and the envelope. The address indicated a Canadian business had sent the letter: Zdzisław Przygoda and Associates.

My thirty-two-year-old mother knew no-one in Canada. She sliced a knife along the top of the envelope and removed a hefty mass of ivory paper – pages and pages. The letter was penned in curved, blue script.

My dearest Joasia,
You must excuse me to call you like this, but I have been silent for so many years, now I use the name as I hold it in my memory . . .

My mother frowned. She knelt to pick up a brown leather folder that had slipped from the envelope. Worn and dog-eared, it contained photos. They were familiar; she had seen them on Alicja's dresser. The first was a picture of herself at around fifteen months old with jet-black hair, tucked into a pram on gigantic wheels, bundled up in a thick woollen coat, hands encased in white knitted mittens. The second photo showed Alicja's sister, Irena, who had died in the war. This was Mum's aunt, dressed in a long evening dress and jacket, clutching an elegant white purse.

Mum stared at Irena's black, wavy hair and her deep-set, dark eyes. She read more of the letter, her own eyes darting back and forth between the photograph and the words. Then something clicked into place.

Hearing my mother shriek, my father dashed into the kitchen. He presumed Mum had cut herself with a knife. Instead, he found her waving a letter. He led her to a chair and told her to sit. 'Read it!' he encouraged.

'I survived the war only because the thought about you gave me the necessary strength . . .' my mother began tentatively. As she read the letter aloud, faces and memories from her childhood in postwar Germany flashed inside her head. She remembered a two-storey villa in the town of Dachau, where she'd lived with Alicja and Mietek and other refugee families.

Your photograph and your mother Irena's photograph were with me all the time. I smuggled these photos through all the camps, even standing naked in Dachau, I hid your picture under my foot . . . I did everything possible to save you and your mother. The Germans killed her – you are the only person I love now and I did love you all the war years and after the war and up till today.

Mum clutched the photograph of Irena to her chest. 'This is my mother,' she said. 'This is my mother.'

My mother kept this letter hidden from me for years. One would think that having been left in the dark, she would be the last person to want to replicate what had been inflicted on her.

But then, much of what transpired makes little sense to me. For example, I don't understand why Alicja would adopt my mother only to treat her so caustically. Alicja nursed her back to health and brought her to Australia where she could have a future. Yet she withheld affection. Why would she treat a child so poorly that her future didn't feel bright at all?

Most families harbour secrets, ordeals we'd rather forget, myths we invent to protect ourselves and those we love. The question is, how to keep secrets and preserve stories of our pasts without lying? And if we don't unravel the lies, how will we ever know the truth?

I may as well begin with the lies. The day after the letter arrived, my father phoned Alicja and invited her to lunch at Cafe Balzac in East Melbourne. The packed restaurant was austere, well suited to Alicja's aura of superiority, but not the kind of place one would want to make a fuss. My father topped up Alicja's wine glass. 'I need to tell you something,' he said. 'Joasia received a letter. From Canada.'

Alicja stared at my father, who calmly described the contents of the letter. Her mouth fell open. 'Zdzisław promised he'd never tell!' she shouted, as men in suits and ties turned to stare at her from across the dining room.

The next day while I was at school, Alicja growled through sprawling suburbs in her fancy car – burlwood dash, bread-slicer grill – past hills dotted with dull green eucalypts, and up the dusty road to the cow-filled paddocks of my parents' home. She slammed the car door and stepped around chicken poo splatted on the brick verandah.

'We were so *good* to you!' she yelled at my mother.

Mum pulled off her vinyl kitchen gloves slowly, trying to calm Alicja. 'But I appreciate you more now I know you adopted me.'

From the couch in our living room, Alicja begged my mother not to tell her grandchildren about the letter. It would only confuse them, she said. We wouldn't love her any more.

Mum thought it over. 'I owe it to you, if this is what you want,' she conceded. 'But I won't lie to them about it if they ever ask me directly.' She dreaded inflicting this pain of betrayal on us.

My mother soon discovered most of Alicja and Mietek's friends and relatives had known about the secret for years. When Alicja learned of the letter, she phoned them and made them swear not to tell her grandchildren. When my mother told Jill, her best friend, Jill burst into tears. She'd known for years, too. Jill had once overheard someone explain that my mother's contrary, stubborn nature was 'because she was adopted and went through dreadful things during the war'.

My mother couldn't believe it. Everyone around her knew. Everyone had tiptoed around the truth for years. My mother didn't feel bitter, so much as stunned. She didn't think it possible a secret could persist in the open for so long. Everyone knew, but her.

A few weekends later, my seven-year-old sister Jacqui and I pulled on our best dresses and buckled our black patent leather shoes. Dad drove us to Nana Alicja's for Papa's birthday. Inside the brick bungalow I thought of as a palace (in truth, a three-bedder in the middle-class suburb of Burwood), a brass mushroom-shaped stool, rugs on polished timber floors and oil paintings lined the entrance hall. One, a broody scene in rich reds and blues, depicted a narrow alleyway in Papa Mietek's hometown of Kraków. I'd asked him about it once, but he'd cupped his hands behind his back and stayed silent. Papa never said much, but whenever he saw me, he'd pull me close and kiss the top of my head.

In a lounge room lined with books and more paintings, adults sipped from Nana's gold-rimmed porcelain, discussed politics and classical music, and gossiped away. I kissed the older relatives and friends first, the ones with more wrinkles. In accented English they called me 'darlink', and the women pinched my cheeks. Shiny specks of silver and gold blinked at me from their teeth whenever they smiled. I could smell coffee on their breath. Ladies splayed their fingers while sipping gingerly from coffee cups, lifting their top lip, placing the cup back onto the saucer. Lipstick still perfect. *Clink, clink.*

Jacqui and I called it the Polish Circus whenever these people gathered together. It was an over-the-top spectacle of jewellery, food, thickly applied make-up and chattering in foreign languages. Most of them pronounced words differently, counting 'vun, two, tree', before singing Happy Birthday in Polish to Mietek. Later, they'd ask me, 'So vot you doo-ink?' I'd say, 'Nothing.' 'Nussink?' they'd repeat. It all felt like theatre.

Nana and her friends even looked like movie stars. They smelled of coconut, of Nana's beauty salon where women sat under metal bulbs and flicked through magazines while steam puffed on their wrinkled faces. Nana would lie on a bed with electrodes plugged to her face before they steamed her. I wanted to try it myself when I grew up. I wanted to be glitzy like her: thin, plucked eyebrows; tanned brown forehead; filigree gold necklace framing the final sculpted product. Compared to my friends' blonde, pale-skinned mothers who crowed 'aaw-yeeah' with an Australian nasal twang, who baked cupcakes and chocolate crackles instead of babkas, Nana and her friends were chic and exotic. My nana was not the kind of woman who would pull on gumboots to collect eggs from our chicken coop. She'd never squelch in clay at the edge of the dam while I caught tadpoles. She and Papa preferred opera.

Aussie parties I attended were nothing like the Polish Circus gatherings. Instead of donning serious faces while debating philosophy and politics, people chugged beer from tinnies and watched footy and cricket on the telly, yelling words Mum abhorred like shit, crikey and bugger. ABBA and AC/DC's electric guitars blared from speakers. Men stood in front of the TV while the women laughed and chatted in another corner. Aussie parties made me feel like a normal Australian. Maybe the tension I felt at Polish Circus parties came from all the effort that went into masking the lies. Or evading the truth.

'Hello darlink,' Inka, one of Nana's best friends, greeted me in her thick, velvet voice. Her gold bangles jingled, her hoop earrings swayed. I did not know then that Inka's husband had been friends with Papa Mietek in Kraków and ended up in the same concentration camp. Years later, my mother would tell me that Inka herself might have been in a camp. The secrets were endless.

Next, Auntie Berta stretched out her arms and wrapped them around me in a bear hug. 'You look so skinny, darlink. Doesn't your mother *feed* you?'

We visited Berta in Caulfield, a suburb my father called The Holy Land because so many Jewish people in Melbourne lived there. Berta would stuff us full of pierogi, goulash and babka because she thought we starved at home. Berta's body was bent over and a hump stuck out of her back. Her face tucked deep into her neck, so when she laughed, she broke into coughing fits. Mum said it was because of the war. When I asked about it, she'd swat me away with her hand. 'When you're old enough,' Mum would say.

Had I learned about the Holocaust at school, I might have interrogated my mother about Berta's husband, who was Alicja's brother. I might have probed her as to why Berta lived alone. I might have hounded her about that hump on her back.

Now I know that after the war, Australia accepted the second highest number of Holocaust survivors proportional to its population[2] after Israel. Around 40 per cent of Caulfield's residents were Jewish.[3] Nana Alicja chose not to live there. Maybe she worried someone from Warsaw who knew my mother's biological father would recognise her and ask questions. I imagine that shops selling potato latkes, pickled herring and onion-filled rollmops reminded her of Poland. If she steered clear of them, she could feel more in control of the new life she was building.

On arrival in Australia, Papa Mietek worked on a poultry farm, though he'd been a lawyer back in Poland. Years later he built a business importing art supplies. From then on, Nana Alicja could live a life of ease. She swung a golf club in her white shoes, donned her bathers on regular holidays to Fiji and lunched with her lady friends. She tossed balls to her poodles in Wattle Park. She wanted to put as much space as possible between her old life and her new one.

In Nana's lounge room, Auntie Stella kissed me on both cheeks. With her undulating waves of Queen Elizabeth hair, Papa's sister exuded warmth and kindness. Her smile melted me.

'What piano pieces are you working on, Karen?' she asked. Stella had been a concert violinist in Poland and now played violin on the radio, in recitals and quartets.

'I'm practising Bach,' I told her shyly, glancing at my shoes.

Dad liked classical music, too. At home, he blasted the *1812 Overture* through monster speakers custom-built into cabinets extending below the floor. The walls throbbed. Dad would throw his head back and swing his arms pretending to conduct the orchestra when he thought no-one was looking.

'So, you've mastered the Mozart, have you?' Stella asked, not skipping a beat, as if I were her student.

I felt honoured. Stella remembered all my pieces. None of my friends at primary school played classical piano. Stella made me feel as if everyone did, like it was the most perfectly normal thing in the world for me to love Mozart and Bach.

I did not know all that Stella was hiding. After the letter from Canada arrived, my mother phoned her, but she already knew. 'Why didn't you tell me?' my mother asked.

Stella had promised Alicja she'd keep her secret safe. She also didn't want the information that Alicja and Mietek were not her parents to upset my mother. She maintained the ruse even when my mother visited her as a teenager, desperate to unburden herself and confide in someone. 'Why doesn't Dad have a number on *his* arm?' my mother asked. 'And why can't I be like normal Australian girls and wear a short dress and stockings to speech night – why do they want me to look Polish and wear socks?'

My mother complained about Alicja's cold and cruel attitude. Sometimes Stella would let my mother stay overnight to give her a break. Arguments at home often died down after these sleepovers.

So, after the letter arrived, my mother went to Stella first for advice. 'What should I do?' she sobbed. Shouldn't Alicja be mad at the man who sent the twenty-eight-page letter? He was the one who had upended Alicja's perfect life, the one she'd painstakingly rebuilt after the war. He was the one who had ruined everything. Yet Alicja blamed my mother. Why?

'Leave it to me,' said Stella.

Instead of feeling betrayed by Stella, the Polish Circus and her friends, my mother felt as if someone had lifted a barbell from her shoulders. She had not hallucinated the grey-uniformed men in black boots she'd remembered as a child, men who'd plagued her nightmares. She had not made them up, as Alicja suggested.

'I'm a somebody, not a nobody,' Mum said.

Her memories finally made sense.

Looking back, it's clear that although my grandparents were hiding details of their past, some of their secrets lived in plain sight. Books crammed their living room shelves with war titles so terrifying I didn't want to touch them, the likes of: *Auschwitz: A Doctor's Eyewitness Account* by Dr Miklos Nyiszli; *Survival in Auschwitz* by Primo Levi and *The Holocaust in Historical Perspective* by Dr Yehuda Bauer.

'What happened to you during the war?' I asked.

Shooting glances at each other, they replied with a terse, 'Not much', or 'We were staying some place where we couldn't travel around', as though at a far-flung spa.

'Did the Nazis do that to you?' I once asked Nana about the dense crimson scar like a giant hand that crept down her cheek and bled into her neck.

'No. It's a birthmark.' Nana touched her neck tentatively.

But friends at school had shown me their birthmarks – mottled patches of pink dots, a postage stamp-sized brown splotch on one girl's chin. Nana's mark was enormous – and it looked inflicted. When she applied make-up in the mornings, I would watch her press powder onto her nose, cheeks and forehead, then spray her hair into a voluminous bob so stiff you could hit it with a stick and it wouldn't move. For someone so meticulous about her appearance, why didn't she dab over the 'birthmark'? Nana mostly wore dresses, even when we drove to the park to play with the poodles. I don't recall her wearing upturned collars or roll neck jumpers, which would at least partially hide the blemish. It was as if she considered the mark a badge of merit. I did not know that after a doctor had suggested she remove her tattoo, she'd told him, 'Never!' She hid the past to protect my mother, but didn't conceal her scars.

'Why don't you know how old she *really* is?' I asked Mum on one of Nana's many fiftieth birthdays.

'Because she lost her papers during the war.'

'She has a passport, though,' I countered. 'Didn't she have to tell them her age?'

'Yes, but when she got new papers after the war, she made up a date.'

'But isn't that *lying?*'

'Enough with the questions,' Mum scolded. 'Go outside and play with the poodles.'

3

My mother taught me that truthfulness is non-negotiable. Yet she'd converted to Christianity when she was fifteen years old, then tried to hide it from her parents. A friend had invited her to dinner. The father read from a Bible and answered my mother's questions, questions she'd found difficult to ask at home. I suspect her attraction to Christianity was precipitated by her friend's buxom mother, who drew her into her arms at the end of the meal. 'My first hug,' my mother says. 'Wonderful, warm flesh all around me.' She returned to that house, not wanting the hugs to stop. She prayed with the family and they held hands around the table. She asked Jesus to enter her heart.

When Alicja and Mietek eventually heard about it, they

yelled at her, despite the fact they didn't believe in God and had never taken her to a synagogue. Science can explain everything, Mietek had told her, wagging his finger. But it was too late. She'd already converted.

Over the years, my mother's faith exacerbated the alienation she felt from her parents. Alicja would fume at Bibles my mother stacked on a shelf in our lounge room, next to books like Billy Graham's *The Jesus Generation*. 'The Jews won't want you because you're a Christian, and the Christians won't want you because you're a *Jew!*' Alicja said.

Maybe Alicja resented my mother's Christianity because she'd found her tribe, one that embraced her optimism. Maybe Alicja worried my mother couldn't carry the legacy of her family's loss if she was Christian.

Every Sunday, my mother would take my siblings and me to Mooroolbark Baptist Church, and years later to a Pentecostal one. 'Lying lips are an *a-bom-ination* to the Lord!' the pastor declared from the dais one week, shaking his fist.

Mum yelled 'Amen!' from the pew, while I blushed next to her. She belonged here. She mattered.

A black leather Bible on Mum's knee was flipped open to Proverbs 12. Wedged between her pink fingernails (matching her lipstick, pink dress, handbag and heels), a silver pen from Micador, Papa's importing business, hovered over her notepad. Mum always wrote down the pastor's lesson, underlining scripture to pray over at home later. She must have wrestled with the line after 'abomination': 'Those dealing in truth are God's delight.' And I'm sure she would have underlined the next verse: 'A prudent person is one who conceals knowledge.'

Before the sermon, I would slip out of the wood-panelled auditorium for Sunday School with Jacqui and dozens of other fidgety children. We sat cross-legged on the floor in a back room, singing as women with thick-framed spectacles and no make-up clapped their hands:

Jesus loves me, this I know. For the Bible tells me so.
Little ones to Him belong,
They are weak, but He is strong.
Yes, Jesus loves me! Yes, Jesus loves me!

The women read from the Bible and we chanted after them: 'Do to others as you would have them do to you.'

Good deeds alone aren't enough for us to enter heaven, the teacher told us. When she asked who could share a story about someone who helps others, I shot up my hand. I wanted the class to know my mum would win extra points in heaven for her good deeds; that she often simmered casseroles in a crockpot on the kitchen bench for a sick mother stuck in bed; that she visited laid-up friends in hospital who'd just given birth or popped in on ill folks from church while we drank Milo after school at a neighbour's house; that she never complained about her aches or pains – like those in her gall bladder that sent her rushing to the loo – nor did she gossip about others, as Nana sometimes did. Every day, it seemed, ladies would drop by our house for advice and for the obligatory cuppa, cake and a yak – ladies from Mum's Bible study group, the Avon Lady, parents from school and neighbours from up the street.

But I wouldn't tell the class about my *angry* mother; how baffling it was that after visitors left, Mum would often screech like a cockatoo. When we disobeyed her or bickered, rage overtook her. We ran. But she would grab us with one hand and break a coat hanger, wooden spoon or hairbrush on our backsides with the other. When she argued with Dad, she'd follow him around the house making her point over and over, to be sure she had the last word.

'Let it go! Stop nagging me!' Dad would yell, wanting to end the hours-long argument. I remember thumps of heavy objects thrown on the floor.

'But I'm NOT nagging! I–I . . . I'm not like that,' Mum would hiccup in between sobs. 'You don't love me any more!' She would trail Dad from room to room, stomping her feet, forever spinning, doubting, desperate for approval. She'd choose death over losing, it seemed to me. After she'd hit us, she couldn't bear thinking we didn't love her. She would run to her bedroom. I could hear her muffled crying behind the locked door. Once, after Mum had been yelling at Dad for a while, he swung a rubber hose at her. I ran screaming with my siblings into Dad's study and we crouched under chairs, sobbing. We never knew what would set off my cuddles-and-kisses mother who didn't know how to accept love. We all laugh about it now, but back then it was as if she was lashing out at ghosts we couldn't see. In my diary, I wrote that Mum would shake me so hard my teeth rattled. She'd yelled at Alicja and Mietek, too, so they'd listen to her. But Dad would not listen. He'd walk out of the room. This only upset Mum more.

Driving home after church in our VW Kombi, Mum reassured me we'd go to heaven. 'We're Jewish like Nana and Papa,' she said, one hand on the steering wheel, the other pressing her hair-sprayed-stiff do, 'but believing in Jesus gives us eternal life.'

Except my grandparents didn't believe in Jesus. They cele-brated Christmas by hosting parties for Papa's business clients. They bought us Christmas presents, which might count for something. 'Does that mean they'll go to hell?' I covered my ears in the back seat, not wanting to hear Mum's response, horrified by the thought of Nana screaming for eternity, roasting in hot, red flames.

'That's up to God,' Mum said, almost cheerfully. 'He'll be the judge, not us.'

This was her stock-standard short-on-details answer when she didn't know, wasn't sure or couldn't bring herself to tell me the truth.

4

Grandchildren are often told things grandparents cannot say to their own children; they become the bridge between generations. Nana hid the truth about the war and evaded my questions, until the day she phoned and asked if I'd take her to see *Schindler's List*. I was in my twenties then, in my first managerial role for a commercial interiors company and living in a duplex around the corner from Nana's. I made a date to take her, but then she saw it at The Rivoli in Camberwell with her best friend instead.

'You must still go,' she pleaded on the phone afterwards. 'The scene in the shower room where they push in all the women, and they look up at the showerheads wondering what is going to happen to them, thinking they will be gassed?'

I paused on the other end, not sure what to say.

'That was exactly what was like for me.'

When I eventually saw the film, I watched guards shout orders in Polish and German at dozens of razor-clipped, shoeless, naked women scuttling into a concrete-floored room. Biting trembling fists, they huddled in groups sobbing, clinging to a mother, a daughter, legs tangled, breast jammed against breast, grabbing the ribs of a stranger while staring up at the pipes. I saw my nana quiver with them. Suddenly the light shut off. Curdled screams turned to a wretched moaning. I heard Nana's cry. For the first time, the Holocaust took on shape and form. I could not speak about it for days.

Nana Alicja suggested we meet at Fiorelli restaurant near the cinema to discuss the movie. We ordered red wine and a rich risotto. When dessert arrived, she described Dr Mengele – known as Auschwitz's 'Angel of Death' – and how his white-gloved hands flicked a whip at women who shivered in the cold next to her on the assembly Platz, how he pushed them from the line, off for killing or experimental, mutilating surgeries and injections filled with poison.

I stared. I wondered why she was telling me, and not my mother, about the vermin-ridden barracks of Birkenau, even though Mum had also seen the movie. Perhaps she didn't want to hurt my mother. More likely, she knew I wouldn't sugar-coat what had happened to her. She knew I'd probe and ask questions.

I wanted the atrocities depicted in the film to help my mother understand why she couldn't recall Alicja hugging or kissing her. I wanted my mother to understand how Auschwitz destroyed Nana's spirit. To my knowledge, having both seen the film, Mum and Alicja discussed only Mietek's cousins and Kraków friends on Schindler's 'list' whom my mother knew, and nothing of Alicja's or Mietek's ordeals. This is what grief does. After it breaks you, the only thing to do is to push it aside and move forward.

My grandparents collected dead things: a taxidermied leopard sprawled across the floor at their beach house whose head I'd squat on as a child, its tongue frozen, with incisors that once punctured and drew blood from my foot; the headless, giant sea turtles that hung on walls; the immovable figurines of scary men carved into dried Balabala fern trees from Fiji that hid in their garden and scratched you when you played hide-and-seek. Dead things remind us we are living.

Alicja's war experiences began weighing on me several years after *Schindler's List*. I was a newlywed. Peter and I moved to Boston to pursue jobs in the booming dot-com economy. But in Sudbury, the neighbourhood where we landed, I found myself for the first time surrounded by Jewish people. Melbourne's Jewish population numbers around 47,000,[4] compared to more than 250,000[5] in the similar-sized Greater Boston area. Neighbours and work colleagues observed Jewish holidays I knew nothing about (Rosh Hashanah, Yom Kippur, Hanukkah), days Alicja didn't observe, although she had a habit of buying matzos when packets of them showed up on supermarket shelves before Easter each year.

Growing up, I knew little about Jews or Judaism. I'd belted out 'Tradition!' while performing in a school production of *Fiddler on the Roof*, but hadn't connected Nana Alicja and Papa Mietek with Jewish names like Tzeitel and Tevye, or with shtetls, or with Anatevka's poor butchers. I always referred to my Chopin-loving grandparents as Polish – not Jewish.

I was twelve when Pastor Finch tipped me back in a water-filled tank at church, next to the dais: Whoosh! When my face burst through the water, I thought I heard angels. The congregation sang 'Follow, follow . . . I will follow Jesus.' I stepped out in my white gown, dripping wet. Baptised. Committed to Christ. From that day on, I thought I needed to save my grandparents from atheism and Judaism.

After an ambulance rushed Papa Mietek to hospital with a heart attack, I gave him my copy of *Betrayed!*, the story of Stan Telchin's Jewish daughter accepting Jesus as the Messiah. Mum tells me Nana Alicja burned the book. Before this, I'd tried to convert him by reading a booklet my church gave me that fitted into the palm of my hand: *The Four Spiritual Laws*. 'You must receive Jesus Christ as Saviour and Lord,' I'd proclaimed to Papa, smiling. 'You can know and experience God's love and plan for your life.'

Papa nodded, but he never said a word.

In truth, I was also committed to changing his and Nana Alicja's 'foreign' habits. I was a child then. I didn't yet know how they'd loaded Papa's father onto a train and gassed him at Treblinka. I didn't know Papa's weakened heart muscle may have been connected to the typhoid he'd picked up in Dachau concentration camp. My mother had concealed from me the fact that after the war, like many survivors, Papa battled with depression. Nor did I know that some calling themselves 'Christian' killed Jews. Given I foisted my religious beliefs on Papa Mietek, now I worry *I* betrayed him.

Years after my water baptism, I yearned for the Holy Spirit to baptise me. Everyone at church, except me, spoke in tongues, a language only God understood. I wanted to belong to this church. This family. Unless God blessed me with tongues, how could I be one of His chosen? Then one night at the end of a service, I lined up in front of the preaching platform. I'd stood there before more than once, waiting for a pastor to lay hands on me. He would move along the line, two hefty men positioned behind the person he prayed over. They would swoon, fall to the floor and lie there sometimes for hours, eyes closed. Peaceful. When the pastor reached me, he placed one hand behind my shoulder, a palm at my forehead. I liked the touch of it. Full of love. As his voice shuddered, his breath warmed my cheek. The men behind me stepped forward. I must have braced myself. Because at the end of it all, I was often the only one left standing, shattered that God did not care for me.

That night at the end of the service, I wanted the Holy Spirit bad. The pastor's wife pressed her lips to my ear. She whispered syllables. She strung them together, over and over, faster, faster. After what seemed like twenty minutes, all at once, strange words came tumbling out of me, un-dammed, liberated. God loved me! For years, whenever I prayed in that strange language, it was as if a power outside myself touched something I did not yet have the language to see.

When I faced heartache growing up, I tended to bury my emotions. I didn't carry a sense of loss as heavy as my mother, but there was a hole, a loneliness. An emptiness lurked in me. I tried to fill it with reading books and scripture, with singing in the church band and praying. I tried to fill it with God. When my husband eventually tried to fill it, I then erected a wall. A crack would appear, a door would open, then I'd slam it shut, retreat and shut my feelings down. Maybe, over the years, I'd desensitised my emotions to combat my mother's pain. Maybe I couldn't process Alicja's.

I left the church before I moved to Boston. Mum called me 'backslidden', as it was labelled by evangelical leaders. I preferred 'curious'. I read books my atheist husband recommended, like Karen Armstrong's *A History of God*, struck by the myriad of religious views one could see through a similar window. Meanwhile, women in Mum's prayer group would sit in a circle each week, praying for me. They praised God, in the hope I would recognise my sin, submit once more and return to Him.

In Boston, Jewish people I met at work were younger, like me. They spoke with American accents, not Polish ones. One neighbour on my leafy street invited me to her son's bar mitzvah. My first visit to a synagogue was not what I expected. In a large, modern hall with stadium-style seating like my Australian Pentecostal church, a cantor tapped her tambourine, leading congregants singing and swaying to minor-key Hava Nagila-style tunes. Another neighbour invited me to Passover. She showed me how to dip parsley into salt water to remember how, thousands of years ago, Jews overcame the impossible. I thought about my family. These experiences with Jewish co-workers and neighbours provoked memories of my grandparents' silences. The brushed-off questions. The hushed conversations. The sound of Mum sobbing through the bedroom wall. This void. This hole. With me since birth. Maybe my mother had passed it on to me.

If someone in Boston asked about my background, I'd say, 'Australian.' That changed after the Twin Towers fell on 9/11. I observed Jews – who had good reason to be sensitive to scapegoating and discrimination – rally around Muslim people. Exclusive access to God by a single religion now seemed ridiculous. When people noticed my nearly jet-black hair and dark-brown eyes and asked if I was Jewish, I surprised myself. I said, 'Yes.'

But I still knew nothing about Jews or Judaism. Eventually, I signed up for an 'A Taste of Judaism' class I'd seen advertised in the *Boston Globe*. I would sit around a table with mostly unmarried couples, where one half were considering converting. When the rabbi, in his forties and dressed in a business shirt and khakis, told us we should cherish doubts, I guffawed. I couldn't believe my ears. Doubt is the key to knowledge, the rabbi said. Doubt leads us to discovery. Doubt is the touchstone of truth.

This was the antithesis of church teachings I'd grown up with; a sin that grieved God. I could happily embrace Judaism for the holiday baking and potato latkes, for belonging to a community, the handed-down traditions and comforting rituals, but doubt could truly win me over. While I treasured the warmth of evangelical churches in Australia (and in years to come even Mum's friends will roll their eyes at the patriarchy), I had never been on board with church-mandated rigid biblical frameworks to answer life's toughest questions. I struggled to blame Satan for man's evil deeds; it felt like a cop-out. The problem was this: scripture could not explain Nana's suffering in Auschwitz.

KAREN KIRSTEN

Or the chasm between Nana Alicja and my mother. To understand, I had to put my faith not in God, but in facts and historians.

One night I phoned Alicja. I asked to interview her.

'It will be your chance to tell me about your life *before* the war,' I told her, hoping I might convince her if she knew she didn't have to discuss the blue-green numbers on her arm.

What I really wanted was for my eighty-one-year-old grandmother to tell me everything. I wanted to crack the lock on her history, and my mother's. I wanted her to give me the key.

A month later, while on holiday from the US, I sat in her lounge room, my mini-cassette recorder spinning. The books that had terrified me as a child still filled her shelves. A sixties sputnik light pointed at us from her ceiling.

It took me days to warm her up, so I broached easier topics first: her favourite foods, why she loved holidaying in Fiji. Then I began asking about the war. Once she dipped her toe into the black sea of memory, we dived as deep as we could, stopping for air when a blank look filled her eyes. If I asked her to clarify a memory, she would sometimes raise one eyebrow, chuckle, then flash her broad smile, even if the memory was grim. Maybe the camps taught her this. Laughing off depravity helps you survive.

After a few days, I asked, 'What was the worst thing that happened to you?'

'They took my nightie,' Nana Alicja said, clasping her fingers together.

She told me she'd traded her ration of bread for tiny scraps of material from other women who'd worked as slave labour at a

34

sewing factory, likely referring to the dimly lit wooden building near Birkenau's main entrance where women endured twelve-hour shifts.[6] She'd sewn the jagged edges of these scraps into a nightdress. The nightdress gave her a feeling of normalcy – you could remind yourself how silk felt as it wisped under your fingertips. After dark, she took off her thin prison uniform and pulled on the nightie, the seams pressing against her protruding bones and unwashed skin. During daily inspections she hid the nightie from the eyes of the SS guards and kapos, the prisoners assigned by the SS to supervise. She buried it in the foul-smelling straw that topped the stacks of wooden bunks, straw bedding soiled by women crushed together like caged chickens, unable to stem flows from starvation sickness. One morning, the SS guards found the nightdress.

'They took your things – you know – like a scarf on your head because you were cold and you had no hair.'

But I didn't know. I shifted my weight in the chair.

'Ach! I cried like anything.' Nana Alicja closed her eyes.

I could not believe losing her nightie was more traumatic than facing Dr Mengele on the assembly Platz, more traumatic than knowing her family and friends choked on Zyklon B in gas chambers. But I did not say this. Her silences and nervous giggles alarmed me more than her graphic descriptions. With Alicja, you knew when to tread lightly. Her voice often had a harsh edge to it, as if telling off a child. She may have left out details too harrowing to recall.

On our last day together, I asked her a final question about the letter from Canada then replaced the tape in my micro-cassette recorder. The streetlights outside Nana's front window flashed on. 'I think everybody's got something inside,' she was saying to me now. 'Yes, there is some evil thing. Not every German was a killer. There were a lot of intelligent, educated people. But they all did the same thing.'

The poodle jumped off the sofa. Nana Alicja looked at me quizzically. 'You think someone will want to know all of this?'

'Yes,' I said. 'I do.'

5

To this day I don't understand completely why Alicja chose me as her confidante. It's true I was the one who took her to symphony concerts. I was the one she asked to take her to see *Schindler's List*. I was the most curious of my siblings, my nose always stuck in a book. Perhaps Alicja knew I'd be the one who'd search for evidence to round out her unbearable memories.

Now in my forties and with no children of my own, I've lived with Alicja's stories for decades. I've stored the tension behind the smiles and laughter that loomed large in Alicja and Mietek's bungalow. All the topics you didn't talk about, the subjects you didn't name. I grew up with an omnipresent yearning in the pit of my abdomen. I grew up learning to seal off the past. Until one day, I no longer could.

It was 2011, 17,000 kilometres from Nana's living room. I was snuggled on my sofa in Boston with my laptop, pounding out work emails. On TV, a young couple on *House Hunters* was deciding between a three-bedroom condo on a golf course and another with ocean views. With one eye on the TV, I googled my mother's maiden name, Dortheimer. Perhaps I needed a distraction from work. More likely, in the back of my mind, I was thinking of Alicja. She'd passed away several years earlier. After interviewing her, I promised her I'd write her story. I'd developed a sense of responsibility to decode my family's buried past and maybe now was the time to act on it.

Google led me to a link. When opened, a US Army film clip launched, shot by Hollywood directors John Ford and George Stevens after the Americans liberated Dachau concentration camp. The camera panned a crowd of men wearing shapeless, dull shirts, numbers stitched at their chests. It zoomed in on one, his face pale and stubbled, rutted eyes and brow, his cap frayed. A Mr Dortheimer. My grandfather, Mietek.

'We are more than sure that no-one is alive from our families,' Mietek says in perfect English.

He stares at me through the camera, thirty-four years old, a striped prisoner's uniform hanging on his 38 kilogram frame.[7] 'We don't know what will be with us. We have no place to go back.'

The epiphany I'd experienced watching *Schindler's List* again overcame me. Except this man wearing the striped uniform belonged to me. Hundreds of curious men with dirt-streaked faces jostle around him. The picture is grainy, the audio garbled. I played it over and over. I strained my ears to jot down what my grandfather was saying.

'Why are you here as a prisoner?' the interviewer asks Mietek.

'Because I am a Jew.'

'Tell us about your treatment in the hands of the Nazis,' the American probes.

Mietek cocks his head. 'In general, it was very bad.' His accented voice sounds dispassionate. 'Yes, they have beaten us. We couldn't escape. Every night and day we were afraid to be taken to the crematorium.'

I shot off an email to my mother and siblings with the video link.

My mother responded with amazement. She'd never seen the video and had trouble making out what Mietek was saying. He'd barely mentioned anything about Dachau, she said.

Alicja never mentioned the video. I doubt she knew about it.

I sent the link to Mum's brother, Tony, and their cousins. It was the first time they'd seen the Dachau interview, too. I couldn't ask Mietek's sister, my Auntie Stella, or any of my grandparents' friends if they'd seen it because they were all dead.

My discovery of the video marked a tipping point. Nearly seventy years after the US Army liberated Dachau, Mietek's assertive 'Because I am a Jew' haunted me. I wrestled with questions: What does it mean to be Jewish when your mother's raised you evangelical? Why do religion, ethnicity or ancestry even matter – when such distinctions only lead to the possibility of someone being hunted, killed or imprisoned simply for looking or speaking differently from the majority or for practising different traditions? For being 'other'?

I was at a crossroads. I could archive Mietek's Dachau video and Alicja's interviews and continue to pursue my career as a marketing executive. Or I could explain why they matter. Pass them on to my family.

I had promised Alicja to write her story, but the story I knew best was my mother's. I knew how the letter from Canada liberated her, released her from feeling like she didn't belong. I knew how it enraged Alicja. But I couldn't stomach how Alicja had closed herself off from my mother. If I could train myself to be more empathetic, I could try to put myself in my mother's shoes. But it was much harder to put myself in Alicja's.

And so, I listened to Alicja's recordings. I jotted notes about gaps in her story. I lay awake at night wondering if I might find answers in Poland. If I were to visit, I might understand how Alicja and my mother survived the chaos of war. I might understand my mother's unwavering faith, how she countered Alicja's conduct with mantras of forgiveness. I might understand how a father could give his daughter away. And why their stories churned inside me.

I booked a flight to Warsaw.

PART TWO

6

On a sunny May morning, I pull out the Warsaw tourist map tucked in my pocket. I study the asterisks and circles marking where Nana Alicja's and my mother's story began. If I had to plot a line to me standing here, it would begin the day I realised Alicja's tattoo wasn't her phone number. It would run through three continents. It would span thirty years. Each revelation along the way blurred my sense of what was true and what was painted over to protect me, not least the discovery that Mietek and Alicja weren't my biological grandparents.

I wind my way through streets on the edge of Warsaw's old city alongside the Vistula River, where ochre-dormered Baroque townhouses line market squares and the Royal Castle has been meticulously reconstructed brick by brick, after the Germans blasted Warsaw nearly flat.

On a wide, cobblestoned street lined with graffiti-scrawled buildings, I stare at number eleven Orla Street. A long, grey, four-storey bunker-like Soviet block, it is set back behind parked cars, flowering white bushes and tall weeds. It was built over the rubble of Alicja's parents' home after Nazis fired mortars at buildings in this neighbourhood, bulldozed them with tanks and then torched them. I count twenty-two sets of double windows: around sixty apartments. From the kerb I snap photographs. A woman peels back a gauze curtain and stares down at me. I feel like an interloper.

The house that once stood here is where Alicja and her sister Irena were raised. It is where Alicja married Mietek, where my grandmother Irena married the man who would break his promise to Alicja. It is where my mother was born. Their stories overlap here. The house connected them, but its destruction shattered them all.

I stop taking photographs and fish out my headset. I pop the buds in my ears. I want the stories I'd convinced Alicja to tell me to guide me around *her* Warsaw. To help me reconstruct her life. To understand how she survived a war. I don't expect I'll understand everything. Especially Alicja's contempt towards her brother-in-law and my mother. But I intend to solve this, to the extent I am able. I aim to layer gaps in the stories with documents, survivor testimonies and historian reports. I will study old photos for clues. I will match historical data with what Nana Alicja told me.

'Our house was in a better area, but a Jewish area,' I hear her say through my earbuds. 'We lived on one of the *better* streets.'

When I recall her modest, Australian, middle-class bungalow, I think she wanted me to know she'd lived in prestige, around the corner from the once stately stock exchange and Bank of Poland. I picture her on Orla Street in 1923; eight years old. I see her poking her head through the third-floor window of the building predating this featureless grey block. Corinthian columns lined her parents' home. Templed pediments. Iron-balustrade balconies. A large abode filled with elegant rooms and countless nooks where a child could hide.

To understand why Alicja hid her past from me, I should begin by telling you about her parents. From one of the few photos that survived, I know that like Alicja, my mother and now me, Alicja's father was a fastidious dresser. And with his thick moustache, bushy eyebrows and plump jowls, Eljasz Mizne radiated a professorial air.

Eljasz was strict with his children. Alicja's brother, Kuba, was fond of dragging stray dogs through the door. Eljasz would toss them back out. One dog hid behind the furniture. At first, Eljasz ignored it, but when the dog took a liking to Alicja, he let it stay. Soon it was following Eljasz around the house, in time even sitting on his knee. 'Such a little dog,' Alicja said, wistful.

Alicja and Kuba could be beastly, teasing and poking their younger brother, Henryk, and sister, Irena, who would turn to their mother, Dorota, for comfort. She was a warm woman with a face as neatly set as a Dutch oil painting, a stocky neck and arms strong enough to pummel dough. But it was Eljasz who would smack them. When he wasn't working, however, Eljasz would play hide-and-seek and burn off his children's energy in parks ablaze with flowers and shimmering fountains.

45

Eljasz ran his leather business from an office at the back of the house. In the mornings, Alicja would watch the workers enter through a side door. Men who tied aprons around their waists carried in the hides, then snipped around long, pointed templates. The room whirred with the din of machines. Women bent over, pushed leather under frantically bobbing needles and stacked the finished gloves in piles.

Eljasz's leather goods were sold in stores throughout Poland, in Europe and America.[8] He imported hides from Germany. He sold them to other factories. As Chairman of the Glovemakers Guild, he attended meetings in the trading streets north of Orla[9] where skinny boys and beefy men wearing caps loaded bales onto drays.

Sometimes Alicja would walk north with her father through the pious quarter where the more observant Jewish people lived, past bathhouses, kosher butchers and shops selling all manner of goods. Alicja would frown at the black-robed Hasidic men wearing fur hats, the boys with peyot sidelocks skipping along the pavement.[10] 'There were a lot of uneducated, very religious Jews,' Alicja said. 'Perhaps that's why people didn't like us? I didn't like them.' These weren't *her* people, her well-dressed, assimilated Jewish friends who easily blended with the Catholic population.

Eljasz's success meant that Alicja wanted for nothing. Although her father forbade it, she could summon a young boy from the factory and send him shopping, or to collect books from her friend. 'You know how it was,' she said, as if everybody employed errand boys.

Alicja gravitated more towards her mother. She would often talk Dorota into shopping outings. 'We did lots of things without my father knowing,' Alicja said with a mischievous smile.

Her parents entertained almost daily. Dorota would serve the main meal of the day at 2 pm, her table laid with crisp white linen, bottles of wine and liqueur in a crystal decanter. 'Good connections,' Alicja said, describing their suited guests, adding that while the family socialised mostly with Polish Jews, Eljasz would also invite over Catholics.

That the family connected with people who made things happen – business contacts; political movers and shakers; officials; good friends – is an important point. Although no-one in the family could imagine that within fifteen years, some guests raising glasses would betray them. Nor could they foresee in one man the heroism that would save only two of them.

On Fridays, Dorota would serve borscht and gefilte fish, even though Eljasz himself wasn't observant. Dorota did keep a kosher kitchen for Passover. 'We'd laugh, because she never was religious,' Alicja said. 'Then suddenly she changed the dishes!'

Eljasz adored his daughter. Many Friday evenings were spent together in their finest attire at the Warsaw Philharmonic Hall. During the interval, Eljasz would ask Alicja about the books she was reading. He paid for her to attend a private Jewish school, a more secular one, where mostly Catholic teachers deepened her love for literature with modernist prose the likes of Jan Kasprowicz. Poetry by Bolesław Leśmian enamoured Alicja, but she hated mathematics. She preferred even Hebrew over maths, yet like her father, Alicja considered herself secular; 'I was a great atheist, I never believed, right from the beginning.'

Alicja refused to walk her mother around the corner to the Great Synagogue on Tłomackie Street where Dorota would sit upstairs behind a wide gate whispering with friends.

'My mother wanted to show her daughter off there,' Alicja told me, scrunching her eyes. 'Now I'm sorry. I should have made her happy. I said I'd never go, and I never did.'

Alicja's single-mindedness, much as it might have hurt her mother, would later save her life.

7

When Alicja made up her mind to tackle something new, there was no talking her out of it. She told me that when she was seventeen years old, she convinced her broad-minded parents she was mature enough to travel overseas without a chaperone.

In 1933, she bounced up the gangplank of a cruise liner destined for England. She stood on the deck gazing at the blue ocean, wind rippling her hair, droplets of salt water spraying her face. As chance would have it, a group of young men was lounging against the rail, laughing and blowing cigarette smoke out to sea. One – the wiry, dapper man with slicked-back hair, nattily dressed in summer trousers – had been telling the joke.

Alicja noted his grin, his charming demeanour. 'It was love at first sight,' she told me.

At the Captain's Ball that night, twenty-one-year-old Mieczysław (Mietek) Dortheimer asked Alicja to dance. Her smile attracted the law student from Kraków's Jagiellonian University, as did her figure-hugging gown and porcelain-smooth skin. Although less educated than his two older sisters, Giza and Stella, the woman whose shoulder Mietek pressed up against as he steered her into a foxtrot, preferred living by her wits.

As they talked late into the night, Mietek learned that Alicja aimed to open her own cosmetic studio after completing beauty courses. He learned of her passion for poetry, for travel, how she loved to promenade on boardwalks by the sea, on streets bustling with cafés, and to shop with her girlfriends for Coco Chanel-inspired dresses. She was a good bourgeois girl who respected her parents yet questioned the rules.

'He wrote me letters every day,' Alicja said of the months after the ship docked back in Poland. In between studies, Mietek visited her in Warsaw where they would walk arm-in-arm admiring the city's palaces. They would eat cake in cafés, sip cocktails in neon-lit nightclubs and tango with the glitterati at the marble and gold bedecked Café Adria.[11] It wasn't long before Alicja's parents invited Mietek to dinner. Eljasz sized up the skinny, confident young man sitting across the table while Mietek tucked into Dorota's fish rolls. Eljasz would have nodded approvingly when Mietek spoke of his father's flourishing wholesaling business dealing in inks, pens and printing machinery. He found Mietek personable enough – charming, even – and in years to come he would make a nice living as a lawyer. But Alicja was eighteen. Far too young to be so serious about this light-hearted boy. Besides, if Mietek were to propose marriage, his daughter would move to Mietek's home town of Kraków. How on earth could he bear losing her?

But Mietek was determined. When Alicja moved to Belgium for a few months to ply women with potions at a cosmetic salon, Mietek wrote every few days.

Like Mietek, my husband also writes to me. On a shelf in my study sits a white box painted with pink flowers, the word 'Treasures' painted on the lid. Folded inside are the letters and Valentine's cards Peter has sent me over the years. Sometimes I curl up on the couch with a cup of tea and read them. Twenty-plus years married and his words still overwhelm me, that even my blunt side endears me to him. More than flowers, words matter. They represent what we miss when away from home – the way my darling turns down my corner of the duvet and flicks on my bedside lamp. Every night. The way he walks my schnoodle when he doesn't like dogs. Love notes he slipped into my suitcase for me to read in Poland.

Alicja lost her love letters. Scattered by bombs. Burned by Nazis who then bulldozed her bedroom. Her treasure box, if she had one, was empty. Perhaps that's why she valued jewellery, property, clothing – things easily replaced.

Despite university quotas limiting Jewish students, Mietek moved to Lwów, 400 kilometres from Orla Street, in 1937[12] to complete his dissertation. Unlike Alicja, who did not attend university, Mietek's sisters had defied the quotas, in Giza's case earning a PhD in organic chemistry, and Stella an MA in musicology and languages.

Mietek was hell-bent on practising law, but Lwów University didn't make it easy. Staff ordered Jewish students to sit on 'ghetto benches' in segregated lecture hall sections.[13] Students herded them into courtyards and slashed them with razors tied to the ends of long poles.[14] 'They were wearing these hats with green ribbons[15] and we knew straight away they were antisemitic,' Alicja said of the Obóz Narodowo-Radykalny (National Radical ONR) students who terrorised Jewish citizens on the streets and in university hallways across Poland at the time.

Mietek kept his head down and elbowed his way to classes. According to Alicja, Mietek would often brush off antisemitic violence. One day, students pushed Jews out of a third-floor window. Mietek said nothing, even though the police and faculty took no action. You can ignore hate crimes until they happen to you.

Nevertheless, Alicja did notice changes in Mietek: the twenty six year old was losing his hair.

They didn't need to read in the papers that the violence and discrimination against Jewish Poles was worsening. Bullies would throw bricks through Jewish shop windows or stand outside and bar non-Jewish Poles from entering.[16] Then they beat up the store owners. They attacked Jews at markets and fairs.

After Chief of State Marshal Józef Piłsudski's death in 1935, Poland had spiralled towards nationalism. The country simmered, abetted by the Nuremberg Race Laws passed in Germany, where they'd excluded Jews from citizenship and prohibited them from marrying or having sexual relations with persons of 'German or related blood'. The laws classified you as a Jew if you had three or four Jewish grandparents, regardless of whether you'd converted, if you were atheist, secular or assimilated.[17]

Everyone in the young couple's circle of friends worried about the anti-Jewish psychosis gripping Poland except for Mietek, even though newspapers had slandered his sister, after Stella had won the *Szymanowski* violin competition and now broadcast widely on the BBC and Polish radio. But newspapers all over the country[18] were attacking Stella and other Jewish musicians for 'poisoning the souls' of Polish radio listeners with 'Jewish values', and 'Jewish world views': 'We do not want to listen to Jews or their songs!'[19] the *Dziennik Bydgoski* newspaper editors wrote about Stella.

'You couldn't really walk on the main Aleje Jerozolimskie street because hooligans could attack you,' Alicja said of the rock-throwing thugs who attacked Jews nearly daily in the streets and public gardens near her parents' home. 'The Polish people were violent towards Jews. There were pogroms,' she said of locally organised, murderous anti-Jewish riots. 'At universities, they beat the students terribly.'

Little did she know that to solve Poland's 'Jewish problem' the authoritarian-leaning government was working on solutions to to encourage 90 per cent of Polish Jews to leave for Madagascar, Palestine – anywhere but Poland.[20] It secretly initiated[21] negotiations with France over the Madagascar plan and scrapped the French proposal only after deeming it economically unfeasible.[22] Then it attempted to strip Jews who lived outside Poland of Polish citizenship.[23] It applied economic pressure to induce Jews to leave, encouraging boycotts of Jewish businesses, and passed a ban on kosher slaughter (although it was only partially implemented). While clergy and right-wing leaders spread antisemitic propaganda, the government ignored violence in universities, too.

Despite this tumult, Alicja and Mietek were in love and engaged like many young couples, but decided to defer marriage until after Mietek finished his studies. The wedding eventually took place on 19 January 1938. Alicja's mother laid out the marriage papers on a table next to the living room window on Orla Street. I picture her lighting candles and tenting a tablecloth with four broomsticks, the perfect stand-in for the synagogue's chuppah.

'I didn't want one,' Alicja said of the wedding. 'I'm telling you, I was against everything. But I couldn't do that to my mother, so we had this wedding at home, because I wouldn't go to the synagogue.'

Mietek's parents, Abe and Toni, and his two sisters watched him slip a ring onto Alicja's finger as he vowed to protect her. A ring she would later trade for a slice of bread. The rabbi intoned blessings, his chants hovering over the modest gathering while God looked down: 'Sos Tasis VeTagel HaAkarah, BeKibbutz Bane'ha Letocha BeSimcha' — *Let the barren city be jubilantly happy and joyful at her joyous reunion with her children.* The rabbi filled the goblet with wine. Alicja tossed back her head. 'I downed the whole glass!' she told me. 'It nearly killed me!'

Mietek stomped his foot on a glass wrapped in cloth. It shattered. Mazel tov! Mazel tov! — *Congratulations!* Someone snapped a photo. Mietek is dressed in a formal suit and white bow tie, his face beaming. He tucks his arm around Alicja's waist, under her bouquet of cascading white flowers. Alicja, nearly as tall as Mietek, looks like a movie star: Greta Garbo pin-curled hair, warm eyes, winged liner, flawless complexion – if her neck bore a birthmark, it is invisible. She is dressed in a long, blue taffeta gown with scooped neckline, ruches and puffs at her shoulders. 'I didn't want a white dress,' she said. Alicja would never agree to anything expected.

I have her taste for fine fabrics. I wanted black silk for my wedding gown, but chose white, to please my mother. Now I think Alicja was encouraging me to not follow rules. To trust my instincts. I should rebel, as she did, against religious and societal expectations.

The thing about surviving a war is that it messes up calendars. Years after her wedding, when Alicja was lying in a makeshift hospital bed recovering from the concentration camps, a Red Cross worker asked her year of birth. She told them 1920. But Alicja was born in 1915. That day, my grandmother split herself into Alicja-before-the-war and Alicja-after. The Nazis had wiped more than five years off her life and this was a first step in reclaiming it.

I have discovered reports, residence documentation, refugee and other application forms that Mietek filled out in the years after the war, where to line up Alicja's younger birth date, he mostly shoehorned into date fields Alicja's high school gradua-tion year and the date she moved to Kraków after they married. On the back of the few family photos that survived (because they were shipped out of the country before the war), Alicja later wrote dates that don't line up with Mietek's documents. In our interviews, Alicja told me she married in 1936. But later, she would tell USC Shoah Foundation that she married on 19 January 1938.

It bothers me that I might not know the true dates. They matter. For example, if I base my timeline on one date, Alicja may have been in Lwów when Jewish students were slashed with razors. They could have pushed Mietek out of a window. But if I use the later date, she is protected, Mietek safe. I never know how much danger they were in, and how close I came to losing them.

8

It's late evening when my train from Warsaw pulls into Kraków's Główny station. I hop into a taxi and whizz by the seven-hundred-year-old walls encircling the city Nana Alicja insisted I visit. 'Kraków University, you should see that,' she'd said, although Auschwitz was first on her list. 'They didn't bomb Kraków,' she told me.

Alicja returned to Poland twice, decades after the war, to visit her only school friend who'd survived. Mietek stayed put, safe in Australia, 15,000 kilometres away. 'He was afraid they wouldn't let him out,' she explained, as the Polish communist government had sent him letters demanding he give up any Polish identity documents and relinquish his right to Polish citizenship.

Passports and visas help you belong. They help you traverse the world, to migrate – to escape. But identity papers can facilitate eviction and violence. Perhaps Mietek stayed away because he couldn't bear to walk the streets where Nazis had loaded his father onto a train.

'What was it like?' I'd asked Alicja naively about her Poland trips.

'It was such a poverty. Terrible poverty,' she'd replied, shrugging her shoulders.

I wanted more of a reaction from her. She'd lost her family and home. I wanted her to be angry. But it touched me that her priority had been to pack her suitcase full of pantyhose and medicine for her friend.

After Alicja married, she lived for a brief time in the light-filled Kraków apartment of Mietek's parents on Potockiego Street, a twenty-five-minute walk to Kazimierz, the Jewish district. The Dortheimer family blended in with the well-to-do Polish–Catholic population, despite the fact Jewish Krakówians numbered around 25 per cent. Most worked in crafts or commerce, like Mietek's father, although one quarter of the city's doctors and half its lawyers were Jewish.[24]

Abe and Toni Dortheimer had blessed their son with a Polish name: Mieczysław – Mietek for short. It sounded less Jewish than Samuel or Abraham. Like Alicja, Mietek's mother and sisters pinned up curls of finger-waved hair, plucked their eyebrows pencil-thin and wore silk stockings. Abe was clean shaven and wore crisp white shirts and ties, not a long black coat.

He spoke mostly Polish, not Yiddish, to his customers. That the Dortheimers strove for professional and social assimilation was cause for hand-wringing in Orthodox circles, but I can find no evidence suggesting Mietek's parents shared Alicja's repugnance of religious Jews.

Music filled the Dortheimer home. During the First World War, the family had fled to Vienna where Stella took up the violin and became a sensation. Upon returning to Kraków, she studied music then travelled solo. The family would gather around the radio to listen to her concerts.[25] But the tutelage of Jenő Hubay and Ede Zathureczky at the prestigious Royal Hungarian Franz Liszt Academy had lured Stella to Budapest, so Giza was the one to soothe Alicja's homesickness by playing nocturnes and sonatas on a piano in the living room.

Alicja was thankful Mietek's close-knit family embraced her, but given Warsaw was six times Kraków's size, the place felt like a village. More accustomed to crowds streaming down the wide avenues off Orla Street, in Kraków Alicja would enter the old city through a medieval tower and wander narrow lanes where men and women brushed past her to duck into churches. She would peer into bookstores and pastry shops. In the vast market square, she inspected long rows of fruit vendors, admiring pears and oranges piled into pyramids, and the twin-towered St Mary's church looming on the corner.

Mietek encouraged Alicja to visit her parents in Warsaw. In Kraków, he took her dancing. He accompanied her to concerts. He hooked his arm in hers and ambled with families who pushed babies in prams around the Planty, a ribbon of parkland surrounding the fortified walls. The two of them would climb the hill to

Wawel Royal Castle, where Alicja could peer over the brick wall, down to the Vistula River's dull, black expanse, piles of garbage dumped on its banks beneath her. In the summer, they swam in freshwater lakes ringed by forests with Stella, Giza and Cousin Igor. They posed for photos on sandy beaches, the lithe young men in belted swimming trunks, the young ladies tanned from shoulder to toe. They hiked in the Tatra Mountains under beech trees and played cards on grassy hillsides basking in the warm sun.

'Yes, I'm very happy here, Mamma, but I wish you would visit,' Alicja pleaded with Dorota on the phone. She didn't tell her mother that she missed her terribly. Sometimes the truth is easier if you don't say it.

At this time, the knot around Jews in Poland was tightening. Alicja and Mietek decided to postpone having children because of the unrest in the air. In 1938, Mietek and other Jewish lawyers were restricted from obtaining licences. The General Assembly of Journalists, the Polish State and the Polish Medical Association passed restriction laws, too.[26] If more than half of Poland's doctors were Jewish,[27] what on earth would happen when people got sick? Given state hospitals rarely employed Jewish doctors, most non-Jewish Poles probably didn't notice.

In Warsaw, around the corner from Alicja's father's business, the Bank Polski adopted rules to exclude Jews. Across the border, in Hungary, Stella, now married, feared for the future. She baptised their Jewish baby as Catholic.

Mietek told his sister Giza over and over that she shouldn't worry. But after Nazis in Germany burned synagogues, smashed shopfronts and murdered Jews, and pogroms broke out in Austria and Czechoslovakia, Giza and her husband Ferdynand left Poland for Australia.

'Australia was very strange,' Alicja would say later about sailing to the backwater nation more than a month's voyage from Europe. 'Giza probably thought it was far enough to be safe. Mietek said maybe we should go there, too. When I told my mother, she couldn't believe it!'

Devastated that his sister had given up on Europe, Mietek kept busy working as a legal advisor for his father's business. Then around spring 1939, Stella broke the news to Mietek. She and Paul, still in Budapest, had obtained permits to join Giza. They would sail to Australia that September.

'It will all blow over,' Mietek said to Alicja after she tried to console him.

I picture Alicja's face, drawn and pale. While she believed in charting one's own path, more than that, she believed in family. She knew Mietek would miss his sisters terribly. How could they visit the mountains this summer without Giza and Stella? Many of Alicja's friends – and now Mietek's sisters – were choosing to leave Poland. Her mother couldn't bear it, but should she and Mietek sail to Australia as well? The first to flee oppression are often those able to pay steep prices to cross oceans. Regardless, it requires nerve to stay. To try to keep things as they are. It also requires courage to change them. The Mietek I am getting to know would have grabbed Alicja's arm, tweaked her cheek and kissed her. 'Let's not panic yet, my sweet.'

When leaders enact segregationist laws in parliaments and boardrooms, some of us take precautions. Others prefer not to notice. We refuse to foresee catastrophe looming. Until it splits families and nations apart, leaving slaughter, ashes and ruin in its wake. A tragedy that ripples through the lives of survivors and transfers the scars to their children.

Mietek would often counter Alicja's testiness with humour, his antidote for serious situations. Alicja told me a story of how, on their wedding day, she was powdering her face and preparing in her bedroom when she noticed Mietek in the doorway, stone-faced. 'I'm not going through with the wedding,' he snapped.

Alicja flew into a tizzy. The rabbi was arriving any minute. 'You can't do that. You have to marry me!'

'I won't,' Mietek said. He ran down the stairs and dashed out the front door. Alicja followed him out into the cold, panting, her heels clacking along Orla Street, around a corner. That's when she saw him, doubled over, laughing.

It wouldn't be the last time he'd fool her. Alicja was Mietek's leading lady, and he her jester. This would be their pas de deux: Mietek winking, pushing Alicja's buttons to hear her laugh, see her smile, to play her off against the incomprehensible calamity thundering towards them.

'Stupid wedding,' Alicja tittered. 'We didn't need a wedding,' she told me. 'We were so happy.'

My hotel in Kazimierz has overbooked my room. They direct me to an apartment across a cobblestoned street lined with restaurants. Diners sit under umbrellas and awnings, ordering traditional Polish and Jewish fare: pierogi, gefilte fish, chicken soup and kreplach. The scent of paprika takes me back to Nana's kitchen. Her tasty chicken giblet soup was a favourite, until she explained to Jacqui and me that she tossed in chicken guts. 'You must use every single bit of the chicken,' Nana Alicja told us, 'not just the good meat.' At the time I thought this strange because my mother didn't cook soup this way. I presumed food was always easy to come by – if you wanted a chicken, you visited a butcher or the poultry farm down the street.

The next morning, I heave open an old, vaulted door to the street, but a man outside blocks the way. I peer over his shoulder, aghast at tour groups swarming in the square. 'Are you trying to come in?' I ask.

The man is a guide, speaking broken English to about thirty people. 'No,' he says, then continues his tour. 'Here is where there used to be a Jewish sign over the door, ah – I'm not sure how you call it – and it was removed.'

'A mezuzah!' a woman in her sixties with grey hair and a deep voice yells out in an oi-veh Brooklyn accent. 'It's a mez*uuuu*zah!'

I will learn later this is a thin case enclosing parchments inscribed with religious texts affixed to the doorframes of Jewish households that act as a reminder of the covenant of faith.

'Why didn't someone fix it?' asks another American woman in a white T-shirt, white sneakers and raincoat.

'Because all the Jews are dead or gone, that's why,' the first woman says, full of sarcasm. I wonder if, like me, she's on a pilgrimage, retracing steps of family she's lost.

Crossing the square towards the hotel for breakfast, I stop and stare. Outside the old synagogue, women hawk Jewish souvenirs: stereotypical figurines of bearded men with bulbous noses hugging violins and accordions. Dozens of golf carts advertising

Jewish tours are parked there. People are queuing to book tours of the former Jewish ghetto in the southern Kraków suburb of Podgórze and the Schindler factory (on the edge of the former ghetto), the traditional Jewish quarter of Kazimierz, and Auschwitz. It's only 9.30 am and Hava Nagila and klezmer music blare from speakers. I wince at the Disneyland atmosphere.

After breakfast, I stroll through Kraków's city gates and head to the Metropolitan Archives. I want to search for Mietek's records, for concrete information to prove he belonged to this city. This place.

Inside, a woman hands me a form. A younger woman in the queue behind me notices my poor Polish and offers to help me fill it out. I wait at a large desk in the reading room, where light streams through a window. The first woman delivers two oversized ledgers, one labelled 1911, Mietek's birth year. I flick through pages of curved handwritten script. Embarrassed, I ask a bespectacled young man next to me if he speaks English.

'A little.'

We find Mietek's entry. The young man runs his finger down the page, explaining what's written in the neat, left-tilted lines. He's stuck. 'Mmmm . . . How you say?'

I look at him, curious.

'They . . . they do this to boys.'

'Circumcision?' I whisper. I make a snipping motion with two fingers.

I hadn't expected a government requirement to note something so personal. My stomach sours when I think about Nazis scouring these registers, how mandating religious and cultural information turned Jewish people into easy targets.

I thank the young man, then make a note to ask my mother why my two brothers were circumcised, when in Australia in the 1970s the procedure was less common.[28] The reason must have been more than medical. If Alicja and Mietek never took Mum to a synagogue, unless Auntie Stella or Giza told her about this Jewish ritual, why would she have chosen to undertake it?

I wander the laneways hugging the old city's perimeter walls. I catch glimpses of the young woman Nana Alicja must have been before the war, sauntering near here in her pencil skirt and heels, carrying shopping bags, eyeing fashionable outfits in store windows. I find myself drawn through a gate leading to the seventeenth-century buildings of the Jagiellonian University's law school. Inside, I run my hand up the balustrade of the stone staircase that Mietek climbed. I listen to a lecture outside a closed door. When it ends, students rush out, chatting loudly, as Mietek did, except these students check texts on their phones. I spill with them into a courtyard where they laugh and smoke cigarettes. An older woman approaches me, scowling. She asks me to not take photographs. She wags her finger in my face. It might appear to her I don't belong here. But the point is, I do.

9

Six months after the letter from Canada arrived – after my mother discovered the Polish Circus already knew about Alicja's secret – after she vowed to Alicja she wouldn't tell her children unless we asked, my mother packed us onto a Pan Am jet to Canada to visit an 'uncle'. 'He's a distant relative from Poland,' Mum explained.

I was nearly ten. Of course, I believed her.

When we landed in Toronto, Mum's cheeks were radiant. She buzzed with ridiculous energy, when all I wanted was to curl up in a ball and sleep. On disembarking, she led us down hallways among throngs of travellers, her Jackie Kennedy bob a perfect black pouf, despite having been wedged against an airline seat for more than two days.

My father, always in charge, led us through enormous doors, my baby brother Alex on his hip. Dad told us to hold hands and not let go, or we'd get lost. He walked up to a stout man in a shirt and tie and navy-blue jacket. He placed a hand on his shoulder. The man spun around. He threw his arms around Mum.

'He's not very excited to see *us*,' Jacqui whispered.

First impressions of this uncle suggested nothing fun or jolly. With deep brown eyes and thick brows, he looked like us, although he didn't have much for hair, a few strands of grey slicked back against his glossy bald head. He was a similar height to my father, a bit taller than Mum. His body was thicker in the middle, like Mum's. He had a full, round face and olive skin, like hers. The one thing that didn't surprise us was his accent. He sounded like Papa Mietek.

Zdzisław – or 'Uncle Dick' as we were encouraged to call him – drove us to his petite 1950s Cape Cod-style house. In the dungeon, as Jacqui and I called the basement where we slept, papers and books covered a desk. Uncle Dick showed me his pipes stacked in a rack that smelled like the straw in our chicken coop back home. Upstairs, bookshelves lined the dining room-turned-study and overflowed with English and Polish titles, enormous books filled with photographs of paintings and sculpture.

On top of one bookshelf sat a black-and-white photograph of a young Uncle Dick dressed in a Polish Army uniform and sporting a huge grin beneath his hard-topped cap. I sat on Dick's knee. I told him how handsome and young he looked.

'Did you ever shoot anyone when you were in the army?' I asked.

'Yes.'

Uncle Dick's sternness and serious glare scared me. He hadn't been around children much. Even his name was severe; none of us could say it properly: Zdzisław (Z-jish-wahv). 'That's why everyone calls him Dick,' said Mum.

Uncle Dick pulled a heavy, white, leather-bound book from the shelf. It was filled with photographs of Polish castles, palaces and stupendously grand buildings. The words were in Polish and I couldn't read or pronounce them, so he read out the names of places in a rumbling baritone: Gdansk, Ujazdów, Warszawa, Piotrkowice.

'Before the war, Poland was important centre of European culture. Now most is gone.' His eyes moistened. 'If you ever go to Poland, Karen, you *must* visit Kraków.'

He emphasised 'must' like my strict teacher did before hitting me or one of my classmates with a ruler. 'The Nazis. They didn't destroy Kraków.'

Uncle Dick told Mum he'd spent his childhood in Russia during a revolution, where his father, Władysław, had worked in the army as a doctor. 'I was born in 1913. From 1895 to 1918 there was no Polish state,' Dick said.

My mother said nothing, which I found strange, because she talked non-stop at home. Dick would reel off dates and details of Polish history, disappointed, it seemed, that Mum didn't expound on them.

'Don't you know about Józef Piłsudski?' Dick asked, referring to Poland's interwar Chief of State. 'Didn't Alicja and Mietek or your teachers tell you about him?'

'Um, no?' Mum said, her voice lilting with an upward inflection. Mum didn't feel attached to Poland. Her heart lay with the teachings of the Church.

One day, we were sitting around Dick's small kitchen table when Mum told him how God had saved my brother Raoul's leg after he'd slipped under a car in a kindergarten car park back in Australia. The car wheel rolled over his leg but left only a bruise. This kind of story – discussing God's miracles and 'sharing her faith', as our pastor called it – was more Mum's domain than Dick's history lessons.

Helena, Dick's eighty-eight-year-old mother with a face like a raisin, had flown in from Florida and slept in a room at the top of the stairs. Her thin plucked eyebrows, shoulder-length plum-dyed hair and Polish accent reminded me of Nana. Mum and Dick had instructed us to call Helena 'Babcia', Polish for grand-mother. Mum and Babcia drank pot-loads of coffee and talked for hours.

'Go outside and play,' Mum ordered, as I clambered up a chair in the kitchen, eager to join their conversation, except it was Babcia who talked most. She was telling Mum about her sewing machine, how she sewed most of her dresses, how before the war she loved wearing the latest fashions to entertain actors, painters and writers at 'salons' in her Warsaw apartment, how it was easier to throw parties back when there were servants to help, how during the war she gave all her jewellery to one maid for safekeeping.

I didn't know that during the war, Babcia Helena had crawled through booby-trapped sewers to escape Nazi tanks and burning buildings. I didn't know that growing up, Mum had yearned for a grandmother, that all her girlfriends had at least one. Her three cousins didn't have grandparents either. And I didn't know that like Dick, Helena was hiding secrets about my mother that she would never reveal.

In Dick's kitchen, Babcia began extracting rings and pendants from velvet bags; including diamonds her maid had returned after the war, jewellery burglars would later steal from our home in Melbourne. The stone in one ring Babcia handed my mother was as blue as the waves at Nana's beach house.

Mum clinked her cup down onto her saucer and flattened her lips. She fixed her eyes on me, until I left the room.

A few days later, Dick drove us to a building filled with corridors and dark rooms. It was a TV studio, he explained. 'Can *I* be on TV?' I asked, tugging at Dick's sleeve.

Mum transferred Alex into some strange woman's arms since Dad had flown on to Europe for work. Mum walked away with Uncle Dick and a man wearing thick glasses and a dark suit. She and Dick sat on the other side of an enormous glass pane talking to the suited man. But if this interview was for the Polish community, as Dick had told me, why were they speaking English?

Dick and Mum waved. They talked to Jacqui, Raoul and me through microphones on telescopic stands. Then suddenly the sound cut out. On our side of the glass it was dead silent.

'What are they talking about?' I asked Jacqui, while Alex crawled along the hallway.

They were discussing Mum's reunion with Uncle Dick and what it was like to live in Australia, the young woman supervising us explained. Of course, now I know this was only partially true, but back then I sensed this was some forbidden adult topic we children were 'too young' to hear.

That evening, Jacqui and I headed off to bed in the dungeon. I lay awake listening to the shadowy mumbles of Uncle Dick's deep voice talking with Mum upstairs. I snuck out of bed, as

I often did during our six weeks in Canada. I crawled up the basement stairs in the dark to the top. I squished my ear close to the gap under the door. I couldn't quite make out what they were discussing. Only the occasional names of Polish cities Uncle Dick had showed me in his books, and Nana and Papa's names. This puzzled me. I couldn't recall my grandparents ever mentioning Dick. But whatever it was Mum and Dick were talking about, I knew it must be important for them to stay up so long, every night.

Three years after our Canada trip, at 11 am the clock at my school struck eleven times. It was Remembrance Day, 11 November, ten days before my thirteenth birthday. I stood to attention with the class, heads bowed, silent for three minutes, honouring those who'd died fighting wars. On Remembrance Day, talk about war at school focused mostly on the ANZACs, members of the Australian and New Zealand Army Corps who fought at Gallipoli against the Ottoman Empire during the First World War. Kids snickered at the 'diggers', the old soldiers you sometimes saw staggering around drunk outside pubs.

After school, Mum picked Jacqui and me up in the Kombi van. The house smelled of Pine O Cleen and cocoa. Mum had baked a chocolate slice for afternoon tea. Jacqui and I stirred cocoa icing and spread it on top. We perched on stools at the kitchen counter and nibbled the slice while discussing Remembrance Day events.

'Why did Nana and others have tattoos on their arms during the war?' asked Jacqui. We knew by then the tattoo wasn't a phone number as Nana had claimed.

'Because she was Jewish,' Mum said. 'They did things like that to the Jews. It was an identity number, like a passport.'

I thought of the crusty, scabbed numbers I'd seen branded on cow and horse rumps in paddocks near our home.

Whenever I asked Mum questions about the war, she guarded her answers, especially when it came to Poland and Nana and Papa. But this Remembrance Day she didn't.

'When you arrived in Australia on the ship, could you speak English?' I asked.

'No, barely a word.'

'Where were you during the war?' I bit off a corner of chocolate slice.

'I was in an orphanage.'

'An *orphanage*?'

'Yes, an orphanage,' said Mum, as if everyone we knew grew up in an orphanage. She paused. She was unusually controlled.

'If you were in an orphanage, that must mean you're adopted,' Jacqui said matter-of-factly.

What a dumb thing to say, I thought. Just because you're in an orphanage doesn't mean you're adopted. It could have been like a holiday house or someplace safe to stay while your parents were somewhere else.

'Yes. I was,' Mum said, then stopped. Uncharacteristically, she stayed silent.

'You're *adopted*?' Jacqui shrieked. 'Aren't Nana and Papa your parents?'

'No.'

'Then who *is*?'

'Uncle Dick is my father.'

'Uncle Dick in *Canada*?' I shouted, my mouth hanging open.

'Yes.' My mother grinned, as if she'd prepared for this moment for years.

'Why didn't you tell us before?' I squealed.

'I couldn't,' Mum said. 'I promised Nana and Papa. They worried you wouldn't love them if you knew they weren't your real grandparents. I promised Nana I would tell you the truth only if you asked me. She didn't think you'd ever ask.'

My head reeled. Nana and Papa's faces spun around my mind as if a wave had dumped them, swirling and sucking them into the undertow.

'How did you find out?' I pressed.

Mum told us about the day she received Uncle Dick's letter, and how on New Year's Eve two months before, she'd prayed and written a list of her 'heart's desires', how she'd asked God to help her figure out why she felt she didn't belong to Alicja and Mietek.

'Why did you hide all this from us?' I was giggling, a strange laughter mixed with hiccupping sobs I couldn't control. 'What did Nana think about us going to Canada?'

There had been a huge hullaballoo, Mum said, when she'd told Nana about the airline tickets Dick purchased for us.

Auntie Stella had intervened before we flew to Canada. The children shouldn't know the truth, they'd all decided. 'Uncle Dick' was the name given to their little white lie.

'So Babcia,' Dick's mother Helena, 'is our *great*-grandmother?' I suddenly figured.

'Yes,' Mum said. Her eyes shone deep with love.

I realised Babcia and Uncle Dick had played a hide-the-truth-game on us kids as well. Every one of Dick's friends we met in

Canada must have been in on the secret. They would have known all about it after Mum and Dick's TV interview. I remembered the night it aired, when Dick's friends – older Polish men and grey-haired married couples – showed up after dinner. Jacqui and I had been eager to tell Dick's friends about our ear-popping ride up to the fifty-fifth floor of Toronto's CN Tower. But Mum had rushed us down the stairs to the dungeon and to bed. In that moment, I should have suspected something. I racked my brain to think of what other signals I'd missed.

I did not feel betrayed that people I loved lied to me. Rather, I surmised that my mother had wanted to protect us. In any event, I knew this was a monumental change to our family. I couldn't grasp the weight of the new information – that Nana's younger sister Irena was my *real* grandmother, and Uncle Dick was suddenly my grandfather.

Jacqui and I weren't sure what to do next. 'Let's write Uncle Dick a letter!' she suggested.

I swiped tears from my cheeks and rushed with her to a cabinet, eager to follow her lead for a change. We pulled out paper and pens. 'What shall we call him?'

'Well, we can't call him Papa.'

'My dearest Grandfather,' I wrote in my neatest handwriting. I wrote about how happy I was to discover I had an extra grandfather. I added that I still loved Nana and Papa. I wrote about how after riding Casper at his barn in Canada, I was taking lessons on my own pony. I didn't ask about Irena. Irena was difficult to conjure. I could recall Dick's deep baritone voice reciting endless stories, but Irena was a mystery. I finished writing and stuffed the pages into a thin airmail envelope.

'Let's keep all this a secret from Nana and Papa,' Jacqui suggested.

We wouldn't tell them for six months, we decided. That way they'd know it made no difference at all – that we loved them, regardless.

My mother watched us. Tears dropped down her face. Her lips locked into a broad smile. Then, she rose to make us dinner. I knew, even then, nothing would be the same.

Four weeks later, two letters arrived from Canada, one addressed to Jacqui and one to me. I slit a knife along the envelope and pulled out my letter from Uncle Dick.

'This discovery of your new grandfather should in no way stop the love you have for Alicja and Mietek,' Dick had written on small pieces of notepad paper. 'You must love them always.'

It's hard to imagine what all this change meant to Alicja and Mietek. Holocaust survivors' children and grandchildren often represent versions of vanished relatives. Fear of losing them sparks the emergence of repressed emotions, of deep grieving for parents and siblings killed without funerals.[29] Perhaps we represented Nana Alicja's victory over Hitler. Perhaps we were her reason to carry on.

10

Once, Dick sent me a letter in which he wrote a sentence or two on Irena, about how they first met. Now, I picture Irena in 1938: swirls of silk black hair like a horse's mane pinned at her temples. She is sipping tea on a shady verandah in the spa town of Otwock. A friend of Dick's father beckons Dick to sit down. Dick bows, hand behind his hip like a butler. He smells of tobacco. He stretches out ink-stained fingers, signet bejewelled pinky, and taps Irena's knuckles with his lips.

But if I conjure Irena, I worry I will botch her short history. I don't know enough yet to actualise the six black-and-white photos of her that survived. I know her teeth are like tiny white dancing Lipizzaners, except for one that spooked out of line. Irena is a phantom. A ghost. I lack words she might have written in letters. I lack words she concealed. I lack her opinion on anything: what attracted her to Dick; how she perceived Alicja's dislike of him; or if indeed this existed then – if Alicja's disdain for Dick crystalised later.

'I didn't want to ever look at him any more in my life,' Alicja said during our interview, after I'd asked about the letter Dick sent my mother. Her body tightened like a wind-up toy, as was often the case when anyone mentioned Dick. 'You could *kill* someone with the shock of this letter. It was full of love to . . . *her.*' She winced; her voice full of sarcasm.

I realised then she had actually read the letter to my mother, even though earlier she told me she hadn't.

'Such a *loving* father. This was not true!' Nana Alicja stressed every syllable. 'Nothing was true.' Her voice tapered off. When I think about it now, this was a signal, a key to understanding my mother's whole, sad story.

Alicja and Irena had holidayed in the spa town of Otwock, 30 kilometres south of Warsaw, since they were children. Their mother, Dorota, would hire a horse and carriage, pile it high with luggage, food, pots and pans, their maid sitting on top, and set off for the summer. Over the years, in summer the majority Jewish town would swell from nineteen to thirty-eight thousand.[30] The 'bazaar' Jews lived in Otwock's centre. These were the predominantly poor butchers, fishmongers, bakers, tailors and shoemakers who hawked wares at the weekly market, bargaining in Polish and Yiddish, some Orthodox, some clean-shaven.[31]

The wealthier, mostly assimilated Jews like Alicja and Irena's family, stayed on the other side of town in balconied wooden villas laced with gingerbread trimmings, and in sanatoriums like that of Dick's father, Władysław's fifty-two roomed abode where he treated his tuberculosis patients.

On this 'better' side of Otwock, as Alicja would have referred to it, she and Irena would saunter past orangeries and fountains and wander through the forest.[32] They could walk to the cinema to watch Douglas Fairbanks star in *Robin Hood*[33] and nibble eclairs in a café afterward. They could dance to five-piece orches-tras[34] in elegant cafés and read books and listen to music on shady verandahs.

When twenty-five-year-old Dick met Irena, he ran a small architectural-engineering practice in Warsaw and was in Otwock designing buildings. Recently back from the Paris Expo, he'd seen the swastika and Soviet hammer and sickles projected magically onto buildings after smoke cleared from fire-works. He'd visited Le Corbusier's office and marvelled at the influential architect's drawings. He'd paid 100 francs to ogle at fleshy sculptures and paintings and a parade of 'working girls' in the bordello of Le Chabanais.[35]

I don't really know what attracted twenty-year-old Irena in that serendipitous moment on the verandah. The first thing people noticed about Dick was his Humphrey Bogart swagger of self-assuredness, his square shoulders, his combed-over light brown hair and almond-shaped eyes. He was built like a rower, a stout neck bulging at his collar, hands strong as a boxer. You wouldn't know it, but he had a quiet side, too. He loved to sketch come-dians such as Pat and Patachon and battle scenes from Henryk

Sienkiewicz's Trilogy novels. Judging by articles he wrote for newspapers and magazines, I suspect his confidence emanated from knowledge. An avid reader, eager to engage in philosophical and political discussions, Dick was meticulous with details. Facts mattered.

It may have been Dick's corporal-officer cadet's outfit that drew Irena's eye. His uniform often came in handy. He'd saluted a dean at Warsaw University wearing his Polish-eagle crested cap, swaying the dean to recognise his 'foreign' Gdansk University engineering diploma.[36] 'He had all these friends from the Polish Army,' Alicja said, furrowing her eyebrows, her eyes full of scorn. 'He wasn't really a Jew.'

But Jewish soldiers in Poland's army numbered 10 per cent, in line with the population.[37] More egregious to Alicja, I think, was that Dick wore his uniform to attract cabaret actresses. This while implying he belonged to the intelligentsia of Polish society. Alicja considered Dick and his beer-drinking friends too rough for her younger sister. Irena could have done better.

I met some of Dick's post-war intelligentsia circle in Canada, during my gap year. Dick had offered to help fulfil my childhood dream of riding horses and competing internationally, and lined up training positions with renowned stables. Nana wrote me letters ending with 'I miss you, my darling'. I'm sure she resented Dick luring her eldest grandchild overseas, although she'd never watched me compete back in Australia. My mother, on the other hand, had been rising at four on weekends to hitch a horse float to her car. She was not afraid to stand near my horse's back legs while I guided it up the ramp. Then, she'd watch me ringside for hours. She wanted to pay me the attention Alicja hadn't given her.

In Canada, during the week I shovelled horse manure. On weekends I would accompany Dick to Polish civic events. A month after I arrived, I attended a Polish engineers ball at a swanky hotel glittering with chandeliers. I paraded in a long white gown and gloves with more than a dozen debutantes on the red-velvet arm of André, a Royal Military College army cadet Dick had organised as my chaperone. I felt like I'd stepped into *Cinderella*. Cameras flashed. My stomach knotted as I curtsied before Ontario's Lieutenant Governor. Dick, in his tuxedo and bow tie, jumped to his feet, cheering and clapping, his face wet with tears.

That night, his grief hit me. Dick had missed out on accompanying my mother to piano lessons, playing the role of tooth fairy, listening to her practise Chopin *Nocturnes*. He'd missed out on moulding her into his Polish daughter. On the dancefloor that night, it struck me: I was in Canada to stand in for my mother.

Dick straightened his shoulders and promenaded me like a show pony. We approached a table, my gloved fingers splayed awkwardly on his forearm. Dick leaned over and whispered, 'Zis is the mayor.' He introduced me to politicians, to judges, to leaders in the Polish community. His expectations daunted me.

On one particular evening, Dick pulled up in his Buick to his Polish Combatants Association club, a rack of medals glinting on his royal blue blazer, including the Polonia Restituta that honoured his service to Poland's army and resistance movement, the Armia Krajowa (AK) underground. I sashayed through the entrance in a mauve silk shirt and skirt that shimmied at my knees – my mother's outfit she'd packed in case I needed formal clothing.

Around our table of starched white cloth, women drew me into conversations about the various committees Dick belonged to. Ever proud of his heritage, he organised monuments to honour Poles: Sir Casimir Gzowski, the former acting Lieutenant Governor of Ontario; Polish officers killed by the Soviets in the Katyn massacre, including his uncle;[38] and mathematician and astronomer Nicolaus Copernicus.

Dick was holding court with his army buddies, discussing life in Poland before the war. He then launched into a joke, as he often did, leaning back, his arms folded, a wide grin on his face. A waiter sidled up to the table and placed the first course in the centre of our settings. When Dick's bowl hit the table, he jerked backward. His nostrils flared. The steam rising from the bowl seemed to assail him. 'What is this?' Dick bellowed.

The waiter stepped back, his face as pale as the white table-cloth. 'Turnip soup, sir.'

Dick looked the waiter square in the eye. 'Take it away!' he barked.

Those at our table immediately fell silent. I knew something was wrong but did not know enough then to connect it to the war.

'Turnips,' Dick snarled. 'That's all they fed us in the camps. Watery soup. Water and turnips. *Never* again will I eat turnips.'

Nana Alicja and Papa Mietek had refused to discuss concentration camps, but Dick seemed unable to stop talking about them. Because my high school didn't teach the Holocaust, I'd learned snippets through books Mum gave me such as *The Hiding Place*, in which Corrie ten Boom's Christian family joined the Dutch resistance and hid Jews in a secret room in their house. But back then, I was more focused on competing in horse tournaments and pleasing God than understanding concentration camps.

On evenings when Dick downed a scotch or two, it was as if we were sitting in a dark, smoky bar, not around his laminate kitchen table. 'Now I tell you about my best friend in camp. He was German, and not Jewish,' Dick would begin across a pile of mail, unpaid bills and a bowl filled with medicine bottles. 'He was put in camp by his own brother.'

Dick described the Vaihingen an der Enz camp where the Germans had sentenced him and Mietek to 'extermination by hard labour'.[39] They'd marched them to an old quarry to shovel and haul stone to build an underground aircraft factory. 'My friend's father had a sewer pipe factory, and the brother wanted to run this factory. He was a very intelligent boy. He got typhus and I was taking care of him. He told me, "If I die of this typhus you have to marry my wife."' Dick's voice rose, as if preparing a punch line. 'Later, after we survived all this, I told his wife. She started to cry, of course.' Dick picked up his glass. 'So you see, Germans were *also* in camp. But not too many.'

I told Dick how the owner of the barn where I rode – a six-and-a-half-foot strapping German man – watched a horse buck me off after it had been cooped up in a stable for three days, how he'd crossed his arms, leaned back and roared with laughter while I lay winded in the sawdust.

'He'd make a good SS man,' Dick muttered. 'But maybe present generation is different.' He stroked his glass. 'The chimneys from Dachau were stinking of human flesh.[40] And the people who lived nearby say they did not know!'

Dick didn't seem to care how his horrible stories might affect an oblivious eighteen year old on her first solo trip overseas. Maybe he would have unburdened himself to anyone willing to listen. But I did not comprehend then what Dick was trying to teach me: that no matter our nationality, race or religion, we are easily manipulated into fearing those who look or believe differently. Dick told me we all are capable of wounding others. Or helping them.

Dick wanted to teach me about his past, but I considered living away from home my education. I wanted to make my own decisions. I wanted to be independent, yet I missed my mother. I wrote to her weekly. She mailed me letters filled with recipes and instructions on how to find the cheapest but best quality fruit and vegetables for cooking. I appreciated my mother's practical side. She told me I should put my sneakers in a pillowcase and wash them on the gentle cycle so 'they won't bang around too much'. She counselled me on the men I seemed to be attracting. Maybe it was my Australian accent, my long hair the colour of Vegemite, my slender figure, but for whatever reason, the men drawn to me were not the born-again-Bible-toting sort my mother hoped for.

But Dick didn't care about religious orientation. One morning at breakfast he turned to me and barked, 'I don't like that boy!' He was referring to André, my debutante ball chaperone whom Dick himself had selected. André was Catholic – and Polish.

André hadn't asked his permission to date me, Dick complained. His fingers trembled so wildly I thought he might snap his glasses. And André had spoken his mind when it came to the silk gown his sister had lent me for his graduation ball. One I'd preferred over the flower-child cheesecloth dress smelling of naphthalene that a grey-haired friend of Dick's had lent and insisted I wear.

'I'm losing interest in you!' Dick glared at me.

My mouth dropped open. I looked at the floor, chastised. I trudged down the basement stairs to my musty room; the dungeon.

Thinking about it now, this was a strange thing for Dick to say given he'd missed out on raising my mother and navigating her coming-of-age. Perhaps I excused his behaviour because he'd survived concentration camps. Or I looked up to him because he spoke like an encyclopedia.

After I told my mother about Dick's cutting words, she suggested that because Dick was expecting to have me mostly to himself, he might be jealous that men closer to my age were showing interest. He might resent André for collecting me on weekends and whisking me away when, 'for so many years Dick had no-one to care for'. My mother has a knack for sticking up for people who feel knocked down. She counselled me to not hurt Dick's feelings, but also advised not to let him smother me.

On weekends, when Dick wasn't regaling me with stories, I wrote letters home while he read books and newspapers by lamplight. *Tick . . . Tick . . . Tick . . .* A clock counting to eternity kept us company, the only sound breaking the silence.

I missed my loud house back in Australia, where high-pitched arguments ping-ponged around the kitchen table: No, no! – I think you should put *more* salt on that, Mum – But I *hate* liver! – Suck it up, princess! – Why *should* I? – You'll *never* guess what my teacher said at school today – But it's *my* turn! Listen to *me*! My mother wanted a boisterous household, full of energy and vitality instead of the sense of despair that hovered in her family home. But none of us really knew how to listen. Perhaps Dick's stories were teaching me how.

Listening to Dick also taught me to ask questions. In Canada, I read the Bible and prayed, just like at home, but I also read books such as *Little Women* by Lousia May Alcott and Jane Austen's *Pride and Prejudice*. I cheered the main character, Elizabeth, for how she challenged stereotypes on men's rights and roles. I began to question my mother's Bible study course, 'Philosophy of Christian Womanhood',[41] where, as an instructor, she taught women to submit to their husbands in all matters. We wouldn't bat an eyelash when my father ordered Mum to clear dishes or fetch dessert. After long days of cooking and caring for children, my mother says a woman should change into clean, attractive clothing and put on lipstick to sustain her husband's interest, that a wife shouldn't infringe on her husband's running-the-household territory (except for cleaning the oven he provides her) lest she quash his God-given ego.

I wanted to please God, but I wanted to chart my own path. I wanted to marry, but not submit to a husband. If children were to restrict me from travelling and exploring different cultures, I didn't want any.

I might have been learning self-sufficiency in Canada, but I failed to meet Dick's education standards. I'd been a straight-A student, but Dick made me feel stupid with his 'fifty-questions' history quizzes and constant lectures.

'In the 1300s, Kazimierz, the Great Polish King, let Jews settle in Poland and protected them with laws. Didn't they teach you this in school?' Dick would start over dinner, in his kitchen that smelled of vegetable oil and burned breadcrumbs.

'No,' I responded, annoyed at his presumption the entire world revolved around Poland. 'In Australia, we learned about Captain Cook.' I twisted strands of my long ponytail between my fingers.

'Poland history is important.' Dick paused. He stared at the wall as if I wasn't there.

Now I realise he wanted me and the world to know about *his* Poland, a cultural mecca brimming with intelligent, creative people, most of whom the Nazis killed. His parents' friends were artists, musicians, doctors and writers. I realise that Dick was trying to say I should pursue this history of his. Because it is my history, too.

II

To make sense of what underpinned Alicja's contempt towards Dick, the best thing to do is visit Otwock. 'The town of pines,' is how Dick described it.

From the train window I stare out at the trees Dick told me about, believed at one time to purify air. Tuberculosis doctors like Dick's father had prescribed their patients to recuperate[42] in the 'velvet air of Otwock'. Besides the thousands of pine trees, I notice abandoned-looking buildings scrawled in graffiti. Tangled vines collapse rusted wire fences. Pot-holed, dirt foot-paths line kerb-less roads. Otwock, it appears, is less a town of healing and more a town of ghosts.

I scan the platform for Zbyszek, the editor of *WIĘŹ*,

a progressive Catholic magazine. As luck would have it, we'd been introduced by email through a neighbour in Boston, who'd connected me to a friend who had grown up in Poland, who, as it turned out, had attended school in Otwock. (My mother says God set up these connections, and I might agree with her.)

Zbyszek picks me out easily on the platform; I'm the only black-haired woman in a sea of blondes, eyes like coffee beans grinding and whirring. We kiss formally on each cheek in the Polish style. I'd expected a deep, booming voice to match his warm emails, but his meek smile suggests a humble man.

He drives me towards the town centre, a mish-mash of small shops with oversized signs and barred windows. We stop outside a palace with cherubic statues flanking Greek columns and stone staircases. 'This was once a bathhouse, café and ballroom,' Zbyszek says.

I picture Alicja dancing here, sipping tea with Irena. I hear the *clink* as Alicja's cup hits the saucer. But Irena still remains fuzzy.

Zbyszek stops his car by a square. He points to where the synagogue once stood, burned down during the occupation. He drives to the other side of the train tracks, through a residential area set between dense stands of pine. He parks outside number five Warszawska Street.

I scramble from the car, and then I stop dead in my tracks. The Przygoda sanatorium was supposed to be a striking building, the way Dick described it. Constructed by his grandfather, Józef, in 1895[43] not long after the Otwock railway line was laid, the fifty-two-room building was once one of Poland's largest timber structures. Intricately laced balconies and enclosed verandahs with circular windows once flanked the grand building's sides.

Now, paint peels off the weatherboard like sunburned skin. Long grass chokes lawns and flowerbeds. The building was converted to apartments after the war and is now home to residents receiving social assistance.

I step into the hallway, treading quietly, a trespasser. It smells musty, of mould and boiled cabbage. Exposed electric cables run naked along dirt-smudged walls. A radio blares from an apartment.

'Let's go upstairs,' Zbyszek beckons, perhaps sensing my disappointment at my family complex's dilapidated state.

I had expected to feel pride that my great-grandfather helped people recover here. I expected to feel a sense of ownership, despite the fact that the Germans confiscated the family building, then the Polish State nationalised it under communism, then the town sold it to new owners. But I didn't expect a wooden structure to provoke the sorrow now coursing through me. It's as if I've woken up the ghosts of my family. They call out to me from their exile, from the vast emptiness left in their wake.

On the landing, Zbyszek points out the last original window. Around six feet tall, its D-shaped pane looks like a smile. 'Most wooden trimmings were torn off the building and burned for firewood,' Zbyszek says of the carved fretwork and balconies. He smiles to make me comfortable, I think, but his voice holds serious weight. 'The Germans cordoned off the sanatorium inside the ghetto. It was allocated as the Judenrat administrative offices,' he says, referring to councils that the Germans forced Jews to set up in towns across Poland to control populations that they soon segregated into areas known as ghettos.

I sidle down the stairs, sliding my hand down the banister, fingers sticky. I wonder if Irena did the same. I recall one photo of her taken near here, pine needles in the background, dressed for snow, hands wrapped in a fur stole, her feet snugged into black boots.

I follow Zbyszek out of the family ruin, down a dirt path a hundred feet or so around the back, to a musk-coloured annex behind a chain-link fence on Długiego Street, the windows covered with lace-embroidered curtains. Dick lived here when Władysław was in residence. It was less formal than their Warsaw apartment in the banking quarter, where Dick's mother, Helena, connected painters to benefactors and threw Saturday dinners for thirty people.

Dick described spirited discussions among writers like the novelist Kaden-Bandrowski, and debates between newspaper editors Marek Turkow of the Yiddish daily *Der Moment* and Wojciech Stpiczyński, editor in chief of the *Kuriera Porannego* paper. Weekdays, mothers would drop children off to Helena's experimental Froebel[44] kindergarten, to dance, sing and play with wooden blocks,[45] that is when she wasn't working with the famed educator Dr Janusz Korczak at his Catholic–Jewish orphanage.

Connections and friendships with prominent Poles were important to Dick. Some of them would save Alicja. Dick mentioned them constantly, but to me this seemed less braggadocios, more a lament. That many of his parents' friends were Jewish was irrelevant. Fifty per cent of Warsaw's doctors were. And lawyers.[46] They were all Polish to Dick.

At Dick's funeral, more than a decade ago, I watched elderly Polish men carry his casket, medal-bearing warriors who saluted the coffin and marched down the aisle in perfect formation. Dick had died from Parkinson's disease, at eighty-three. We'd talked more frequently after I moved to Boston. I'd convinced him into accepting help with bathing and transportation to medical appointments. I suspected his poor health was connected to what he'd endured in concentration camps.

On our calls, we also discussed the memoir he'd published with a small press. A few years earlier, he'd mailed me typed and handwritten pages documenting his life. His tone was unsentimental, academic even. I retyped everything and sent him back a printed manuscript scribbled with notes where I'd corrected his English, along with questions and suggestions: 'How did you *feel* when the bombs started falling?' 'Can you describe your relationship with your wife, Irena?'

'Please type exactly as written. No changes,' Dick wrote back.

A rabbi and a priest led Dick's funeral. He left me no instructions about arrangements. Although Jewish by birth, Dick said in his later years that 'Our Lord' had saved his life. 'I would not be alive without my Polish friends,' he'd told me, over and over, referring to his Catholic army buddies and friends of his family. Some Christians attending were angry a rabbi was present, and some Jews were furious about the priest. But I know my grandfather would have wanted this. In death, as in life, he saw no reason why Jews and Christians could not live side by side.

Zbyszek interrupts my ruminations and points at long weeds, obscuring a cranking handle poking from a well. If I ventured towards it, I'd expect to see snakes and pieces of broken crockery.

'It's rumoured that after the invasion, the sanatorium's medical equipment was swiftly buried somewhere here, to protect it from being stolen.'

I jump back, startled when pigeons flap out from the old eaves. A chained-up dog lying in the dirt whimpers. Its eyes hook onto me. I walk back to the car in silence, dodging puddles.

In a café filled with young families, we meet Barbara, a retired journalist. From a folder, she pulls out articles she's written about the Przygoda sanatorium and Dick's life in Canada after the war. She hands me old photographs. Years ago, she tried to track down my mother, sending letters to various addresses. Mum will say she couldn't read them. I wonder if she avoided translation help from Polish relatives – if the past is easier to live with if you pretend it doesn't exist.

I poke my fork into a slice of sernik cheesecake. Barbara reads me a sentence from the article she published: 'One day a child or grandchild will come here from Australia.' She puts her paper down and smiles at me. Yes, I'm here. I fulfilled her prophecy. But why me, and how did she know?

A sense of responsibility drew me here. A need to disentangle Alicja and Dick's secrets and their intertwined meanings. I am the only one in my family who lived with Dick. In some respects, I knew him better than my mother. But I thought the task I've set myself would be easy, that I would unearth facts to explain Alicja's dislike for Dick and my mother. I thought I could fix Mum's pain. I thought by shedding light on her past I could help her make sense of it. Yet the truth differs depending on whose point of view I consider: an optical illusion. Multifaceted. Erratic. Dizzying.

My shoulders tighten when I listen to Barbara, Zbyszek and others who revere Jewish citizens like the Przygodas, because seventy years ago, some townspeople in Otwock and across Poland turned in their Jewish neighbours.[47] When furs and jewellery belonging to Mietek's aunts and uncles ran out, neighbours who had hidden them called the Gestapo.

After coffee, we drive to Przygoda Street. In the 1970s, Dick visited Otwock and lobbied town officials to memorialise his father's contributions to the town. I imagine the pines must have closed in on him and the air felt anything but velvet. Today, Przygoda Street is a dirt road riven with potholes. I stare at the dense pines. I wonder if in 1942 I could have survived hiding out here.

'It's all gone now,' Alicja had said about Otwock, a blank look on her face.

I find it difficult to envisage her carefree summers here, all the laughing and twirling, when dozens of blistered wooden buildings around me threaten to collapse; abandoned, decayed and scattered. The town feels dark. The pine trees, the dirt roads, the decay – it all spooks me.

Zbyszek pulls up at an unremarkable spot in the forest. A modest memorial stands in a clearing. 'This is where around two thousand Jews were buried after they escaped the round-ups for Treblinka,'[48] he says matter-of-factly. 'The Germans hunted for people hiding in the forest and in cellars, then shot them here.'

I wind down the car window. The air reeks of mint and pepper. Pine needles rustle in the breeze. Whenever I see forests in Poland, I imagine Jews crouching in the shadows, wondering when they'll be shot.

I could never have predicted that in years to come, I and thousands of others – townspeople, a few Holocaust survivors, a rabbi and priests – will march past the Przygoda sanatorium to this remembrance stone. Zbyszek organises this annual procession with others who raise money to protect the wooden buildings and the memory of Otwock's Jews. We will lay flowers at this very monument. We will light candles. I will cry when a survivor's son tips his head back and sings 'El Malei Rachamim' to remember and protect the souls of those killed here. His Hebrew words of mourning will cut me. They will stir my bones. And bones of those buried beneath my feet.

Zbyszek drives me to the Hotel Śródborowianka, an enormous stucco building flanked by gargantuan columns, as if White Lady ghosts guard this place. Once known for its magnificent ballroom, the hotel is now home to a Jewish social-cultural association. Jewish people travel from around the world to study and holiday here. As Zbyszek turns off the engine, I roll down the window to watch young men and women chatting outside.

'There is only one Jew left in Otwock that I know of,' he says out of the blue. Both of us turn wistful.

I wonder if Dick and Irena ever danced here, if this is where Dick dipped on bended knee and proposed. If that's why he wanted me to dance at a debutante ball.

I do not know that Dick's aunt, his mother's sister Gustuwa, and her husband built this hotel. I do not realise that as a teenager, Dick sipped drinks here, smoked cigarettes and flirted with girls.

I wish I'd pushed Dick to tell me more about Irena before he died. What made her laugh and cry? Was she as kind-hearted and trusting as my mother? Could this be perhaps why Dick gave her up? Maybe we all erase memories of those we lose to help us carry on.

Dick's selective amnesia might be why Alicja turned up her nose at him. What is certain is that Otwock connected them all. What remains in doubt is what exactly tore them apart.

12

On a warm July 1939 morning, Dick and Irena carried their suitcases across Warsaw airport's departure hall. Dick pulled two sets of airline tickets from inside his jacket. Standing at a pre-arranged spot, he waited for the tour group with his fiancée, Irena. He lit a cigarette and scanned the hall.

People rushed by, their heels *click-clacking*. They chattered in French, German, Hungarian, English, their voices high-pitched and hurried. All the talk of war was fuelling a growing sense of panic. ALL MEN UP TO 50 YEARS OF AGE MUST CLARIFY THEIR MILITARY STATUS[49] [50] the *Gazeta Polska* newspaper declared. But last-minute travel bargains still lured a few wary vacationers to Poland's empty beaches.[51]

Dick checked his watch. They would have to fly to Budapest alone. Before they knew it, it was time to climb the stairs of their plane. The door closed. Propellers whirred. It was exciting to think about flying, about what awaited them, about the hotel room all to themselves. The aircraft pulled back and taxied away from the terminal. Dick and Irena were taking off.

On the tranquil shore of Hungary's Lake Balaton, near Siófok, Irena lay in the sun next to Dick. He told my mother that Irena was unlike any other woman he'd dated, that she was thoughtful, warm-hearted and drawn to people. I assume Irena initiated conversations with strangers – women in Budapest dance halls, swimming-capped ladies soaking in Siófok's thermal waters – and that she discussed Nazi leader Albert Forster's threats to annex Danzig, Dick's university town.[52]

Every day, tourists packed up and left. In nightclubs, dancing revellers dwindled. Fewer sailboats crossed the lake; the normally crowded shores emptied. Dick told me later that he worried they'd get stuck on the wrong side of the border if the Nazis followed through on their threats. He inquired about flights back to Poland, but they were all booked. Grasping his officer's card, he stood in a long line at the Polish Embassy. Countless phone calls later, an official offered Dick two seats.

On Kraków's market square, Dick and Irena dined with Alicja and Mietek at Havelka, where patrons spontaneously belted out patriotic songs. They raised vodka glasses and whooped, 'A toast to Poland!' Vodka helped mask the Hitler jitters, and besides, Dick wasn't eager to rush home.

Three days later, Dick and Irena feasted in Myślenice on the town's famed bacon. They soaked up the sun in the rolling hills near the resort town of Raba Wyżna, the Tatra Mountains looming behind. In a photo that he will smuggle through Auschwitz, Vaihingen and Dachau, that decades later will slip out of a letter he will address to my mother in Australia, Dick reclines on a rock. He nuzzles Irena's cheek and whispers in her ear. She leans back into his chest, slim and tanned in her swimming costume.

'The world seemed so beautiful and peaceful,' Dick wrote of those love-filled summer days. 'The danger of war did not seem real.'

For my mother, this photo marks the beginning of a life that grounded her. She had discovered her parents. Her roots. Today when I look at this photo, I see a woman with a heart as big as my mother's, eyes as deep. Perhaps this is key to me knowing Irena. To turn her from ghost to flesh and blood. It strikes me that if I am to truly understand Alicja's grief at losing Irena, I must look more at my mother.

But the funny thing about that photo is that Mietek snapped it, according to Dick. The two men came together debating Freud and Kant. In this way, at least, they were alike. Dick valued books over nice things but fell for pretty girls, cabaret and bawdy theatre. Mietek preferred symphony, dancing in hotel ballrooms and playing cards while picnicking with his parents. When Dick laughed, it was a boom; Mietek had more of a gentlemanly chuckle.

Alicja mentioned that Irena had visited her once in Kraków, but she said nothing about Dick accompanying her. She said nothing of Mietek driving Dick, his new friend, to the mountains in his sporty car. Nothing about Dick's friendship with Mietek and how they kept each other alive in the camps. Perhaps Alicja simply wanted to forget.

By August, Alicja was sweating in Kraków's stifling heat. It was so hot, men and women dipped in the Vistula River to stay cool, then walked home through the streets in bathing suits.[53] While German troops ringed Poland's borders, overheated merrymakers partied in nightclubs. They swayed their hips and danced to 'The Lambeth Walk', snapped their fingers, shouted, 'It'll be all right – just wait and see!'[54]

On 22 August, City Hall ordered everyone to dig air-raid shelters. Men, women and children shovelled through the sultry night, digging up squares, parks and vacant lots. Mothers sewed address tags onto children's clothing.[55]

On Friday 1 September, Alicja heard gunfire. People rushed to their windows. The Germans dropped bombs on Kraków's train station and army buildings along Rakowicka Street.[56] Alicja sat glued to the radio in a daze.

'And then it was the war,' she would tell me years later. 'That was the end, really.'

This, of course, is an understatement. Her way of toning down what happened next.

On 1 September at around five in the morning, Dick yawned and stepped out onto his balcony. The night before, revellers had packed into jazz clubs, cabarets and cinemas despite German bombs dropped near the airport. In Otwock, the Luftwaffe had bombed targets near the Przygoda sanatorium, killing seven children at the Centos healthcare clinic.[57]

Dick had heeded government warnings – he'd crisscrossed his apartment windows with tape to prevent them from shattering. Others carried on as normal. Outside Warsaw's five-star Bristol Hotel, guests reclined in wicker chairs and ignored the air-raid sirens.[58] Butlers kept up a flurry of cocktails, carrying out trays loaded with drinks. Around the corner from Dick's apartment, people lined up to withdraw cash at the Bank Polski. Others rushed off with large bags to butchers and grocery stores to stock up.

On the balcony, Dick tensed. Air-raid sirens revved and swelled to a bone-chilling yowl. Dick heard planes droning. He looked up at the sky. He thought they were Polish,[59] then spotted black swastikas on the tails. He rushed inside and ducked under a table. Warsaw was under attack.

That morning and for weeks after, explosions thudded after a shrill whistling in the sky. Bricks, glass and concrete exploded into the streets. 'I immediately took my motorbike and drove to pick up my mother,' Dick would write in his memoir, thinking Helena – who lived alone after Władyslaw's sudden death the year prior – would be safer if he delivered her to Otwock, away from Poland's capital. Meanwhile, his fiancée, Irena, was shaking behind blacked-out windows at her parents' apartment a kilometre from his. Perhaps his mother merited first place because she was older. Regardless, he left Irena with her family.

Ashen-faced women fleeing Warsaw streamed down Otwock's main road. They pushed prams and tugged children by the hand. When Dick parked his motorbike at his Aunt Gustawa's Hotel Śródborowianka, she begged him to stay. Vats of soup were simmering in the hotel's kitchen. Helena and Gustawa dished out bowls to tired families lining up outside.

Dick left his mother, jumped on his motorbike and headed back towards Warsaw like a fish swimming upstream. Cars blared horns on roads jammed with fire engines, taxis and ambulances.[60] Refugees from the west headed towards Warsaw. Those fleeing aerial bombardment swarmed out of the city, bent over carrying sacks and suitcases. They walked beside bicycles. They dragged dogs on leashes. They tugged the odd cow on a rope.

Dick heard a rumbling in the sky. It turned in to a roar. He swerved his motorbike off the road, then ran, leaping for cover. He heard shouts and screams. German planes were tracking the ground, diving low, propellers roaring. Dick covered his ears as machine-gun fire strafed the road. A plane banked over an open-sided train loaded with women and children. He heard the bomb shriek as it plummeted.

'There was complete chaos,' Dick wrote in his memoir. 'Earlier there had been an order for mobilisation. The order was then postponed under pressure from Poland's allies, France and England. Mr Chamberlain had led a futile campaign to appease Hitler, resulting in a horrible mess.'

Dick reported for duty. Before the government fled on 6 September, Poland's President and Commander in Chief, Marshal Śmigły-Ridz, had ordered men to travel east to launch a counteroffensive.[61] As an army officer, Dick had sworn allegiance to his now imperilled country, but some Jews, understandably, found uniting under the Polish banner difficult given the state's discriminatory laws.[62]

Dick marched with thousands of young men, next to his cousin, Aunt Gustawa's son, Henry Plucer-Sarna. When German panzer tanks closed on the Polish cavalry, Dick's garrison moved south, past scorched fields and smouldering truck remnants. Seventy kilometres from Warsaw, in Garwolin, Dick dove into a haystack, dodging Nazi gunners firing from planes. The planes and German infantry set fire to Garwolin. Wherever the Lufwaffe flew, it walloped Poland's cavalry and outmoded tanks. Batteries of howitzers were trucked across Poland's border.[63] German troops surrounded Warsaw and mortared it, a viciously effective campaign augmented with thousands of bomb-dropping sorties.[64] The dome of St John's cathedral fell into a heap. The Philharmonic Hall where Alicja had taken piano lessons and attended concerts with her father crumpled into rubble and dust.[65]

Dick's unit disbanded. Returning to Warsaw, he stepped around broken glass and dead horses tethered to overturned wagons,[66] bloodied men and women splayed on streets. He passed red-brick chimneys poking above debris left after walls had crashed down. Photographs of smiling movie stars hung eerily on one exposed living room wall. It was difficult to breathe. A rotting stench cut through the dust.

When Dick reached his apartment, he stared at bricks protruding through gaping holes in the facade. A bookshelf teetered on the edge of his caved-in floor. Where was his drawing desk? Where was his engineering slide rule, his bed?

Dick reported to the Warsaw Command and crossed the Vistula River. He organised civilians who'd heeded official radio pleas to construct barriers.[67] The soldiers stopped men on the streets and handed them shovels. Hundreds of civilians joined in the digging. They shovelled deep trenches[68] in solidarity, for the most part – not a whiff of antisemitism.[69]

Dick and the diggers aimed to stop German tanks from entering the city. Soldiers tore up tram tracks and converted them into rows of protruding steel pylons to snarl tank treads. Meanwhile, doctors across the city struggled to tend to the over fifty thousand critically wounded, the hospitals having been bombed and levelled.[70] 'The only glimmer of life came from the Polish Radio broadcasting the news from a basement location,' Dick remembered.

On 1 October, Hitler's Wehrmacht troops marched into Warsaw from the west.[71] Trams stood abandoned in empty streets. The Germans allowed no-one to leave. There was no water, no electricity, no gas. Cobblestones were stained red as garnets.

13

While bombs pummelled Warsaw and Kraków's airport, railway station and army buildings,[72] Mietek dug in his heels. 'He didn't want to leave when the Germans came,' Alicja said. 'He didn't believe that what was happening would last more than a few days.'

On 6 September, German soldiers marched into the city and circled Kraków's Rynek Square.[73] They zipped around on motorbikes, handing out lollies to children, filming the scenes to send back to Germany.

Black trucks and tanks festooned with the white Balkenkreuz[74] rumbled into Kraków.[75] From the south, soldiers in drab, grey Nazi uniforms strutted in columns, boots rising, heels slamming down: *Rapt! Rapt! Rapt!* Bystanders glared, stone-faced. A Jewish Krakówian with a long beard stood mute on a street corner, his eyes boring into the ground.

The next day, posters went up decreeing an early evening curfew for Jews. Despite Alicja's religious ambivalence, she would have bristled when the Nazis ordered synagogues to close. And when German officers evicted wealthy Jewish families from their homes and moved in, rolled up carpets and carted out valuable oil paintings for the Reich,[76] Alicja would have been furious.

But Mietek had already snapped. Around 2 September, after the Germans had captured Polish soldiers on Kraków's streets and citizens began looting shops and smashing into municipal warehouses for sugar, cigarettes, canned food and vodka,[77] Mietek crammed their suitcases into his car. He and Alicja hatched a plan to drive 330 kilometres to Lwów.[78] Mietek's father, Abe, accompanied them. His mother had died from surgery complications earlier that year. Mietek hoped his university contacts in Lwów and Abe's business connections might help him find work.

Abe and Alicja squeezed into the car between suitcases and satchels. As Mietek inched forward, thousands jostled in the streets alongside them carrying bags, women grasping children's hands. When Mietek finally reached Kraków's outskirts, two Polish officers waved their arms, gesturing him to pull over.

'You can't drive this car,' the officers sneered, perhaps intending to commandeer it for their own escape.

Mietek showed the officers his registration papers. Everything was in order, Mietek told them. His name was noted as the owner. He'd polished the car's headlights and bonnet so shiny you could see your face if you leaned over it. But it didn't matter. 'Officers saw the car and Jews in it,' Alicja said later. 'They took the car away!'

While Alicja stood on the roadside fuming, Mietek lifted out their suitcases. What should she carry? A trinket from Mama? A favourite pair of shoes? How about the photos? This is how loss feels. Choosing what's important. Should she take the poetry book? Maybe a coat?

Hours later, blisters bit into Alicja's toes. She rubbed at her ankles. The ache in her shoulders turned to searing pain. She put down her suitcase and shook out her fingers. Switching the case to her opposite hand, she wondered how long Mietek's sixty-two-year-old father would last.

Alicja plodded on, as if in a trance. She bumped against children hoisted on mothers' hips, some strapped in cloth slings. With no radio or telephone, she worried about her parents. Passing through villages, she'd picked up news snippets and learned of the bombs dropping on Warsaw. Had her family fled, too? By train, on foot? Were they alive? Where would they go – to Otwock? Alicja passed another cabbage field. Potato patches. A small village.

A few miles further, Mietek noticed a farmer standing next to a horse hitched to a wagon. 'How much would you take for your horse?' Mietek tipped his hat at the farmer. If his father could stretch out in the dray, he might make it.

Alicja scrutinised the horse. Swaybacked, it looked old and underfed. Its hipbones protruded like coat hangers. She listened as the farmer assured Mietek the animal was placid, that it could easily manage hauling their load. Mietek knew a lot about cars, Alicja told me, nothing of horses. But in that moment, the horse was the most beautiful thing Mietek had ever seen. He settled on a price, counted out złoty notes, then hoisted their suitcases into the wagon. He guided Abe up the step, into the passenger row.

Back on the road, Alicja walked slowly beside the horse, while Mietek pulled at the reins, coaxing it to move forward. 'It was an old, sick horse that wouldn't walk properly,' Alicja said.

Miles later, she heard humming and looked up. She saw black swastikas painted on aeroplane tails, a gunner in the glass cockpit looking down. Mietek was tugging at the terrified horse, begging it to move it off the road. Then a plane banked and plunged. People screamed, scattered like ants, leapt into ditches and dashed towards trees. Mietek and Alicja dived into the long grass.

The sky howled. Planes circled, swarming like wasps. *Rat-tat-tat-tat-tat!* Bullets ripped into men, children, women. 'And cows,' Alicja said later. 'They shot cows so people wouldn't have food.'

She lay in a ditch and waited until the buzzing faded, the planes disappearing into black dots in the distance. But then they turned. The bombers were coming back. Corkscrewing like hawks, they plummeted towards her and strafed the ground. The staccato of bullets nearly deafened her.

Eventually, Alicja and Mietek stood up, shaking. Mietek yelled out to his father, relieved when he saw Abe's head pop up in the field. Around them, bodies lay flecked with blood and dirt.

Days later, the horse slowed to an alarming hobble. It lowered its head, then refused to budge a step further. Mietek unhitched the horse from the wagon, while Alicja rummaged through their bags. She culled what she could stuff into pockets and sling over her shoulder. Trudging towards Lwów, she looked back at the horse on the roadside. She thought it might just topple over.

After they staggered into Lwów, filthy and exhausted, Abe and Mietek had trouble tracking down business acquaintances and college friends. It turned out that after Soviet soldiers on white horses[79] with a penchant for rape and plunder had trumpeted social liberation for the toiling masses, subsequently business owners, professors, aristocrats and lawyers – the kinds of people Abe and Mietek had hoped to connect with – feared being carted off to Siberian gulags.[80] They'd vanished.

Before Germany invaded Poland, the Soviets signed a non-aggression pact that sanctioned manoeuvres across a vast expanse of Europe – Poland, Romania, Lithuania, Latvia, Estonia, Belarus, Ukraine and Finland – in return for advantageous territorial realignments. Soon, the NKVD Soviet secret police,[81] would be knocking on doors across Lwów offering rewards for neighbours to turn in their neighbours.[82] People hid their jewellery and fur coats in attics and cupboards so as not to appear wealthy. They ripped holes in their clothing and invited family and strangers to move in with them.

But when Mietek knocked on doors, he was told, 'There is no room here.' With night closing in, Mietek persisted. Finally, the widow of a Jewish dentist led him inside. Mietek counted out notes. Then the woman handed him a key to a small room in a tenement building.

'We came in with nothing, just what we had on,' Alicja explained. 'So this woman thought we were beggars. The people there treated us very badly, because we didn't belong. *She* was just the same, this woman,' Alicja sneered.

To picture the Alicja I knew, coiffed hair and painted finger-nails, petticoated chain circling her rose-scented neck. To see her like this: standing in the doorway of a slum building in Lwów, face streaked with dirt, dress and stockings torn – her humiliation mortifies me.

14

Three hundred kilometres from Lwów, Basia the caretaker unlocks the enormous steel gate for me. I follow her into the Jewish cemetery, behind an eighty-seven-year-old man I've only recently met. Wearing a tan baseball cap and coke-bottle glasses, Fredek walks gingerly along the mown grass trail, wrists clasped behind his back, jeans and an oversized shirt billowing off his reedy frame.

Fredek is Mietek's cousin. When I arrived in Nowy Sącz a few days ago, he was evasive. He skirted my questions about Mietek. Instead, we toured the medieval market square. We drove to a spa town in the Beskid Mountains. We visited cafés. It might have been when we were licking ice-cream cones when Fredek remembered that, as a boy, he'd hurtled along a back road near Kraków in Mietek's aerodynamic, dorsal-finned Tatra. Buffed shiny, the car looked part Batmobile, part VW bug. It zoomed at up to 150km/h.

Mietek's obsession with cars lasted a lifetime. When I was a girl, a new car would show up in his garage every few years. Before he let me squish into seats that smelled like my saddle, my grandfather would make me wash my hands. But later, during the weeks, he would sit in his blue velvet chair as still as a hummingbird, his memories whirring while his beloved car remained stationary. Oil seeped from the engine and stained the garage floor.

Two days after I arrived in Nowy Sącz, Fredek finally began talking. We were drinking tea on his townhouse balcony with his companion, Dorota. Fredek pointed out aunts and uncles in old photos. A car sped by. Birds twittered. But then mid-sentence, he stood up and went inside.

'He fears the neighbours will hear,' Dorota whispered.

I learned that in 1939 when the Germans entered the town of Sanok, halfway to Lwów, Fredek's parents urged him to flee. Aged fourteen, he ran for the forest and crossed into Soviet territory. Later he tried joining the Polish Army who were cooperating with the Soviets to fight Germany[83] but they denied him on the grounds he was Jewish. Ultimately, Fredek joined Commander Zygmunt Berling's Polish forces in exile by switching his last name for one that included the letters 'szcz'. A Slavic name. The name he still uses today.

At war's end, people in Sanok chased him from town. Upon learning his parents were gassed in the Belzec extermination camp, he moved with the army around Poland. But Fredek had disappeared. From then on, everyone knew him as Edward.

During my visit, his moods varied. This morning, my last day, he brimmed with a strange energy. He recommended I read Jan Gross's *Neighbours* about the 1941 Jedwabne massacre of Polish Jews by their non-Jewish neighbours. 'If you want to understand Poland,' Fredek said, 'you have to understand the history of the Jews.' Then he announced he wanted to take me to the cemetery.

Now we amble among the graves. Fredek says he used to come here with his survivor friend Jakub.[84] Although Fredek is not religious, the few occasions he celebrated Jewish holidays were with Jakub, whose two sisters the Nazis had shot. They lie buried somewhere here, along with young men and women the Nazis similarly murdered in the cemetery.[85]

In a far corner of the field, Basia opens the door of what appears to be a small temple with arched windows of dark glass screened with steel mesh.

'An Ohel,' Fredek whispers, as if we are still sitting on his balcony.

Inside, it smells of rotting leaves. Basia offers to take a photo in front of a famed Hasidic rabbi's tombstone. Fredek shakes his head and waves her away. But as we begin to leave, he changes his mind. I hand my camera to Basia.

In the photo, Fredek turns his head to me, his eyes wide. Behind us, hundreds of small pieces of paper that look to be prayer notes are scattered on a shelf. Fredek is beaming, my arm at his shoulder, his skin hanging loose on thin, albeit untattooed arms.

Three years after Basia snaps this picture, soldiers wearing black berets will stand to attention in a Catholic church, and escort Fredek's remains out for burial. But the name carved on his tombstone will not be Fredek. It will be EDWARD.

When I look at this photo, I sense Fredek handing his past off to me, like Dick and Alicja did. The weight of what they endured distresses me. What should I do with their stories tossing inside me? They sunder me. They flip me in different directions. *Look under that rock; take a train here; read this book; watch that video.* This while my husband emails from Boston: 'Just been to Costco to get a new humidifier and installed it in the basement.'

At times, I dread returning home to Boston. I am fortunate for many reasons. My husband is working. I have unused annual leave and no children to support. When I return home, I trust I will find a job with hours that allow me to keep researching. But I also know I will have to examine my notes and discoveries. Sift them for clues. Toss out what's noise. Look deeper. Despite my rigorous searching in Poland, there are things I don't know. Mysteries I may never unravel. Who are these people I love, *really*? How did their resourcefulness, their pain and their courage shape them? How did it shape me?

I'm not sure I fully understand yet why this is so important. Maybe I am searching for me.

15

In October 1939, Dick stood in a long line outside a Warsaw municipal building feeling wretched. It was cold. He'd been waiting for hours. A month after Germany invaded, the phone lines were still cut, so he didn't know if his mother had survived the bombings. He was desperate to cycle to Otwock to find out, but the Germans now required permits for travel outside the city.

Every day the occupiers imposed new rules. Hitler installed his personal legal advisor,[86] Hans Frank, as Poland's Governor General. German troops prowled the city streets, grabbing men and women, bundling them into trucks headed to labour camps. Officers ordered Jews to clear roads of debris.[87] German officials took over Warsaw's public and private institutions, the railways, building offices, the schools. Weeks earlier, elegant women had shopped at fashionable boutiques along Nowy Świat and Aleje Jerozolimskie. Now people waited in long lines outside soup kitchens. They crowded pavements selling pots, pans and household goods – anything in order to buy food.[88]

Dick overheard two men ahead of him in the queue speaking in animated tones. A well-dressed civil engineer[89] and a Warsaw Building Department inspector were gesturing at a German officer. Always on the lookout for contacts that might come in handy, Dick pushed his way closer. 'Kann ich Sie helfen?' — *Can I help?* he asked the officer.

The officer nodded, relieved he'd found someone who could speak German. He explained to Dick he wanted the building repaired for his soldiers. After translating for the men, Dick handed out three business cards, then shrank back to his place down the line.

A few days later, he was stepping gingerly around rubble that was once his apartment, rummaging for items he could save, when he heard someone yell his name. The building's janitor poked his head through a hole. 'There's a German downstairs looking for you!'

Outside, a German in uniform stood waiting.

'Zdzisław Przygoda?'

'Yes.'

'Come with me.'

Dick climbed into a car with the German, who drove to a large building that had been damaged by bombs. Dick noticed a convoy of trucks and a gang of men unloading sheets of glass.

'You will help restore this building, and others, for our men,' the officer told Dick, pointing out the newly requisitioned soldiers' quarters.

Dick felt lucky. One of the business cards he'd handed out while standing in the queue had made its way to Warsaw's mayor, Major Stefan Starzyński, commander of the failed defence of Warsaw. Dick's networking, brazenness and cocksure attitude that Alicja so detested had proved in this case a godsend. The officer explained that Dick would function as Starzyński's liaison engineer between the Wehrmacht's Warsaw military commander,[90] General Karl-Ulrich von Neumann-Neurode,[91] and the Building Department.

The next day, Dick showed up to work. The irony that his job in the now German-occupied city was located in a Polish Army building wasn't lost on him. He shook hands with the civil engineer he'd met standing in line, who ushered him into a room and directed him to a desk. Next door, the sixty-three-year-old General von Neumann-Neurode and his aide-de-camp worked their phones. Dick could observe the constant flow of German officers and Polish officials who dropped by for appointments.

At the building site of the new Wehrmacht headquarters, von Neumann-Neurode pointed to long-bearded glaziers.[92] 'The glassworkers are all Jewish,' Dick told the general, who looked surprised. 'It's a tradition! It's the same with the electrical workers. But don't worry,' Dick grinned, 'the carpenters are all Catholic.'

Caught completely off guard, at first the general was silent. According to Dick, the general assumed[93] all Jews were rich and corrupt merchants. 'He was typical Prussian officer,' Dick said of the general's political and militaristic astuteness. 'He didn't like Hitler,' Dick remarked, having listened in on the general's conversations from his office next door. 'He was not a bad man.'

Von Neumann-Neurode watched the glaziers studiously measuring and cutting glass to fit the blown-out windowpanes. When the Nazis later declared rationing, the general would double the glazier's food.

If Dick's advocacy for Jewish workers caused von Neumann-Nuerode to suspect he was Jewish, the general gave nothing away. He'd issued Dick a bona fide work card even though in mid-October the Nazis had frozen Jewish bank accounts.[94] Despite these financial limitations, Dick considered himself fortunate. His chiselled, slender nose, fine eyebrows and lighter hair helped him pass as Polish–Catholic. He 'looked good', as was the expression used to describe Jews of Slavic appearance.[95] Dick represented the minority of Warsaw's assimilated Jews who spoke Polish with no detectable trace of Yiddish or Hebrew.[96] Regardless of Dick's linguistic credentials and perfect German, every day he risked exposure.

One day, Dick walked into von Neumann-Neurode's office to exploit a loophole. He convinced the general to stamp exit permits in ten passports belonging to his father's medical friends, available only to those holding Italian or Japanese visas. Perhaps the general was too busy to scrutinise names, or there were none like Goldberg or Samuel: names more easily recognised as Jewish.

On another occasion, Dick was walking to work when he noticed his parents' friend, Dr Janusz Korczak, leading a column of his orphans. Korczak had taught four-year-old Dick to speak Polish during the Russian revolution[97] when serving at a field hospital in Ukraine with Dick's father, and was revered for his revolutionary teaching methods to elevate children. Korczak was a pseudonym for Henryk Goldszmit. Like Dick's parents, he was Jewish, and assimilated.

Dick watched as Korczak's children snaked around armoured vehicles and machine-gun-wielding soldiers towards the Unknown Soldier's tomb at the Saxon Palace. Korczak knelt at the tomb. Dick stood back. He watched the children laying flowers. Moved by this provocative act, Dick whispered to Korczak, 'I can arrange papers for your escape from Poland.'

'Are you crazy?' hissed Korczak. 'I would never leave my children. Go and help someone else!'

Dick knew people who could secure papers for Korczak, but I find it odd he did not use those same connections to secure papers for himself and Irena.

'This was the last time I saw Korczak,' Dick would write later. 'He was gassed in Treblinka together with his two hundred children.'

Remorse can be a powerful editor. That Dick was fond of his parents' friend and wanted to save him is without question. More than fifty years later, Dick would send me books about Korczak and books written by him, such as *King Matt the First* that's still read in Polish schools today. He would write me letters explaining Korczak's teaching methods, stressing his selfless sacrifice. But I find his devotion to Korczak and the fact he abandoned his own child – my mother – difficult to reconcile.

❋

In October, the German security police ordered the establishment of a Jewish Council of Elders, the Judenrat, headed up by engineer and former senator Adam Czerniaków, and for it to conduct[98] a census. In all, 359,827 Warsaw Jews were counted. Then on 4 November, an event occurred that would change everything. SS-Standartenführer Dr Rudolf Baatz announced General von Neumann-Neurode's decree: within three days all Jews must move into a concentrated, mapped-out area.[99] To speed up relocations, the SS snapped up twenty-four Jews and held them hostage.[100]

The next day, Dick watched three Judenrat leaders walk into the general's office, hats in hand, clearly bypassing the SS and police. He strained his ears to listen.

'I never issued a decree of this kind,' the general said to the portly Czerniaków,[101] after hearing details of separating thousands of families and the epidemic risks from living in such crowded conditions. 'It must be a mistake, this is barbarism!'[102] Von Neumann-Neurode then rose to consult with the Gestapo.

Later, he returned to the room. 'It was a misunderstanding,' he said, avoiding the Jewish leader's bespectacled eyes. 'I did issue the decree, but not like that. Please go home, don't worry, and tell your people there is nothing to fear. Let everyone stay where they are, calmly.'

But Dick wasn't calm. That evening, he relayed the valuable news to Irena's father, now that he and his mother, Helena, had moved into Irena's parents' apartment. When Eljasz heard about the segregation plan and of the thirty thousand Jews desperately seeking apartment floors to sleep on, he brushed it off as rumour – Irena and Dorota would be perfectly safe staying put in Orla Street.

The next week,[103] Dick's qualms eased. The SS released the hostages. But two weeks on, they erected barbed-wire fences at street entrances to the Jewish district. Signs appeared: Infection. Entry banned to soldiers.[104] News of the fences spread like wildfire.

It never would have occurred to Dick that he would marry Irena in the dark. At number eleven Orla Street, the shutters were closed and the curtains tightly drawn. After the 9 pm curfew, Nazi soldiers would shoot at any windows emitting light.[105]

Dick tried to block out thoughts of the Germans. Outside, the streets were a sea of white bands bearing the blue Star of David wrapped around people's right arms.[106] The occupiers had marked shops with yellow stars. If Irena had wanted to pronounce her vows in the synagogue around the corner, she couldn't. It would draw too much attention.

In the apartment, Dick would have smiled at his mother. But what of Alicja? Had she been able to send letters from Lwów, or managed to get through by telephone?

Maybe Irena, a twenty-one-year-old bride, wore a long dress, a two-stranded pearl necklace on her neck. Any photos taken that day did not survive. Not a single one.

'The ceremony was witnessed by both our families,' Dick would write later. 'It was the last occasion I saw my family all together.'

One evening in December, Dick handed a wad of cash to a Polish police officer, watching as he hastily stuffed the notes into

his jacket. He hoped the friend who'd tipped him off was right about bribing this man. The following night, wrapped in a warm coat and gloves, Dick waited with Irena as the policeman had instructed. The frigid air stuck in his throat. With electricity and gas supplies damaged during the bombing not yet fully restored, darkness blanketed the street.[107] Dick scanned around for looters, and for German police patrolling in the shadows.

When a car pulled up to the kerb, Dick peered inside and locked eyes with the policeman. Dick signalled to Irena. She slid into the back seat.

'I'll drive you over the border, to the Soviet zone,' the policeman said.

Dick kept his face straight. Days earlier he'd failed to cross the border with Irena, at Malkinia station around 100 kilometres northeast of Warsaw. Only his work card had helped them escape the Polish-speaking Silesian–German soldiers who beat Jews with truncheons.

Now, as they neared the edge of the city, Dick wondered what General von Neumann-Neurode would think when he didn't show up to work. He hadn't dared ask the general for exit visas; von Neumann-Neurode might suspect him as Jewish. Irena's parents may have downplayed the fences and armbands, but Dick, on the other hand, feared the worst. He'd observed the SS manoeuvring around the general's perceived softness towards concentrating Jews into a ghetto.[108] Dick knew that his influence, along with the general's, was waning.

The police officer pulled over and dropped them off at the edge of a forest. Ankle-deep snow soaked Irena's shoes.[109] Frozen pine needles crunched underfoot, unnerving them. The recently wed couple crouched under the pines and watched as the car drove away.

When they emerged from the trees, it was eerily quiet. Dick was carrying a bag, Irena a loaf of bread, maybe kielbasa sausage wrapped in brown paper. With these meagre supplies they hustled in the direction of the border. But on the horizon, head-lights suddenly lit up the road, splaying wiry shadows on the trees. Dick froze. He singled out not one set of lights, but a long convoy of vehicles. Black trucks were growling towards them. Dozens of soldiers seated in the back clutched their guns.

Soon, Dick was lying flat in a ditch next to Irena, their hearts pounding like horse's hooves. The lump in his throat wasn't fear, it was fury – the policeman hadn't dropped them over the border at all! His friend had been wrong. The policeman had conned them.

On the long walk back to Warsaw, Dick dragged his feet. He wracked his brain. Whom could he trust now to plot a new escape? Rumours abounded in Dick's circles. You thought someone was your ally, but then non-Jewish friends switched allegiance, thanks partly to the Nazi propaganda machine dis-seminating newsreels with stories of Jews collaborating with the Gestapo. The Nazi-backed *Nowy Kurjer Warszawski* newspaper splashed preposterous headlines across its front pages, featuring pictures of enormous-nosed men unearthing caches of machine guns from coffins.[110]

Dick was known as a man of his word. He was proud of it. Tonight, a Polish policeman had swindled him, but it could have been worse; the officer could have taken his money and reported him to the Gestapo. He'd need to sharpen up.

It didn't take him long. A few days later, he sat on a train next to Irena. Once again they were speeding towards Malkinia, near a branch in the line leading to a tiny logging station called Treblinka. Dick's best friend's brother, Janek Stamieszkin, sat on his other side. If Irena's dark hair and eyebrows shaped like lilac blossoms were a slight giveaway, Janek's enormous nose and big ears gave Dick the jitters. But Dick had promised his friend he'd look out for Janek.

When the train pulled up to Malkinia, there was mayhem. SS soldiers screamed at the panicked crowds. They poked them with weapons. 'Links!' — *Left, go left!* an SS officer yelled, ordering Jews to one side. Dick led Irena and elbowed his way from the carriage. In the melee, people stamped on toes and kicked shins. 'Stick close to me,' hissed Dick to Janek.

On the platform, an SS officer hooked eyes on Janek. He pointed his stick. Dick turned back. He pulled his work-identity card from his pocket. 'Dieser Mann arbeitet für mich!' — *This man works for me!* With one hand, he pointed at Janek. He shook the card with the other.

The officer took the card, glanced at Dick then snapped to attention and handed Dick the card back. He motioned Janek to go to the right.

Outside, Irena, Dick and Janek tried regrouping, but thousands pushing and shoving swept them into the crowd. Everyone was headed for the same place, to the border crossing a few kilometres away, in no-man's-land, as the refugees referred to the long strip between German and Soviet lines. It would be easy to become trapped there. They could starve or freeze to death, if soldiers didn't shoot them first.[III]

The mob heaved around them like cattle trying to squeeze through a narrow gate. Soviet soldiers charged their horses at the crowd. The screams were deafening. Men and women fell, bones cracking. Army dogs gnashed teeth and snapped at legs. Troops drove the mob back from the border.

Hours later, Dick grabbed Irena's hand just before the swell sucked him back in. The crowd surged once again. Dick found himself fanned towards the edge. He stumbled. He ran with Irena until sweat dripped down their backs. Until the border was in the distance behind them.

In the dark, they picked their way through shrubbery and over logs. More than a day later, they walked into Białystok, exhausted but relieved. Germany had conceded the Polish city to the Soviets under the Molotov-Ribbentrop pact.[112] Now the streets teemed with unbathed refugees like Dick and Irena, many itching from lice. Dick asked around for directions to his university friend's apartment. When he knocked on the door, his friend clasped his hand and beamed. He pointed them to a bed. Dick crawled under the sheets with Irena and closed his eyes. Tomorrow, he promised her, they would catch a train to Lwów. Tomorrow, Irena would hug her sister.

16

Picture with me if you will the reunion in a third-floor, low-ceilinged Lwów tenement room. Alicja clutched Irena's shoulders while Mietek slapped Dick on the back.

'Ma? How is she really?' Alicja asked Irena, blinking back tears.

This was a pivotal moment – Dick and Alicja linked for life, like silver melted into gold – despite Alicja's reservations at Irena's rushed marriage.

Irena, too tired to notice the worry lines on Alicja's face, pulled her arms from her coat. 'Father told Mama not to be anxious, so she says she's fine.'

Alicja shifted her eyes. She hoped Irena didn't sense her alarm. On the road from Kraków she'd watched Germans shooting from planes killing women the same age as Mama. What's more, the papers were full of stories of violence against Jews. Tens of thousands of refugees streaming into Lwów every day from Warsaw, Łódź, Kraków and Radom recounted horrific stories.[113]

Alicja hung Irena's coat in a cupboard that loomed large in the small room that smelled of earth and beetroot.

'So, you found work?' Dick asked Mietek. He was keen to rekindle the camaraderie of their escapade near Kraków, joking over whiskey, puffing cigarettes, debating Nietzsche.

'I have a very difficult job,' said Mietek. 'All the thinking gives me a headache.'

Alicja rolled her eyes at her husband and reached for a pot on the stove.

'I'm a chauffeur for a Dr Lachs,' Mietek told Dick. He explained how he drove the doctor around town in his car, often choosing longer routes to avoid the NKVD who'd been arresting Polish officers and policemen.[114] Intellectual 'elites' like his boss would be next.

Dick wondered if he'd have to settle for manual work, too. He planned first to track down his father's friends in Lwów, to plot their escape to Australia. Before the Nazis invaded, with Irena's sister-in-law's words ringing in his ears, he'd applied for visas, but the nearest Australian consulate was in Romania.

'I'm taking classes at the Lwów Household Academy.' Alicja poured tea. A family friend had helped secure her a spot. 'I wash all our clothes now,' she added, smiling, lifting her chin. Perhaps she neglected to mention the shimmering evening frocks she'd left in Kraków, and the sensible woollen dresses she'd left on the roadside like a shed skin, a few hundred kilometres from Lwów.

At the Academy, Alicja would remove laundry from her bag and collect water in a tub. They taught her how to scrub garments between her fists, how to pull then push the clothes to the bottom. She would carry the dried folded clothes home together with the occasional leftovers from cooking class, along cobblestoned roads and alleyways, up the stairs to her and Mietek's dark room.

As Alicja described this, Irena's mouth fell open in shock. This wasn't the sister who sent a boy from their father's factory to fetch books, the sister who asked the maid to cook her favourite borscht.

'It was my idea,' Alicja said. 'I really learned something: how to do the housework and how to cook. But later, there was nothing to cook.'

In March 1940, Mietek ripped open a letter sent via Moscow[115] from Stella in Australia. By now, his father, Abe, had left for the mountains to live with his sister-in-law.[116] Dick was at work, driving a truck filled with vodka for the J A Baczewski distillery. So the two couples squeezed into one room, like matchsticks in a box, although Mietek longed to leave for the mountains to be closer to Abe. Instead, he'd been running around town begging for work, as his boss, Dr Lachs, had left Lwów, possibly fearing an NKVD round-up.[117] Poof! Just like that: no more Dr Lachs, no more job! Mietek was willing to dirty his hands even working on a farm or in a factory, but thanks to his father's connections, he'd just landed a new position as manager for Kankprom, a chemical cooperative.[118]

Mietek devoured Stella's letter, eager for news. He read that Stella's husband, Paul, a lawyer like him, had found work as the director of an arsenic and toilet paper factory. Stella did not mention his and Alicja's Australian visa applications. Fifteen thousand spaces[119] had been allocated for Jews fleeing Europe – that's how Stella and Giza had sailed there. How could Mietek convince the immigration authorities to admit them, too? A job reference, English fluency, something else that might bolster their case? Mietek grabbed his coat and bolted out the door. He rushed to the telegraph office.

Back at the apartment, he penned a letter to Stella on lined graph paper. 'I've given up being a chauffeur,' he wrote. 'I'm supposed to engage myself in a chemical factory (inks, etc.), as assistant to the previous owner and current director. As a long-time worker for Pelikan [fountain pen and ink manufacturer], I am completely qualified, and besides it is less tiring work.' He was qualified to work at Paul's toilet paper factory in Australia, too.

Mietek kept his tone flat, not a trace of fear. He didn't mention the piano in their Kraków living room that SS officers were in all likelihood now playing. He didn't mention bombs and books crashed on the floor. He didn't want to scare Stella. 'Too bad we don't have a big enough radio to hear your violin concert today,' he teased, given the Australian authorities had denied his sister Sydney and Melbourne Symphony Orchestra positions. As a 'refugee alien' they allowed her to perform only on radio.

'My Dear!' Alicja saluted Stella underneath Mietek's curvaceous script. 'No change with us . . . I'll soon be a certified chef. It's too bad you can't taste my excellent tea cakes and biscuits etc.'

'PS,' Mietek added, as if to say: a small inconvenience you shouldn't worry about too much, my dear Stella, but please help get us out of this mess: 'Please contact Mr M and Uncle Z. They can do a lot about our matter.'

Stella's silence on Australian visas may have been intentional. Maybe she couldn't bear breaking the news to Mietek that after Hitler's attack on Poland, Australia's Jewish visa program had ground to a halt.

In Lwów, my grandmother adapted. On early spring mornings, Alicja would arrange her hair in waves, pull on her stockings and fire up the wood stove to make Mietek coffee.

Mietek loved that his clever wife had found someone on the black market to sell her coffee, a rarity. He admired her new street savvy and verve, how she stood in alleyways picking up snippets of gossip. You never knew what she would bring home at the end of the day. But if the NKVD caught her, they would deport them both to Siberia.

After breakfast, Alicja left the apartment and hurried past shuttered shops, their shelves stripped bare back when Soviet soldiers paid with roubles or stole boxes and sacks full of produce. She joined glum-faced people in a queue that snaked around the corner of the block.

Alicja lined up for rations for only two, since Dick and Irena had moved to a Franciscan monastery in the Polish spa town of Morszyn in the Carpathian foothills. Thanks to a meeting with a friend of Dick's father, Dick was building gas lines for the Soviets.

'Mustard,' a woman further up the queue mumbled.

Alicja's cravings for eggs were dashed. 'You had to stand in a queue all day and sometimes night for one thing,' she said later.

The ration lines were exhausting. Often she would leave empty-handed. She tugged at her fur coat. The cold numbed her toes. She bunched up to women in front and behind her to lessen the draughts.

By summer, Lwów's heat frayed tempers. It strained access to fresh water. It scorched Alicja as she lined up for bread. The heat exasperated tens of thousands of refugees, crammed ten or more to a room. It was impossible to ignore the foetid smell of septic, un-showered bodies wafting up from the street into the crevices of their quarters.

Summer blurred into autumn. Alicja, like almost everyone in Lwów, thought about food. One evening, Mietek returned from work and found Alicja lying in bed, her teeth chattering, the covers pulled up to her chin. Mietek touched her arm. Her skin was so hot he flinched and pulled back his hand. Alicja could not sleep. The next morning the sheets were soaking wet. Her head pounded. Her distended stomach hurt. Mietek dressed and hovered over her. He pulled on his coat and left to fetch a doctor.

A week later, Alicja lay in a hospital bed in a long room, fading in and out of delirium, her body speckled in a red rash. She opened her eyes to see nuns in white linen habits sponging her forehead with cool water.

Meanwhile, NKVD men paced the streets. They asked refugees eager to return home, and others who'd refused Soviet citizenship, for their names and addresses. At night, the NKVD knocked on doors. Mietek went into hiding. Alicja's Household

Academy friends didn't. The NKVD dragged some of Alicja's friends off to Siberia.

Luckily, the NKVD feared typhoid more than Hitler, and didn't dare barge into Alicja's hospital ward.

'They knew that I am Jewish,' Alicja told me about the nuns and doctors at the hospital.

'How did they know?'

'I suppose they just knew somehow . . .' She seemed puzzled I'd asked.

'That would have made you afraid?'

'No. It was all right,' she said, her voice resolute, as if the Soviets were pussycats.

She was surprised I would ask such simplistic questions. What did I know about hiding one's identity?

'If it had been the Germans, I wouldn't have survived,' she said, raising her voice. 'And I survived, as you can see.' She laugh-snorted.

I found her deference towards the Soviets confusing. She had subscribed us both to season tickets at the Melbourne Symphony Orchestra, but on the few occasions a Russian conductor was visiting she'd refused to go. She told me: 'I don't listen to Russians, because of the war.'

But we listened to German orchestras, and she owned a Blaupunkt TV. When I asked, she'd refused to elaborate.

17

With Alicja sufficiently recovered from typhoid, Irena and Dick were eager to check on her. Dick had negotiated one week away from work. In June 1941, he strolled along the tree-lined boulevard of Lwów's Legionów Street, the domed Municipal Theatre at one end soaring like a palace over the park.[120] He knocked elbows with Polish- and Yiddish-speaking citizens and refugees teeming along the thoroughfare. His eyes lit up at their chatter.

While the small spa town of Morszyn where Dick worked reminded him of his father's sanatorium, Lwów's city bustle energised him. In Morszyn, the Soviets had converted dozens of boarding houses into sanatoriums to treat stomach maladies.

The fact they fitted one out in luxury for Stalin's officers and Communist party officials appalled Dick. Meanwhile, the same Soviets were paying him to construct a theatre. He'd witnessed their tilt away from the masses to favour the elites. Officials had spared no expense chauffeuring a prima ballerina to Morszyn from Moscow in a white limousine!

Dick glowered at the Stalin and hammer-and-sickle banners afixed to Lwów's Municipal Theatre.[121] He marvelled at ornate gas lanterns and copper-topped cupolas casting shadows on market squares. Fountains crowned with statues reminded him of carefree days flirting outside cafés in Warsaw, but the sight of children begging in filthy, ripped trousers and pinafores and women hawking clothing to buy food unsettled him.

He was walking on Łyczakowska Street[122] when a display in a small food shop window caught his eye. He stopped and peered through the glass. Instead of jam jars and biscuit boxes, Dick noticed gold-trimmed Guenter Wagner fountain pens, a stack of drawing paper, a bottle of black Pelikan ink. Dick thought of the woodcuts he liked to print before Germany's bombs and tanks had bulldozed Poland apart, and of his drawings, how ink bled through the nib as he pressed it to paper, that solid feeling of stroking a pad with his pen. The weight of it. Dick pushed the door open and wandered in.

That night, Dick awoke startled, in a cold sweat. He heard a staccato rattle of machine-gun fire. Was it a dream? Then Irena rolled over and rubbed her eyes, her curls tousled. She heard gunfire, too.

'Wake Alicja and Mietek, then give me your papers,' Dick whispered.

Soon, their identity documents lay on the cramped apartment's table. Dick reached for the brown paper bundle holding his purchases from the previous day. He pulled out the black bottle of Pelikan ink.

He pointed at the official writing inside his Soviet passport. Black ink. 'Here,' Dick said. 'Where it says "nationality", I will scratch out the word "Yevrey". Instead of Jew, I will write Polish.'

Minutes ticked by. Dick scratched with his fingernail. He erased one letter. Another. Moved onto the next passort. The night passed slowly. Dick practised the curves of Cyrillic characters with his new fountain pen. When he felt ready, he pressed the pen against the first passport. Hours later, after altering the fourth set of papers, Dick wrapped up the ink bottle. He stashed it in a safe place.

Around 4 am, Dick jerked awake. He heard planes roaring overhead. The building shook. Windows shattered outside. You could barely hear the *pop, pop* of Soviet anti-aircraft fire against the thundering German artillery and Luftwaffe.[123]

The railway station went up in flames, killing hundreds. Words flew across hallways inside Alicja and Mietek's building, and all around town. 'We are finished now,' people said. 'The Russians are gone!'[124]

'They're shooting Jews!' one neighbour whispered.

Mietek and Dick would have sat by the radio, listening in between the static for news, but there was too much interference. For days, they kept the door locked. No-one dared step outside – Ukrainian Nationalists were shooting civilians from rooftops. Gangs looted shops. All over town Jews were hiding in basements, in workshops and in warehouses.

After the Soviets torched the Brygidki Prison, rumours spread quickly: 'Jews murdered the prisoners!' people claimed. Any sense of law and order evaporated. Young men wearing the Ukrainian militia's yellow and blue armbands soon roamed the streets, some emboldened to hack Jews with axes.[125] As the last of the Soviet troops evacuated the city, Ukrainians hopeful of winning back independence glued up posters calling for people to 'Smash the Jews and the Communists!'

It was morning when Dick heard rumbling outside. Wehrmacht units riding motorcycles buzzed down the avenue. Daimler-Benz tanks motored by, rattling windows,[126] acrid petrol fumes[127] seeped through the frames. Ukrainians lined the street yelling and cheering. Women rushed at German soldiers and thrust flowers into their arms.[128] Behind the Germans, Ukrainian Nachtigal battalions marched singing nationalist anthems. Then a mighty roar went up from the market square. They toppled the Soviet red star from the City Hall tower and in its place hoisted a swastika flag alongside the Ukrainian blue and yellow flag.

When Dick heard someone rapping on the door, he froze. Two Ukrainian militiamen wearing berets burst in.

'How many of you live here?' one barked.

Dick caught a flash of the dagger hanging from one man's belt.

'Four,' said Mietek, his face pale.

'Show us your papers!' The Ukrainian held Dick's papers up to the light. The tie of his uniform crimped his neck.

Dick gritted his teeth. He focused his breathing. The Ukrainian handed back the four sets of papers. Then the man saluted him.

Not long after, a door slammed across the hallway. Dick, Irena, Mietek and Alicja could hear loud thumps. Screams from apartments upstairs. Gunshots rang out. Ukrainian militiamen and civilians were dragging their neighbours onto the street.

Below their building and throughout town, children wailed. Men pulled the children's mothers by the hair and stripped off their clothing.[129] One man ran through the crowd striking Jews' heads with a metal cane[130] and poking their eyes. Boys in shirts and ties who should have been at school beat Jewish people with sticks. Women with hair neatly tied in buns laughed as they, too, beat Jews. Men pushed girls to the ground. They hitched up their skirts.

Two days later in the dark of evening, it was eerily quiet in Mietek and Alicja's building. Dick's clever forgery had saved them. Thousands of Jews had been killed.[131] Ukrainians led some to prison yards where they beat them. The SS shot others. Most of their neighbours had disappeared. 'They never came back,' Dick would later write in his letter to my mother.

Except one. The next morning, Dick heard shuffling in the hallway outside their room. He heard a muted gurgling, then a groan. He opened the door, just a crack. He saw a man spread across the hallway floor, writhing in pain. A thick red puddle pooled around him. The man gripped his stomach. His eyes bulged like marbles. Dick gaped at the glossy organs where assailants had slashed open the man's stomach. Then, the man was still.

It wouldn't be the last time Dick witnessed someone's eyes fade and roll back. It was a sign of what was about to happen to people he loved.

✳

When I was nineteen, my father recorded Dick in our lounge room telling us his story.

'Well, I treat you all as students. I make the chairman Roger,' Dick said as he peered over his notes at my father. 'Mr Chairman, ladies and gentlemen!' Dick bellowed, as if he were speaking at the UN. My thirteen-year-old brother squirmed in his chair at Dick's dignified baritone. 'I tell you a bit about my life, so you know a little of your heritage.'

About halfway in, Dick told us about those bloody July days in Lwów when over six thousand Jews were murdered.[132]

'The drawing ink saved our lives,' Dick said, stressing the word 'lives'. He paused. I noticed that faraway vacant stare. But then, he flipped the page and carried on.

I'd repeatedly asked my father to find those four cassette tapes. When I announced I was taking off for Poland, my cautious, methodical father didn't think me patient enough to endure such research. Eventually, he sent them. Now when I listen to Dick and Alicja's taped stories, they drain me. Even though they are dead, I feel a need to protect them both from pain.

I try to separate the historical events from the emotions their voices provoke, but walking the streets where they walked in Poland, when life was so unbearably hard, it's as though I've swallowed a bucket of lead. It presses hard on my stomach, turns my legs to rubber.

Before my trip, I'd emailed Aunt Giza's son to inquire about letters Alicja sent her. 'Enjoy your visit to Poland, but be careful not to get depressed there,' he wrote back. 'And do PREPARE yourself emotionally for your visit to Auschwitz. It is incredibly harrowing, and the experience will haunt and stay with you for YEARS.'

What haunts me more than my upcoming visit to Auschwitz, however, is the question of why Alicja turned against Dick when he'd saved her life and the life of her husband and sister that night in Lwów.

'I didn't know him much,' Alicja once said. Yet they had lived in the same tiny apartment. In the months and years to come, she and Mietek would be bonded to Dick. They would rely on him. They would beg him for help. Notably, Alicja told me about the drawing ink – one of the few times her account matches Dick's.

Alicja would never be able to admit Dick saved her. Maybe in her mind, the pain of Irena's death cancelled any good he did. Maybe it blocked out the memory of his bravery. Maybe Alicja could remember better how Dick's temper would later force her into horrible choices she would have to make. But that's another story, for later.

Alicja did tell me about what followed the Nazis' entry into Lwów. They mandated 'Kennkarte' for all residents, a grey passport document that included a photograph, fingerprints and stated the holder's 'religion'.[133] Applying for one would require a birth certificate – a dead giveaway revealing Alicja as Jewish. The Germans ordered Jews to wrap a blue Star of David around their upper arms.

'Ohhh, it was frightening. Terrible!' Alicja said. 'You were afraid not to wear the star.' She paused. She looked down, wanting to move the conversation on, it seemed. Then her eyes lit up. 'You know what I did? You *know* what I was doing?' She smiled like a child boasting about the 'A' they'd received at school. 'For a while, I was selling. You had to have job good enough so they don't send you to a camp. A good job was to sell old iron, because that was for German Army. I sold old pieces of things, kitchen things, all different things,' Alicja said, her voice lilting upward. 'So, I had this big sack on my arm – you know – holding like that with a few pieces, all this rubbish.' She guffawed, lifting her hand over her shoulder to demonstrate. 'And you could walk with this on the street. It was safe, because you were working for *German* Army!' She laughed, again.

My jaw dropped. I couldn't fathom *my* Alicja, *my* nana – who wore a gold filigree necklace around her tanned neck – picking through piles of rubble. She had no Kennkarte; her sack was her passport – freedom to roam. And a feeling of purpose.

I know nothing about how she found this job, what she had to do to get it, and if the German she managed to persuade knew she was Jewish. This was war. I know nothing about war.

With Germans guarding the border, Dick and Irena couldn't risk returning to Morszyn. Before leaving for their holiday, Dick had packed his General von Neumann-Neurode-issued work papers in his bag. In Alicja and Mietek's room, Dick began writing letters to army friends and to his father's contacts, applying for jobs in Lwów. Finally, he landed a job at the municipal sanitation department that managed the sewers. 'This enabled me to receive from the Germans an apartment,' Dick would write later. He and Irena packed up their few clothes and moved across town. Dick was now stuck in Lwów, 400 kilometres from home.

18

Early one autumn morning, Alicja kissed Mietek goodbye and scuttled down the street with a Jewish man she barely knew. Mietek had paid the man a hefty sum. The trip Alicja was about to take would last two days and cover 400 kilometres by coach and train. Gestapo men were everywhere. They would shoot her if they suspected she were Jewish. They were stopping people at roadblocks. They boarded trains and inspected papers. Alicja's courier told her that if the Gestapo approached them, he'd slip away and leave her alone. But none of this mattered. Alicja wanted to see her parents.

'It was really foolish,' she said later when she told me this story. 'But I believed in this fellow.'

Folded in the man's jacket pocket was his counterfeit Kennkarte. Alicja carried only her Soviet ID documents – the passport Dick had altered. Despite her courier's reputation for trafficking people along the dangerous route to Warsaw, Alicja wondered if she'd make it there, let alone back.

From the train window, she gazed at narrow roads weaving through rolling hills where she'd once driven with Mietek to hike and picnic, to kiss in meadows sprinkled with wildflowers. Maybe she thought about the look on Mietek's face when he kissed her goodbye. It struck her that she might never see him again.

The hours passed slowly. Alicja looked away from men holding hats on their knees, their drowsy heads bobbing. She avoided engaging with women nibbling sandwiches. Whenever the train pulled to a stop at a station and Gestapo with guns prowled along the platform, Alicja willed calm into her face. Into her hands.

Outside Warsaw's central station, Alicja stepped into a horse-drawn carriage with her courier. They clopped along streets where she'd walked with her father to concerts and plays, and with her mother to shop. But everything looked different. Nazi decrees blared from 'barkers', as people referred to the loudspeakers strung up on posts.[134] The Germans had sliced off sections of the city for the ghetto, making it difficult to manoeuvre. Chłodna Street, Warsaw's main road leading to the east, cut like a long knife between the 'small' and the 'large' ghetto now encompassing Alicja's parents' home on Orla Street. A gate choked traffic at Żelazna and Chłodna Streets, where Gestapo patrolled for smugglers, anyone trying to escape, and anyone risking their life to pass a starving child some bread.

Alicja kept an eye out for uniformed Nazis. But then a gang of young boys ran towards her carriage. They jumped and whooped. 'These are Jews, these are Jews!' the boys yelled, pointing their fingers.

Alicja's heart skipped a beat. She feared her guide would leap out and leave her. 'We probably looked like Jews. You were frightened all the time. You could see it in your face.'

Passers-by turned to look. Others scurried past, staring at the ground. Luckily the Gestapo was busy elsewhere.

By evening, Alicja found herself crouched in the dark, four storeys above ground, perilously making her way along a roof. Clutching the edges of clay tiles, she tried to balance herself. Had she dared to look down, she would have seen the streets she'd skipped along to school, where she'd scoffed cake in cafés with her father. But with eyes straight ahead, she inched one foot, then the other. Her guide stooped low ahead of her. He dipped his eyes and scanned the street for Polish police[135] and for German units patrolling on foot, by motorbike or in cars.

Ahead of her, Alicja's guide knocked on a tile. Alicja saw a trapdoor lid tilt upwards. A hand poked through. Her guide slipped through the roof, into an attic. Alicja grabbed his hand, slid down through the opening and tumbled into a dank-smelling room. She held her breath at the sour scent, stepping around men, women and children sleeping back-to-back in rooms and hallways. She followed her guide out a door, up some stairs and into another dwelling. She clambered onto the roof again. Down into an attic, through a door, into another building, then up onto the roof, Alicja scrambled across slippery steel and roof tiles.

'Well, you couldn't exactly go through the front entrance, could you?' Alicja chortled, years later.

The path she'd taken was frequently used by food smugglers.[136] They would lug sacks brimming with chicken, buckwheat cereal and lard to sell to middle- and upper-class Jews.[137] The Alicja I know feared heights, but she crawled across roofs to see her parents. That day in Warsaw, she broke in.

When Alicja's fifty-four-year-old father opened the door, he nearly fainted. Eljasz squeezed his daughter and kissed both her cheeks. But Alicja hardly recognised him. His double chin and plump jowls had disappeared. Loose skin hung at his neck. His legs swam in baggy trousers pulled tight at his waist. His jacket drooped off his bulky frame.

I picture Alicja running down the hallway to hug Dorota, her mother's cheeks dripping with pearlescent tears. And a profusion of listless eyes peering around the corner to see what all the fuss was about.

A German directive had ordered every dwelling in the ghetto to take in strangers; on average six to seven people squatted in each room.[138] The thin-faced men and women lying on blankets strewn across the living room floor had been marched in from towns near Warsaw – more than 400,000 squeezed behind the three-metre-high brick walls[139] into an area of 3.37 square kilometres.[140] Mietek had even encouraged his father to move in. He thought Abe would be safer with Alicja's parents. Dick's mother, Helena, slept in one of these rooms, too.

Early the next morning, Eljasz and Dorota left Alicja at the house while they walked to work at the German-controlled labour 'shops'. Eljasz passed the main gate and the nearby

Krasiński Palace, where years before he had meandered with Alicja through the acres of gardens inhabited by peacocks. But now he assembled brushes for the Wehrmacht at the Brush-makers' 'shop', a German factory at 34 Świętojerska Street;[141] brushes for polishing the black-top boots worn by German soldiers, brushes for grooming German horses. Eljasz's labour added extra calories to the 184[142] allotted on his ration card. He might have been able to purchase bread if his employer did not extort his rations.[143] He and Dorota could sip a thin soup for dinner, better than the watery 'spitter soup' gruel Jewish agencies dished up for the poorest ghetto residents in the crumbling tenement buildings north of Orla Street.[144]

There was one man who kept Eljasz and Dorota from starving. In his early forties, he owned a modest glove shop on a grand boulevard graced with boutiques and jewellery stores outside the ghetto walls. Before the Germans confiscated Jewish businesses, froze bank accounts and forbade Jews to produce and trade textiles, Eljasz had given another man, a Mr Karłowicz, one of Warsaw's largest leather shop owners, most of the leather from his warehouse for safekeeping. The plan was this: Mr Karłowicz would sell the leather hides to feed Eljasz's family. To the man with the glove shop, Eljasz had given a smaller amount of leather and boxes of gloves.

Eljasz heard nothing from Mr Karłowicz, despite the fact that telephones functioned inside the ghetto and mail was being delivered.[145] He didn't see a single złoty from the leather his so-called friend had squandered. Yet every month, the more modest man with the glove shop would find a way to smuggle a small amount of food and money to Eljasz. He would walk by posters plastered on brick walls outside the ghetto warning of the death penalty for anyone caught sheltering a Jew.[146]

The man's name, I would learn later, was Roman Talikowski. Alicja never mentioned him. She vaguely referred to someone who'd smuggled food and money. I learned about Roman from Dick.

That night in the ghetto, Alicja pleaded with her father. 'You must leave here,' she begged. Eljasz looked away. Deals were being negotiated all over Poland: jewels for food, money for squeezing through a hole in the wall or into the sewers, a fur coat for a loaf of bread. Alicja's brother, Kuba, was safe in Brussels and knew people who could help.

'Nothing will happen to us; we have work – don't worry,' Eljasz told his daughter.

But Alicja had seen the swollen-stomached children on the streets holding out bony hands. She'd choked on dense odours wafting from wooden carts. Yet outside the house, a veneer of routine seemed to quell her father's fears. Musicians from the Warsaw Philharmonic, Polish Radio and Opera Chamber orchestras performed free concerts. Across the road, a fortune teller forecast prosperous futures. A bookseller near the corner of Orla and Leszno streets offered sparse pickings. Orla Street housed a laundry, haberdashery, ambulance service, hairdresser and manicurist, a tailor and a matchmaker. Perhaps the Nazis turned a blind eye to prevent Jews whipping up hysteria.[147]

Eljasz outlined his reasons to stay. The formal curtains were gone, the sofas, the oil paintings, the silver, the porcelain and crystal, but Orla Street was where he'd raised his children. Where he'd built his now shuttered business. Where Irena and Alicja had married. Where they would start over after the Germans left. 'This can't go on forever,' Eljasz assured Alicja. 'It will end soon. You'll see.'

Alicja's throat tightened. Her patience was waning. She tried talking to her mother, but Dorota brushed off her husband's stubbornness, though Alicja could see the worry in her fifty-one-year-old mother's eyes.

A few days later, Alicja's guide returned. Alicja kissed her parents goodbye. She left that day bearing a horrible pain that would intensify and metastasise. It would ravage her as she fought for decades to deaden it. It would destroy her relationship with my mother.

'My parents didn't want to move from the ghetto,' Alicja told me, pursing her lips. 'They didn't believe in the need to go, you know, they didn't *believe* it. My father thought: "Look at the Germans! Look at how they are taking this and taking that. They can't win – it will soon finish, this war . . ."' Her eyes dropped to the floor. I wondered then if she was angry at herself for not persuading her parents to leave.

Then she looked back at me. 'That was the last time I saw my father,' she said.

In my hotel room, I listen to Alicja through my headphones describing the ghetto.

Two am. Four am. Still. Wide. Awake. In Poland, my mind often plays movies of my grandparents. Falling asleep scares me.

The next day I walk along Nowy Świat – the Royal Route running between the Royal Castle and the seventeenth-century Wilanów Palace – past a Nespresso store, then a Starbucks. Ahead, a man begs on the footpath, his oily clothes covered in grime. I cross the road.

Further on, my stomach suddenly lurches. In a flash, everything turns hazy: I'm inside the ghetto walls. Children lie dead on the road, the man on the footpath behind me is begging for food. Yellow oozes from boils on his feet. Then suddenly, a dog straining at its leash like my schnoodle at home snaps me back.

It horrifies me that, yes – in 1942 I might have ignored the hundreds of thousands starving – you could see them through windows fronting the ghetto wall, as many Polish people would have. I might have turned away.

But this strikes me as naive. I am Jewish. I would have been locked in there, too. Nonetheless, I just snubbed a man begging. Worse, I crossed the road. There are no death penalty posters threatening me. No Nazis patrolling with guns. I have no right to judge bystanders who chose, back then, to not lend a hand. If there was ever a moment when I failed my family, it is now. Given what they endured, I should be stronger.

19

On 8 November 1941, in Lwów the Nazis issued a declaration: all Jews must leave their homes and relocate to the city's poorest streets.[148] Gestapo and SS men knocked on doors and quarantined Jews behind barbed-wire fences.

Without a German Kennkarte ID, Alicja feared she'd be trapped. She and Mietek crossed the city to Irena and Dick's apartment. During the day, she would crouch in a wall cavity. Dick had manoeuvred a large cupboard to cover the small opening he'd cut into a wall. In the evenings, Dick and Irena would bustle around, talking loudly. While Irena swept the floor or clanged pots, Dick would carefully slide the cupboard back. Alicja and Mietek would emerge.

By January, Lwów's 'ghetto' brimmed with around 120,000 Jews.[149] Some had been stripped naked, thrown onto trucks, driven into the forest and shot.[150] Others were shot in broad daylight for their furs and sweaters. Every day, hundreds of the elderly and poor mysteriously disappeared. Behind the cupboard, Alicja and Mietek plotted to leave.

'There was a woman,' Alicja remembered later. 'She said she'd make papers for us and provide a job, in Tarnów.'

People in the know whispered about fake Kennkarten available on the black market.[151] One of them would have to leave the apartment. Or, Dick could help. But they would have to hand over enough money to buy a small car.[152]

They scraped up a sufficient amount for the woman to provide fake birth and marriage certificates; 'Alicja Darewicz' the married name written on Alicja's. It flummoxed her how authentic it looked. Now they could apply for Kennkarten. 'I had to go to the Polish police to get that,' Alicja said, possibly referring to the required fingerprints. 'I went by myself.'

I don't know what questions the officials asked the terrified woman, or what lies Alicja told to secure the identity document dictating her right to live or die. Either way, it was time for her to move to Tarnów, 250 kilometres away.

Irena and Dick were leaving, too. Irena was pregnant. In the dimly lit Lwów apartment, Alicja wrapped her fur coat around Irena's shoulders. Dick checked his pocket for the train tickets to Warsaw that his German boss had purchased for them, and for his papers. He always carried his General von Neumann-Neurode-issued work card, but the Gestapo could easily nab Irena. Yet she had made up her mind and there was no talking her out of it: Irena wanted to go to her parents.

In some ghettos the Nazis forbade Jewish women to bear children, compelling pregnant women like Irena to abort.[153] Maybe Irena was imagining Dorota singing her future grandchild – my mother – lullabies. Maybe she was picturing Eljasz pushing a pram. I like to imagine Irena choosing to grow the seed of my mother inside her, despite the army of brutish men proclaiming her child's fate. That in her quiet, stubborn way, Irena resisted. I like to think her decision to leave Lwów was key to my mother's survival.

Alicja threw her arms around her sister. The fur coat tickled her wrists. 'Keep it, my dear,' I picture Alicja saying while squeezing Irena's shoulders. Alicja hoped her sister could sell the fur in the ghetto, or smuggle it to the 'Aryan' side[154] to buy food on the black market. Little did Alicja know that a year earlier in Warsaw, the Nazis had issued a decree: 'Jews of Warsaw must hand over furs, winter coats, wraps and fur collars, on penalty of death.'[155]

Alicja did not know this was the last time she would ever see her sister.

A day or so later, behind the court building on Leszno Street, Dick's stomach was in knots. Irena was standing next to him. He'd just slipped money into a man's hand. Now the stranger was tugging at loose bricks in the ghetto wall. When the man waved at Irena, she crouched down. She lifted a leg through the hole where the bricks had been. In a flash, she vanished.

Dick's friends had told him about the holes smugglers knocked into the ghetto walls. They threw food sacks over them at lightning speed to feed those starving inside – 43,000 dead so far.[156] They could throw over a hundred sacks in less than fifteen minutes.[157] Dick's friends had suggested the holes were a safer bet than bribing guards at the entrance gates. These were patrolled by six guards: two German policemen, two Polish and two Jewish. The Jewish policemen would broker the bribes and distract the German guards who could be 'worked', even though talking to them was forbidden.

On the ghetto side of the wall, Irena barely had time to dust herself off before vanishing into the crowd. The macabre smell was hard to ignore. Unbathed men and women draped in filthy clothes bumped her along jam-packed streets. It was as if Irena were swimming and swept up by a rip, as if the Jews of Warsaw were carrying her to Orla Street.

Two hundred kilometres away from Irena's parents, in Kielce, Dick presented his Danzig German Diploma to a German architect. The architect hired him. On weekends, Dick would travel back to Warsaw and hide behind a shelf in Roman Talikowski's glove shop. He would sneak out at a pre-arranged time to hand food and some of his wages to a courier to deliver to Irena and his mother, Helena, in Orla Street. Sometimes he crawled through the wall to check on Irena himself. Sometimes he paid a bribe at the gate, or at the back door of the municipal courthouse near where he'd smuggled Irena in.

With Jews starving within the ghetto walls, Dick's nerves frayed. At any minute, someone could call the Gestapo to drag him off, despite his new falsified papers Roman and other friends had helped him obtain. Dick worried someone in his office might suspect he was Jewish; someone on a streetcar; neighbours in

Kielce or Warsaw; even an old friend might turn him in. Zdzisław Przygoda was considered a truly Polish name, unlike Jewish ones like Shmuel or Goldfein, yet he worried. His brown-blond hair combed upwards in a light wave and his almond-shaped eyes helped him blend in, but betrayal was always on his mind.

Hiding was becoming increasingly difficult. Alicja's father-in-law's family had been hiding, but after handing the last necklace and earrings over to their neighbours, the neighbours sent word to the Gestapo. All over the country, the Granatowa policja – the Polish Blue Police now under the leadership of the German Order Police[158] – and truncheon-swinging SS showed up in villages, towns and cities responding to calls from so-called Jew-trackers[159] and neighbours. Maybe the 'hyenas and jackals', as some Jewish Poles referred to the traitors, were hungry. Maybe they'd lost mothers and fathers, too. But often, if some people fancied the pretty curtains, the extra room, the larger fireplace, they crossed town. They picked through the leftovers and moved in.[160]

Inside the ghetto, Irena and her parents ignored the rumours. 'We'll be deported to Romania!' neighbours muttered. The numbers of 'unproductive elements' to be deported were said to be 150,000. Then 200,000. 'Bah! It's Polish merchants spreading such nonsense,' some countered. 'They want us Jews with anything left to sell off our things!'[161]

Eljasz preferred this version. What's more, the Judenrat assured protection for anyone with jobs at German factories, like Dorota and him.

In March the Germans had changed the ghetto borders. This only helped to fuel deportation speculations. They'd evacuated the Great Synagogue in Tłomackie Street. The Central Judaic Library due east of Orla Street. In April, when four thousand new Jews arrived from Germany,[162] the smell from overcrowding became intolerable. People wondered where they would sleep if the ghetto was already elbow to elbow.

News from Lublin would have rattled Alicja's family: 40,000 Jews had been expelled and slaughtered.[163] Then after dark on the seventeenth, truckloads of SS and Gestapo roared into the Warsaw ghetto. They fanned out into squads, rushed into buildings, shooting and bellowing. The SS came for a baker on Gęsia Street. The frantic wife ran after her husband. They killed her, too. Fifty-two were shot,[164] including Polish Underground members.[165]

Reports of deportations from Kraków reached Mietek's father at Orla Street. All over Poland the Nazis were winding down ghettos. The plight of the Jews was clear, but Eljasz could not see it. A civilised race that had produced brilliant composers and writers the likes of Schiller and Goethe surely could not commit such atrocities.

Meanwhile, my mother rolled and kicked inside Irena's womb.

On 17 June 1942, the pains in Irena's back and belly burned and pounded. Someone ran to fetch Dr Gordon from an adjacent apartment. I picture Irena in the kitchen, sprawled out on the table, her body slippery with sweat, Dorota bent towards her daughter, stroking her forehead with her now ringless fingers. She coaxed Irena to muffle the screams she so desperately wanted to let out, to keep the Gestapo away from their door.

Dick was there, too. He'd slipped through the ghetto gate by ducking into a column of labourers. Now, he paced around until finally, when Irena couldn't push a minute longer, a shock of black hair emerged, the baby's eyes like black sapphires, absorbing all the light. They named her Joanna: graced by Yahweh, God is gracious. Informally, Joasia.

'I blame the table I was born on for my Pirellis,' my mother says, referring to flab rolls that ripple around her middle.

Like me, whenever she bakes, Mum always slips herself a second slice of cake. And a third. Unlike my mother, Alicja could eat cake every day and not gain weight.

To this day, that table in Orla Street looms large when my mother tells her story to Christian women's groups. The table connects her, I think, to Irena; her way of rationalising that she is 'short, plump and wide' compared to Alicja's slim frame; the woman she'd thought was her biological mother, but wasn't.

On 22 July, a few weeks after my mother's birth, a light drizzle fell. It dampened hair into sad, angry curls. Overnight, Polish Blue Police and German auxiliary units of Lithuanians, Latvians and Ukrainians had surrounded the ghetto perimeter walls. Inside the walls, the SS waited in cars. Strauss's waltzes mewled from a gramophone.[166] In the morning, a few blocks from Orla Street, SS Sturmbannführer Hermann Höfle's staff gave the Judenrat an order for the so-called resettlement.[167]

Around midday, posters were plastered on buildings:

All Jews will be resettled to the east, regardless of age and sex.
With the exception of:
– Jews working for German institutions or companies
– Jews working for the Judenrat
– Jewish hospital staff.
Each person is allowed to take 15 kg of luggage and all valuables:
Gold, jewellery, money etc.

Jewish police rounded up street beggars in torn clothing, refugees from homeless shelters,[168] and prisoners held in a lockup. For weeks, ghetto policemen protected from deportation if they met Nazi quotas, blockaded streets. Armed SS and auxiliary units ran in the rain and heat into foetid buildings, their boiled woollen uniforms smelled of wet dog. They demanded to see work documents. They 'shook out' housing blocks,[169] shoved women and children down stairwells and onto the streets. Alicja's parents held Dienstausweisen,[170] or 'life tickets' as the identity papers were known, distributed to employees like them who worked in the German-owned factories. For now, at least, they were safe.

The SS aimed their weapons at those weak from starvation and the bedridden elderly. Women ran from courtyards screaming. Old men hobbled. Some carried bundles, suitcases, a precious pair of shoes, a shawl, soap, a spoon. A confused toddler stood alone and cried for his mother. Children told mothers they should go on without them, not to worry, they would find somewhere to hide.[171] People hid in sofas, attics, cellars, under beds.[172] The streets seethed as the SS, auxiliary units and police whipped crowds and thrashed them with truncheons, pushed them in rickshaws and drove them in wagons[173] towards the Umschlagplatz, a large square on Stawki Street.

A week of rain and wind did not delay the train loadings. 'Where's the round-up today?' people would ask in a panic. Dr Gordon, the gynaecologist who'd attended Irena's birth, vanished.

For those who made it to the Umschlagplatz alive, barbed wire and machine guns stopped anyone with escape ideas. Thousands waited, often overnight, begging for water, forbidden to move. There were no latrines. They pushed Mietek's father, Abe, towards one open cattle car. Lithuanian and Ukrainian troops beat him, Alicja's aunts, uncles and her cousins. You couldn't block out the deafening screams, the wild, crazy fear in people's eyes.[174] Troops filled sixty boxcars in less than an hour.[175] Five thousand to ten thousand a day.[176] If the Jewish Police were short on quotas, their own families were loaded on, too.[177] Eight police-men suicided the first week.[178]

Mietek's father, Alicja's aunts, uncles and her cousins might belong to me. But they belong to us all. As was the case in the 1920s and 30s, it is easier for us, step by step, over years, to accept small acts of discrimination. Laws can change so gradually that the dominant majority either does not notice or simply lets acts of prejudice slip by. It is like the apocryphal story of placing a frog in a pot of cold water, heating it up ever so gradually to a steaming boil. Despite legs able to launch it from a pond to snap mosquitoes, it does not jump out, because it does not even realise what is happening.

In each cattle car, one hundred people crammed on top of one another.[179] Mothers suffocated children. Some succumbed to asphyxiation from the lack of air and chlorinated lime sprinkled on the bottom and then on the corpses,[180] the living clambering on top of the pile, desperate to reach the small grate at the top. The shrieks of terror became so piteous, the SS and Ukrainian guards poked their weapons into the vent. They didn't aim. They just fired.

Alicja's sister-in-law – my Auntie Berta with the gravelly laugh – was herded onto a boxcar. I don't know if it happened during the Gross-Aktion of July 1942, or if it was later. The legend goes, that on the way to Treblinka, Berta jumped from the train and scrambled away.

I read an account of what was thought to be one of few break-outs from an Umschlagplatz train. Around January 1943, a boy sawed off the narrow grate with a tool hidden in his shoe. As luck would have it, the Germans had posted no roof guards. When the train passed over a sandy embankment, a woman named Chaika Spiegel – the grandmother of a woman whom by chance I would befriend years later in Boston – and seven others jumped off.[181] Now I wonder if Berta jumped with them.

Three years after Berta rolled down that embankment, she would scour lists of dead and find her husband Henryk's name, Alicja's brother. When my mother told me that Berta hurled herself from a third-floor window of a building and crashed onto rubble, I knew why, when I was a child, she could not tell me about that hump on Auntie Berta's back.

❋

In Warsaw, I walk down the steps of the Jewish Historical Institute, my hands shaking. I'd just watched a video filmed inside the ghetto. I purchased a copy thinking if I could immerse myself in it, I might find words to describe what happened to my family.

'*Schindler's List* is prettied up,' my mother told me once, which I find interesting given she didn't discuss Auschwitz with Alicja. (Dick told me he'd been unable to stomach the movie.) Maybe she'd read more about the camps than she let on to me.

There is nothing pretty about this ghetto film. I watch it over and over on my laptop in my hotel room. A child with match-stick-thin forearms begs for food, her swollen bare head and cheekbones pressing pallid skin. These are not animals starving to death. These are women and children we see every day, on the school run, at a neighbour's house – these are people we know.

All this time travelling sends me to dark places. The film clips and survivor testimonies pull me down, down, down. Sometimes I cover my mouth to stifle nausea. But then I think of Alicja. Berta. My mother. This is so awful, I must put my worries aside and find the strength to finish their stories.

When I return from Poland, when my husband and my friends reach out to hug me, I will sometimes recoil like a beetle retreating into its carapace. I worry I'll break if they touch me. I might admit to the nightmares that jolt me awake in the dark. Some will ask if my trips to Poland are fun. They mean well, but it makes me want to scream.

'Yeah, the Holocaust is hilarious,' I will say in jest to one woman. When she takes a step back, I want to take back my words.

Those not my closest friends no longer know how to engage with me. I don't know how to either.

Many suggest books I should read about the Holocaust. Novels like *The Nightingale* by Kristin Hannah and *Those Who Save Us* by Jenna Blum, books not written by survivors that provide the distance I need, and a vocabulary that allows me to analyse my grandmother's stories. The authors' words help me make sense of the horror I watch in the videos. Words that as a child in Australia, I was unable to hear.

While deportees staggered towards the Umschlagplatz in their tens of thousands, Dick crushed two sedatives. He pushed the bitter mixture into my mother's mouth. The doctor who'd given him the pills had warned him two might kill a baby. Joasia was asleep and limp in Dick's arms when he tucked her into a backpack. He left a tiny opening for air. He lifted the straps over his shoulders. He pulled the belt tight at his waist.

Every minute counted, but Dick was savvy enough to slow down. He must have been rehearsing what he would say if a policeman or SS officer pulled him out of the crowd, what he'd do if they poked a gun at his pack.

Dick squeezed Eljasz's hand. After Irena released her mother, Dick kissed Dorota's cheeks. He did not know that in eighteen months' time, a selfless deed Dorota had arranged would save the child on his back. But he and Irena might have suspected it would be the last time they would ever see Dorota again.

Near the Leszno Street checkpoint gate, Dick lingered for a moment. He passed a pre-arranged bribe. Then he and Irena slid into a column of haggard, sunken-eyed workers whose names did not appear on the deportation lists, those deemed strong enough to labour on the Aryan side. Dick and Irena marched out of the ghetto.[182] The rucksack with my mother inside rested warm on his spine.

On the other side of Leszno Street, Dick passed another bribe. Dozens of szmalcownicy blackmailers swarmed like locusts scanning for darting, nervous eyes, for dark hair pushed under hats: frightened Jews to extort and rob.[183] Dick glanced across the street at a man standing on the kerb. He singled out Roman's slender face, fine hair and kind eyes. The two men traded looks.

Roman began to walk away, down the footpath. Dick fell in, not far behind. They rounded a corner. Dick followed Roman to an apartment. He crouched with Irena behind a bookshelf in the dark.

20

Early each morning, Dick would pull on his hat and coat, kiss Irena, and without waking Joasia, rush off to catch the Warsaw train. The Okrężna station lay on the outskirts of Grodzisk Mazowiecki, near Milanówek, 36 kilometres from Warsaw's central station. From there, Dick would stride into town, climb onto a tram and rattle to the other side of the city to work, a full two hours later. Roman Talikowski was the one who'd arranged Dick's job with a Polish contracting firm constructing warehouses for the Germans at the Warsaw–Gdansk railway station.

While Dick was at work, Irena would keep close to the place Roman had found for them: an attic room in a chalet-style wooden villa with a steel roof. Set between beech trees at the end of a long driveway, acres of woodlands screened the house from prying neighbours. When it was safe, Irena could sit under the shade of an old apple tree with her baby. She could watch feathered heads of rye grasses bow in the wind. She could pick wild strawberries in the field next door.

The villa was owned by Maria Kaczyńska, a feisty, heavy-set, hospitable woman who governed her house with strict rules and a quick temper. Along with Irena, Dick and Joasia, two other women rented rooms. The women took turns cooking in the kitchen. In the summer they picked vegetables from the garden. In winter, when food was scarce, everyone ate together. They would peel and shred potatoes, stir them into batter then scoop the crisp pancakes from a baking sheet with their fingers. Each evening, Dick would return to the house to his nine-month-old daughter, her eyes the colour of dark rye bread, her gurgles a balm for her parents' grief.

After Irena and my mother's escape from the ghetto, the Treblinka deportations had continued into August. One day, the Germans had shown up at the factory where Irena's mother, Dorota, worked and ordered all women outside. The SS shoved them into line. They whacked them with rifle butts and forced them to run. Women wheezed and fell to the ground. The SS shoved Dorota and a handful of her colleagues to one side. The rest they sent back to the factory.

Irena and Alicja's cousins, aunts, uncles and many friends had all disappeared. Dick heard how his friend, Dr Korczak, had led four columns of his orphans onto the boxcars holding the hands of two children while staring up at the sky. Now the ghetto was relatively empty, with only 35,000 'useful' Jews left. Alicja and Irena's father, Eljasz, were among them.

Some mornings on his way to work, Dick would walk alongside the ghetto wall. On his way home, he'd march through the ghetto gate with a group of bricklayers who maintained the walls to meet Eljasz. But after the Germans emptied buildings in the Gross-Aktion, they moved the ghetto boundary. Now number eleven Orla Street was on the Aryan side. Eljasz had been evicted.

Spring 1943. It was dusk when Dick slipped into the column of labourers. His eyes bored into the neck of the man walking ahead of him, papers folded inside his jacket. Dick lowered his cap to avoid the gaze of the Gestapo. He scanned the street and doorways. When it was safe, he darted down a side street, towards where he'd arranged to meet Eljasz.

The plan was this: Dick would show Eljasz his name masterfully forged on identification papers that once belonged to a retired railway worker; he'd convince Eljasz this was his last hope. Eljasz would agree. Then they would walk to an appointed place along the ghetto wall. Then they would run for the Aryan side.

But things did not go according to plan. Eljasz asked for a few more days to consider his options. Dick had been through this routine before with his father-in-law. Negotiation was his talent. He could be convincing, intimidating if necessary, but always respectful of others' wishes, particularly if pride and honour were at stake.

Shortly before 9 pm – minutes before the curfew would send everyone scurrying indoors – Dick hesitated, then squeezed

Eljasz's hand. He looked left and right, then scrambled up a ladder where moments before, smugglers had been tossing parcels. Dick swung his leg onto the three-metre-high wall and leaned over. He flung himself off.

In the split second before his feet hit the ground, Dick saw the back of the German policeman's hat – he was so close the scent of the man rushed up Dick's nose – a sour mix of sweat and cologne. Dick unfurled himself off the cobblestones, feet scrabbling. He sprinted along the road. The bicycle taxi driver he was trying to reach had seen the German, and now he was pedalling away frantically. As the taxi neared full speed, Dick leapt into the passenger cart. He heard gunshots cracking behind him. When they reached Roman's glove shop, Dick clambered out and dashed inside. He pushed the shelf to one side and slid in.

Not long after this near-miss, on Monday 19 April 1943, Dick alighted the tram at the wide road near Krasiński Square. It was a warm spring day, Passover eve. Daffodils bloomed in the Saxon Gardens. He heard someone yell through a megaphone from the ghetto side of the wall.

'We are uprising against the Germans and we will fight them! We ask the public to stay away from the ghetto walls to avoid the unnecessary loss of human life!'

Dick stood transfixed. Wehrmacht soldiers and Waffen SS[184] filled the square. Troops blocked the trams. Passengers were tumbling out of them onto the street. Dick watched cannon[185] fire over the ghetto walls. Shells boomed, blasting holes into buildings. Dust powdered Dick on the Aryan side.

Where was Eljasz? Where was his mother? A Catholic teacher

friend had helped Helena escape, but given she was teaching children in underground kindergartens, she could be on the wrong side of the wall.

Fighting continued throughout the day. The Polish Underground under the command of Captain Józef Pszenny tried to break down the ghetto wall at Bonifraterska Street. In buildings outside the ghetto, you could hear cannon booming and rifle fire. The city buzzed with stories. People talked of hundreds of dead Germans, wrecked tanks and wounded soldiers carried to hospitals. In Żoliborz – the middle-class suburb where Jews hid among the Polish intelligentsia – crowds gathered at a safe distance to watch the spectacle of Jews rebelling against the occupiers. Women cried. Some citizens praised the Jews for their heroism.[186] Others said, 'Let them burn.'

That evening, as Dick sat in a tram making his way back across the city, he wondered if his father-in-law was still alive. Dick listened to passengers around him talking, most admiring the Jews for taking a stand against their common enemy.

'The ghetto is burning! The Jews are burning and we will finally be rid of them!' Dick heard one man across from him exclaim. Some passengers rushed to hit the man, who ran for the door and jumped to the street.[187]

The Jewish resistance surprised the Germans. SS General Jürgen Stroop took charge, sending fresh troops to quell the rebellion. Underneath buildings, men and women hid in a lab-yrinth of shelters and bunkers they'd been constructing for months; in cellars and beneath cellars, outbuildings and court-yards.[188] Fighting was fierce in the area of the brushmaker's factory where Eljasz worked. Some aid trickled in from the

Polish Underground, but it was too little, too late. The rebels were vastly outgunned by the Nazis.

The following week, the Germans set fire to houses and smoked out the Jews. A Jewish mother holding her son leapt from the third-storey window of a burning building. A woman in the crowd outside the wall covered her eyes with her hands, 'Jesus, Jesus, have mercy! After all, they are human beings.'[189]

German troops deported thousands to the camps. A few Jewish people survived by dropping into the sewers. Germans tossed in hand grenades. The hunted emerged through manholes only to be handed over by fellow Poles. But other Poles whisked some away into hiding. Including Dick's mother.

Unbeknownst to Dick, his mother had been hiding in the rubble. A Mrs Gośeiej smuggled Helena and a second woman out to the Aryan side. She hid the two women in her apartment at 56 Wspólna Street, close to the central station and would later pay off a szmalcownik – *blackmailer* – who threatened to denounce Helena to the Gestapo.[190]

On 16 May, three days before they declared Berlin Judenrein – cleansed of Jews – the Germans blew up the Great Synagogue on Tłomackie Street around the corner from Orla. Stroop pressed the detonation button himself.[191] It was the final and official signal: there were, at least officially, no more Jews in Warsaw.

Years later, citizens will have to block out images like these. All over Poland, they will have to remove photos, clothes, mementos from homes they move into. They will have to hang bedding outside and air rooms. They will have to exorcise scents of Jewish people who once lived there. Ghosts who would never return.

❀

Alicja never mentioned Dick bringing Eljasz false papers. 'My father was in the camp with my brother,' she said, referring to Henryk, Berta's husband. 'We heard they had been deported. But if that's really true or not, I don't know.'

Alicja never read Dick's memoir, in which he described how he'd tried to persuade Eljasz to leave the ghetto. I regret not asking her why. When I repeated a few details from it to her, she'd quipped, 'Oh, did he say zat?'

Dick published his book after Mietek died. Maybe Alicja couldn't bear to read about Dick and Mietek's shared camp experiences. More likely, I suspect she didn't want to know the truth about Dick because her anger towards him helped to mask the grief of losing her family.

Dick assumed Eljasz was killed in the uprising. Maybe he was. Maybe it was later, in the camps. I want to capture history correctly, but there are moments when I wonder why location even matters.

'I knew they had died,' Nana Alicja said. 'Because everyone did.'

The day of 22 May 1943 was the last time Dick saw Irena alive. That morning, he left the villa in his hat and suit. When he disembarked the train that evening, neighbours were waiting for him on the platform. Their faces told him something terrible had happened. Dick ran towards the villa, up the long driveway. As he drew close, Dick heard his daughter wail.

The Gestapo had showed up that day on a mission. Someone had told them about people living in Maria Kaczyńska's villa. They killed three women, including Irena.

As Dick threw open the front door, his heart pounded. He saw Joasia dragging herself across the floor like a wounded animal, her eyes red and swollen. She gripped one of Irena's bras in her fingers. It smelled of soap and potato cakes.

Dick knew the Gestapo could return at any moment. He scooped up Joasia and grabbed Irena's bra. He could not afford to let it go.

21

On the station platform in Warsaw, I point to my schedule and ask strangers for help. I join a ticket queue behind a slender man in his mid-twenties with cropped brown hair. 'Milanówek?' I ask.

'Mmmm. Yes.'

His English uplifts me, like finding a lost ring under a sofa.

'We will go past Milanówek. Follow us and I will tell you when to get off the train.'

On board, passengers fill every seat. We stand near the doorway, gripping the handrails.

'Why you going to Milanówek?' the young man asks. 'Tourists don't go to such a place. It is unusual.'

'I am going to the cemetery.' I pause for a second, wondering how I can censor a murder story. 'My grandmother is buried there.'

'You are Polish?' he asks, his eyebrows arching.

'I live in America; I'm Australian. My mother was born in Warsaw during the war. She was born in the ghetto.' In Poland I speak in shorter sentences, to give people time to interpret.

'You Jewish? Really? Jewish?' He squealed as if he'd won the lottery.

I nod. I'm not a 'real' Jew, I tell him – not Orthodox or practising, just born Jewish through my mother's bloodline.

In our house, my mother connected everything to Jesus. She taught me Jesus was Jewish, and because we didn't practise the Jewish faith, we were Jews by birth only.

When Dick eventually shared his story with my siblings and me, my sister Jacqui, around eighteen at the time asked him, 'Did you ever speak Jewish?'

Dick spoke neither Hebrew nor Yiddish. 'I was brought up Polish,' he said.

'So are we genetically—?'

'Yes, you're Jewish, because it comes from the mother,' Mum interrupted.

'So we can marry a non-Jew and be Jewish?' I chimed in. 'That makes no sense.'

'Yes, that's the way it is, biblically,' Mum insisted. 'Don't you remember Jesus's line came through the women? It started with—'

'How can *we* be Jewish when Dad's *not*?'

We were all talking at once, as is normal in our family, but this overwhelmed Dick. 'Don't be like Hitler!' he barked. 'Only Hitler made people a quarter or an eighth of a Jew. Only Hitler did that!' He was so angry, his face flushed red. 'I considered myself a Pole. It was just I was of Jewish religion.'

But my mother is Jewish. Her religion is Christian.

Back then, I naively assumed nationality and birthplace eclipsed ancestry. Besides the Polish Circus, I knew no Jewish people. I connected the babka cakes, the dill pickles, the bickering and the gossip to being Polish. Both my parents hold Australian passports. I considered myself Australian, but half Polish because my mother was born in Poland, and half Swiss given my father's heritage.

When I first moved to the US, it shocked me that when filling out government and medical forms I had to check boxes noting skin colour and physical features, instead of ancestry. Now I know this American term of 'race' originated from slavery and the subsequent caste system that ranked people in the United States based on appearance.[192]

I always hesitate checking boxes that define race. Most social and biological scientists agree race is largely a social construct.[193] We share 99.9 per cent of our DNA with each other.[194] I especially worry about what Dick said when I fill out medical forms that ask if I'm Ashkenazi, since descendants of Ashkenazi Jews carry genes that put them at higher risk for contracting diseases such as breast and ovarian cancer, and Tay-Sach's disease.[195]

My discomfort intensifies when after seeking Alicja's records in a Warsaw archive, a guard escorts me out after I tell staff she was Jewish, and in years to come after speaking in schools in Otwock, someone sprays swastikas on a Jewish memorial. Noting race or religion on an identity document resulted in horrible consequences for my family. Governments singled them out as 'other' and questioned their loyalty. It will take years for me to tick an Ashkenazi box.

On the train, the young man peppers me with questions. 'Why do Jewish graves have lions and three candles on them?' he asks.

I panic. 'I didn't grow up Jewish, so I'm not entirely sure, but I think the lion is one of the tribes. I'm not sure about the three candles, but the menorah has nine candles. Or is it twelve?' I lower my eyes, embarrassed. I make a mental note to check this later.

'Why do they place stones on the grave and not flowers?' he persists.

I vaguely recall having seen pebbles on Jewish headstones, perhaps when Mietek was buried. 'I don't know,' I admit, ashamed I know so little about the traditions that marked my relatives as subhumans to be exterminated.

The young man asks about my mother. I don't know if it's because he seems to know more about Jews than me, but I decide to tell him about the ghetto, about the shootings that killed my grandmother near Milanówek.

'This is the first time I have heard such a story from a person in Poland,' he says, shaking his head.

His reaction is perhaps understandable, given the chances of him meeting a Jewish Pole are slim. Fewer than ten thousand Jews live in Poland today compared to more than three million before the Holocaust.[196]

'You must have a story, too,' I say. Given Poland's history of brutal invasions and communist oppression, many people I meet tell me about family members raped by Russian soldiers, sent to labour camps, and those who were arrested and tortured.

'Maybe. But no-one asks and no-one tells.'

'What about your grandparents?'

'No-one wants to talk about the past, even the past before communism.'

In several years, Poland's far-right nationalist government will censor museums, historians and academics to re-write history.[197] They will pass laws to incarcerate anyone who suggests Poland was complicit in harming Jews and modify them only after an international backlash.[198] They will depict foreigners and non-slavic refugees as 'others' they do not want within their borders (but welcome millions of Ukrainians after Russia's invasion). They will encourage patriotic posters, videos and memes that incite mobs to rail against Jews and LGBTQI+ people.[199]

The young man tells me he discusses Poland's past with his priest and wants to do something to change things. He glances down for a second. Then his eyes are at me. 'I like that you are choosing to do something.'

But what am I doing and for whom? It doesn't seem a big deal that I'm in Poland chasing down my family's history. I have no choice but to pursue the crazy questions spinning in my mind. I am heir to a legacy of hate implanted inside me before I was born.

The train slows. 'You are young and can do anything you want with your future,' I say, wondering if someone with his mindset would have joined the Underground in 1940. 'Do something important,' I say. The train's brakes screech. I stretch out my hand and clasp his. 'I'm Karen.'

'I'm Simon,' he says.

I rush out the open door. As the train pulls away from the platform, I wave.

Near the station, a roughly shaven man sits in a car reading a newspaper, the word 'taxi' printed on his door. We agree on a price. Soon I'm spinning along a road lined with grand villas – some old, some new – set back behind entrance gates. Milanówek was a fashionable summer resort in the 1930s. Established at the end of the nineteenth century, wealthy Varsovians would take the Warsaw–Vienna train to stroll through lush forests and grassy fields. But it's the dilapidated buildings with faded paintwork and rusted steel roofs I see through the taxi window that interest me most. Is this where it happened? Was Irena shot there?

The cab driver drops me off at the cemetery's brick entrance. The office is closed. I'd hoped to buy flowers. Across the street I spot a hedge with maple-shaped leaves. I look around to check no-one is watching. I pick some and fashion them into a green bouquet.

I walk through the abandoned cemetery entrance, over-whelmed by ten acres of headstones arrayed around me. Mum had emailed me photos of Irena's: a large rectangular slab, a Christian cross etched to the left of her name. I wander up and down narrow pathways and avenues that smell of damp. I scan for tell-tale hints from the photo to anchor me: the grey, concrete cross behind Irena's plot, a wiry iron cross next to it.

I hear a swishing sound. A woman in her sixties clad in an apron and gloves dips a brush into a bucket of water and scrubs black mould and dirt from an old headstone. Thinking she might work here I quicken my steps. 'Dzień dobry' — *Hello*.

She nods, brushing.

I hold up my iPhone and point to the picture of Irena's grave.

'Proszę' — *Please*. 'My Babcia?'

'Nie, nie, przepraszam' — *No, no, I'm sorry*. She shakes her head.

I walk down the gravel path, disappointed. The rhythm of her scrubbing brush echoes in my ears.

It was 1977 when Dick returned to Grodzisk Mazowiecki, near Milanówek. He'd wandered down narrow dirt laneways searching for the wooden villa where, years before, he'd found a terrified Joasia dragging Irena's bra across the floor. Just as he was ready to give up, he noticed an old woman carrying two pails of milk. He asked if she knew about the place where three women were executed during the war.

'The house is right behind you,' the woman said, pointing. She told Dick that Germans had forced neighbours to dig a grave. The women, she said, lay buried in the backyard. Dick thanked her and offered money. 'Jesus would punish me if I take your money,' the woman said.

Dick reached for her weathered hands. He drew them to his lips and kissed them. Then he strode up the driveway to the house he remembered. The fancy fretwork had been stripped off. The wooden spread-eagled Polish coat of arms, gone. Dick knocked. Zosia, daughter of his former landlord, Maria Kaczyńska, opened the door. She stared at him. Dick stared back at Zosia's grey hair, at the deep lines on her face. Last time he'd seen her, she was rocking Joasia in her arms, crooning lullabies.

Zosia led Dick inside. Eighty-four-year-old Maria lay in bed, sick. 'Where is your beautiful long hair?' Maria quipped.

In 1977, Dick was close to sixty. He'd lost his Cary Grant, side-swept mop. His middle was thicker than when Maria had last seen him, when there was little to eat.

When Maria grew tired of talking, Zosia led Dick outside. He followed her to behind the house, through long grasses, under the old apple tree branches, to a corner of the yard. Zosia pointed. After the war, the husband of one of the executed women exhumed only his wife from this spot under the trees. Irena and the second woman still lay there under dirt and leaves.

Of course, I knew none of this when I first met Dick in Canada, and it would be ten more years before he told me the bones of this story. Now I'm here in Milanówek to dig up the rest. Although Irena was killed in 1943, I figure her grave would be lined up with others buried around the same year as Dick's visit. After he left Poland, his friend organised Irena's exhumation and reburial somewhere near where I stand.

I turn back towards the cemetery entrance, beleaguered by the thousands of headstones I will have to scan. But twilight dew on my nose spurs me on. I zig-zag up and down cul-de-sacs and dirt paths. I turn left onto a dark grey cobblestoned trail lined with light-coloured bricks. Then I see it: a long, rough-hewn bluestone tomb. Mottled from sun, rain and moss, low-slung weeds border Irena's stone, and tiny white flowers. Imprinted on the headstone is the tall thin cross I'd seen in my mother's photo, and S.P. for Swietej Pamieci – *Holy Memory*.

Irena Przygoda
Executed
22 May 1943

Here lies Irena, the grandmother I know so little about. I perch on her granite slab. I whisper to her. I list the names of my brothers and sister in Australia. I tell her my mother survived the shooting. I tell her about Dick's letter, how I met him, and now, I am finally here. My tears drip onto her tomb, staining it with grey splotches.

I feel strange talking to a grave, but this is the closest I get to physically touching her. Because Dick never visited the cemetery, I am compelled to fill Irena in on everything. I long to know her. But I have no sense of her character, her outlook on the world, what pleased or soured her.

If Irena were alive, I would take her to the symphony. I would bake her cakes. We would sip tea and listen to each other's stories, and I would watch my mother lean in to kiss her. Then I would smile. To see my mother happy like this would mean more to me than this whole, lonely quest. If Irena were alive, Alicja would be in the picture, too. She would be my mother's aunt. I see the four of us together, Alicja leaning in to kiss my mother.

But that story is an illusion. I have never known Irena. I have only a few photos of her, two that Dick smuggled through the camps. I will never know the whole truth about their relationship and why Alicja resented it. Secrets have a way of rippling through generations. I want it to stop here.

The sun fades. A chill prickles my arms. I switch on my phone and google the Jewish tradition Simon asked about on the train. I learn that because stones last forever, Jews place them on graves, unlike flowers that will wither and die. I scout the cemetery until I've collected a handful of round, smooth stones. I place them on Irena's grave and nudge them into a heart shape. I lay my ragged bouquet of leaves underneath. I kneel and kiss Irena goodbye. I glide my finger along her tomb and walk away.

Dick wasn't forthcoming with specific details on what happened after he scooped my infant mother from the floor. I only know he headed to his Aunt Justyna's in Wawer, near Otwock. Dick thought Joasia would be safe there, since his aunt had false papers. He neglected to say how Justyna would hide a black-haired child baying for her mother.

War can numb you and suffocate your emotions, yet when Dick left my mother and disappeared into the dark night, desperate thoughts must have tortured him. Where would he live? He couldn't return to his Warsaw job. The shock of Irena's murder could blow his cover. But if Joasia could hide with his aunt for a few weeks, perhaps he could inquire about help for the child from his father-in-law's friend, Roman Talikowski.

He also planned to contact Alicja, who was living on false papers 400 kilometres from Warsaw. Dick would call Alicja. She would know what to do.

22

The train's vinyl seat sticks to my sweaty legs. By the time we rattle through Kraków's outskirts, a breeze flows through the open windows. Heads loll. I think about Alicja and my mother, and why I'm on this train.

When I interviewed Alicja, she told me Dick paid a Catholic woman to take my one-year-old mother from his Aunt Justyna's to Alicja's apartment, in Tarnów, 400 kilometres away. 'Everyone was afraid to keep her,' she explained. 'So, *I* took her. And this was really for us a terrible thing to do. She was very dark – dark eyes and dark hair. And for the people living in Tarnów – well, how do I have suddenly this child? So, I told them a story, that her mother was taken to Germany to work, because they *were* taking people off the streets, and that for the time being I keep her until my brother-in-law finds something else. And that was that. But we were frightened terribly.'

It's not that keeping my mother would inconvenience Alicja. More that the Nazis could kill her and Mietek for it.

A month after Irena was murdered, Dick joined the Armia Krajowa (AK – the Polish Home Army military arm of the Underground) and swore an oath: 'I pledge allegiance to my Fatherland, the Republic of Poland.'[200]

I can't imagine what ran through Dick's mind, other than joining the AK to avenge his wife's death. It is the oath's last line that startles me: 'I pledge to resolutely keep secret whatever may happen to me.' In years to come, Dick's silence regarding his Underground missions would compel Alicja to construct narratives that blamed Dick for harms inflicted on her. I wonder, if Dick had broken his AK pledge, maybe Alicja would have been less bitter towards him, and towards my mother.

With my mother concealed in Tarnów, Dick took a job as technical manager for a plant manufacturing insulation panels. Three weeks after Dick sent my mother to Alicja, the Nazis swept up Jews in Wawer. They shot Aunt Justyna. If they caught Alicja carrying the child, they would shoot her, too. So, whenever she pushed my mother's pram through Tarnów's streets, she was careful to hide her face under a blanket. But one day when she was out, the Gestapo knocked on their apartment door. 'They are looking for you,' the landlady reported to Alicja.

That night, Mietek phoned Dick. Dick came up with a plan. He hastily arranged an interview in Warsaw with a supplier. Mietek and Alicja packed a small bag and travelled to Alicja's home town, leaving fourteen-month-old Joasia behind, inside the Tarnów ghetto on the Catholic hospital campus with Alicja's friend, a nurse.

Twenty minutes into my train trip, the carriage lurches and stops. I stare out the window at grass verges. Fifteen minutes pass. Every minute, a broad-set man across from me wearing a white singlet lets out a heavy, drawn-out sigh. I count down a full hour by his sighs.

Eventually, a yellow diesel engine draws close. Some passengers crane their heads out windows. Most keep reading their books and magazines or make phone calls.

Another hour and a conductor flits by muttering. 'We take another train,' a passenger explains to me in broken English.

People grab suitcases, shopping bags, babies. They jump off the step, landing on gravel next to the tracks. I grab an older lady's hand and help her down. Then my stomach lurches.

Hundreds walk ahead of me along the tracks. Behind, people are still clambering out of the carriage. In my mind I see Alicja, my grandmother, stepping onto the platform at Auschwitz-Birkenau. Yesterday, I walked beneath the ARBEIT MACHT FREI gate and toured only a fraction of the 191-hectare compound.[201] Last night, Alicja's voice tormented me while I dreamed. It is almost sinful that a broken-down train triggered the images now flashing in my brain. Am I hallucinating? I see the SS prodding Nana Alicja from the cattle car with rifle butts. *Where is my husband? I've lost him.* She stumbles. *Look, Karen, can you see me?*

I arrive in Tarnów two hours late and alight at the most beautiful train station I have ever seen. Wood panelled ceilings and walls lead towards an art exhibition. A curve of copper tops the Art Deco entrance. Classical music serenades me from speakers. I can't help recalling Alicja describing violinists playing at Auschwitz's gates.

In Tarnów's town centre, old dwellings of ochre and apple-green line a spectacular main square, the Gothic town hall rimmed with pinnacles and a red-brick tower. It is as if I've stepped into a fairy tale. If I bite into a door or poke a wall, gingerbread might fall off.

Around a corner, I see what's left of the Old Synagogue. Set ablaze in 1939, the centre of the prayer hall, the bimah, is the last remnant standing. People walk their dogs around it, letting them defacate on the grass.

When Alicja and Mietek sought refuge here, the population swelled from 25,000 Jews – around 50 per cent of the population – to 40,000.[202] Of those taken to Nazi camps, only 700 survived.

At the interview in Warsaw, Mietek's head for business and numbers landed him the job. They appointed him administrator of a sawmill in Suchedniów, 48 kilometres from where Dick worked. Alicja would cook for the factory's men.

After overnighting in Warsaw, Dick's driver sped them to Suchedniów in the company car. Dick left Mietek there, then

Irena and Alicja, Warsaw.

Kraków, 1937. Rear from left: Mietek Dortheimer, his mother Toni (vel Taube) holding Mary, and his sister, Giza; front, from left: Alicja, Paul Nemet, Stella, Abe Dortheimer.

Mietek and his sisters, Orla Street, Warsaw, approx. 1938.

Alicja and Mietek on their wedding day, Warsaw.

Passover dinner, Warsaw, 1939. Rear, at second left is Irena, and at right, Alicja; front left: Dorota and Eljasz.

Irena Przygoda,
nee Mizne.

Irena, Śródborów
on the outskirts of
Otwock, 1935.

The leather folder made by a Dachau prisoner that Dick sent with his letter to Joasia. *Top left:* Irena. *Top right:* Dick and Irena in the village of Raba Wyżna, summer 1939. *Bottom:* Joasia, Suchedniów, 1943.

Mother Superior Serafia Adela Rosolińska with Joasia, early 1944. *Photo courtesy Siostry Najświętszego Imienia Jezus, Suchedniów*

Joasia, Dachau, summer 1946.

Top: Dr Władyslaw Przygoda's turberculosis sanatorium, Otwock, 1926. *Courtesy Ilustrowany Kurier Codzienny / Narodowe Archiwum Cyfrowe*
Middle: Maria Kaczyńska's home in Grodzisk Mazowiecki, where Irena, Zdzisław and Joasia sheltered in an attic room after escaping the Warsaw ghetto. *Right:* Still from the documentary *From Hollywood to Nuremberg: John Ford, Samuel Fuller, George Stevens* of Dr Mieczysław (Mietek) Dortheimer, Dachau concentration camp, 6 May 1945.

Zdzisław (Dick) Przygoda, Germany, approx. 1947.

Meeting 'Uncle Dick', Toronto airport. From left: Dick, Jacqui, Joasia, Raoul, Roger holding Alex, Karen.

Sister Honorata with Karen in Poland, on the phone with Joasia in Australia.

Above: Joasia returns to Suchedniów, and is pictured here between Sister Honorata (left) and Sister Zofia.

Left: Karen and Joasia in Poland 2012.

Joasia and Alicja at Karen's twenty-first birthday.

At the march to remember Otwock's murdered Jewish citizens, August 2021.
From left: Father Marek Nowak OP of the Polish Council of Christians
and Jews; Zbigniew Nosowski, chairman of the Citizens' Committee for
Remembrance of the Jews of Otwock and Karczew; Karen and local parish
priest Father Bogdan Sankowski. *Photo courtesy Przemysław Skoczek, editor Linia Otwocka*

Karen at the Righteous Among the Nations medal ceremony for Sisters Serafia
Adela Rosolińska and Kornelia Jankowska, 2014 Polish Bishop's Conference.
Courtesy the press office of the Polish Bishop's Conference

headed for Tarnów with Alicja to pick up my mother from the Catholic hospital.

But that morning, SS Hauptsturmführer Amon Göth – the notorious Kommandant of Płaszów Concentration Camp portrayed in *Schindler's List* – roamed Tarnów's ghetto. He ordered all Jews to gather clothes and valuables and to assemble, and shot anyone who protested.[203] He shot those who complied, too. He killed children hidden in rucksacks. Then he shot the mothers. Midway through, he ordered a bowl of water to wash his hands, wiping the perspiration from his forehead.

Dick and Alicja stopped on their way to Tarnów and heard news of Göth's Aktion. Dick decided Alicja should wait in a hotel in Kraków, 85 kilometres west of Tarnów. He and his driver would drive on to rescue Joasia.

When Dick's driver, Kazimierczak, pulled up to the Tarnów SS checkpoint, he passed his papers through the car window to the officer with Dick's German-issued ID documents. 'We're headed to the hospital to collect a child receiving medical treatment,' Kazimierczak explained in fluent German. The SS man flipped through their papers. He waved them on.

Szpitalna Street cut awkwardly down the ghetto's middle. Amid Göth's Aktion, Jewish people were running towards the car, jamming the street. Some walked, ashen faced. Others limped, blood soaking into their clothes. Kazimierczak stopped at another checkpoint. An SS officer craned his neck to look at Dick in the rear.

✼

It's a long walk to find the hospital. I cross a busy road and glimpse the Jewish cemetery. The town has rebuilt the stone walls around it. Inside them it is eerily silent. I read in my guidebook that during the Aktions, they marched thousands of Jews through the gates here and executed them.

I take a left down a main road lined with grey, communist-era apartment blocks and past derelict factories. I stop a man in his seventies and point to my map. 'Szpitalna? I'm looking for Szpitalna Street.' I smell vodka on his breath.

He waves down a passer-by. They banter and finally agree: I'm walking in the wrong direction. I cross the double-lane road again and retrace my steps back into town.

Soon, I notice rows of dilapidated two-storey buildings behind a wire fence. My heart beats faster. The roofs topped in a rusted steel betray their age. Next, I notice a re-clad building, three storeys high. A kitschy Soviet-era building to the left with a blue canopied entrance looks like it could be a hospital. The complex comprises several wings. A shot of adrenalin hits me.

'Catholic Spital?' I ask an older man walking towards me. He looks at the stocky woman with him, then turns back to me.

'Tak' — *Yes*.

I point to where I'd written '1943' on my map, then to the older building behind us.

'*Ghetto* Spital?'

'Tak, tak, tak!' the man replies, his crooked, smoke-stained teeth highlighting his broad smile.

My heart is thrumming so hard my lips tingle. I point at my chest. '*My* Mama. Here.' I point at the hospital. 'Nazis!'

He says something in an upbeat voice, then pushes the woman

at me. She leads me to the hospital's wooden entrance door. Did Dick run out this door clutching my mother?

The hallway's high ceiling has rounded corners that melt into the walls. No-one is around; there's an air of calm. Was there shooting *inside* the hospital the day Göth unleashed his Aktion? Could my mother hear the screams?

I follow the woman into a fresco ceilinged chapel, an altar with Jesus hanging on the cross up the front. Did my mother hide *here*?

The woman drops quietly to her knees. She crosses herself.

A wave of nausea hits me. I reach for the first pew directly to her right. I squeeze every muscle to dam my breath in. 'Thank you,' I sniff in Polish in a contorted whisper. I fix my eyes on the altarpiece, the blur of Jesus's arms splayed on the cross. I sense the woman's presence beside me for a minute longer. She rises quietly. When the door closes behind her, I let go.

After I visit Tarnów, I talk with my mother. I reiterate the story of Alicja hiding her there. I hope now she will realise Alicja loved her.

'No-one wanted me,' Mum says light-heartedly, as if horrid things don't matter if you turn them into cartoons, like calling Alicja The Dragon. Alicja risked her life to hide her. But my mother still feels the sting of rejection. 'What should they do with Joasia?' Mum says, as if she were a package shuttled by FedEx hither and thither. It is too light a turn of phrase for her life-and-death ordeals, but my mother has always been a pragmatist, not one to linger over spilt milk, always spinning negatives into positives. Yet no matter how often I share fresh information and explain the many chances Alicja took to save her, Mum cannot see. I wish I knew how to show her Alicja's love. I wish I could change her mind. But this is arrogant and naive of me.

I remember as a girl during hot summers, I'd lie on the cool bricks on our verandah and watch skinks skitter by. Once, I picked one up and stroked it. It blinked, twitched, lungs shimmering beneath scaly skin. Suddenly, a tail shaped like a bullet arched and gyrated. It tickled my sweaty palm. I dropped it, and watched mortified. Half a skink scampered away. For weeks, I watched out for that skink. I noticed others, their stumps wiggling. Over time, they rebuilt cartilage. Regenerated their skin. Eventually, you couldn't tell them apart. They'd amputated themselves in an act of self-preservation – no scar. You couldn't tell their tail had been severed at all.

23

In autumn of 1943, Alicja and Mietek moved with my mother into a long, wooden building in Suchedniów – the Arbolit sawmill at 35 Bugaj Street. By that time, the leaves on the trees lining the roads had turned chestnut orange. Undulating grasslands and woodlands surrounded the village. Hills loomed in the distance. Across the street, trains rattled by hauling German troops and supplies. During the day, you could hear Arbolit's saws and grinders mewling. Beyond the warehouse, behind a back fence, you could see cemetery headstones scattered.

Their Arborlit room was larger than the ones in Lwów and Tarnów. It included a bed, a cot for Joasia and a small kitchen. Alicja cornered off a small section to prevent Joasia from burning herself on the stove. At fifteen months old, my mother was growing curious and could haul herself up from the floor. She'd stumble forward, grabbing onto Alicja's hand.

Alicja took great care with her job of preparing food for the labourers. She simmered vats of soups and goulashes. She tried her hand at cakes and breads. Baking smells would waft through the building, beckoning men from the factory after a hard morning's work.

'Good day, Mrs Darewicz,' the men greeted Alicja as she dished up lunch, the main meal of the day.

She nodded, accustomed now to the strange name written in her papers. She knew they valued her not only for her cooking but her creativity. Food was becoming increasingly scarce with ever stricter rationing. German authorities seized grain from Polish farms and suppliers to ship to Germany. They sequestered vegetables, milk, eggs and poultry for Wehrmacht troops and hospitals nearby.[204] But Alicja had developed connections with local farmers and stores. The rest she sourced on the black market. She collected milk from farmers and strained it through muslin to form twaróg, a peasant's cheese she baked into rich sernik cheesecakes. She mixed onions, spices and vegetables into the twaróg to form a soft, tart spread.

As Mr and Mrs Darewicz, Alicja and Mietek blended into town life like octopuses mimicking sand to deter predators. Instead of city-girl heels and hip-hugging dresses, Alicja wore shapeless shirts and an apron over her skirt, diverting attention from her slender cheekbones and beguiling smile. She would bundle my mother into her pram, cover her face with a blanket, and close the apartment door behind her. She would amble past the ceramic and iron factories, along peaceful roads lined with small homes, past animals grazing in fields. With the town behind her, she would pull the blanket away. My mother's eyes were a death sentence, dark as bitter-sweet chocolate, her hair ink-black.

On weekends, Alicja would perch on a pew in church, touch her forehead and tap her chest in the sign of the cross. She would bow her head and mutter the liturgy. 'The peasants listened to what the priests said,' Alicja told me later. 'That Jews steal, that everything bad comes from Jews.'

The rhythm of her clandestine life anchored her, as did autumn turning into winter; the days filled with more wind, more rain and fewer hours of daylight. November turned to December, the fields white with snow. Andrzejki – St Andrew's Day – passed, then it was Babórka – St Barbara's Day. On 6 December Alicja may have placed a small apple under Joasia's pillow for the feast of St Nicholas. As was the Catholic tradition, she would have told those around the dinner table that next year, her child would be perfectly behaved. She would have done so even though in her heart it was impossible to conceive of the year turning when Mama, Papa, Irena and Henryk were all gone.

Dick often visited on weekends. He sometimes brought Alicja freshly killed chickens and turkeys. He'd also been slipping the birds and hefty quantities of vodka to the German major who oversaw his plant for the Rüstungskommando – the Armament Command. In return, the major signed papers confirming he'd received insulation panels to transport to Russia.

Instead of shipping the panels to the Eastern front, however, Dick sold them on the black market, mostly to farmers in exchange for food he distributed to the plant's workers. It was a delicate balance, the size and timing of the bribes, and managing the major's suspicions. Dick told me that some evenings, Jews and POW escapees would ring the Radom factory doorbell.[205] Dick or his AK comrades would lead them to the warehouse where they would sweep back wood shavings and lever up floorboards. They would hide the men in a cavity below, in the dark. A few days would pass. While the major snored on a sofa in a drunken stupor behind Dick's office, AK members would pull back the floorboards and hand the thin, hungry men their freshly minted false identity papers. The men would then climb out and abscond like rabbits into the night.

At Arbolit, Alicja took Dick's poultry and cooked up soup with dumplings. She breaded cutlets and boiled potatoes, filling their room with a smell like wet toast. Men ambled into the house from the sawmill, dusted wood shavings off their clothing and sat around the table. 'All they talked about was Jews being killed here and there,' Alicja said. 'And we had to listen and say: "Oh yes, that's good." All the time, that was the main conversation.'

One weekend when Dick visited, winter sunlight beckoned them outside for a stroll before sundown. The air was turning cold. Alicja buttoned my mother's dark-blue woollen coat, pulled on her mittens, placed her into her pram and tucked a white blanket over her feet. She pulled a white hat over Joasia's head. Lingering in the yard behind the warehouse, my mother sat up.

Someone snapped a photograph of this moment, a black-and-white portrait that, decades later, Dick will mail to my mother in Australia with a letter. Someone waved at my mother. I picture them singing her a Polish lullaby:

You have pretty eyes
To whom do they give such beautiful eyes?
Such beautiful eyes . . .

Joasia smiled back at the camera. I recognise those dark eyes. I recognise the dimpled cheeks. They are my dimples, too.

24

Early one midwinter morning, a car sped towards Dick's factory. Gestapo officers scrambled out. They ran into the warehouse, swept back wood shavings and levered up the floorboards. They barked orders and hauled a man out. Then the Gestapo men ran to fetch Dick. They snapped handcuffs on Dick's wrists and led him towards the car. They shoved Dick and the fugitive into the back.

Dick said this is how it happened. The rest I must reconstruct with help from documents and Dick's prison files an archive sent me. I ask one historian who wrote a book about Radom Prison dozens of questions. I read eyewitness accounts he collected, of interrogations at the notorious Gestapo headquarters on Kościuszki Street 1.5 kilometres from the prison, where the

Germans directed their fight against the Polish resistance,[206] and where they took AK members like Dick.

The building was intimidating. The Reich had confiscated it from the Catholic church. Five storeys high, the colour of vomit, its long torso stretched an entire block. Nothing could prepare Dick for the murder and madness behind its enormous wooden front doors.

Dick was registered on 14 January 1944, his religion officially recorded as Roman Catholic. His profession: architect. Marital status: widowed, his address the Arbolit Sawmill: Suchedniów, Bugaj 35.When asked about his 'partner', his brother-in-law Mieczysław Darewicz, Dick kept a straight face. It mortified him that Mietek and Alicja might have been implicated. But if the Gestapo were using Mietek's false name, Dick thought, maybe they didn't suspect Mietek as Jewish.

On line twenty-three of his paperwork, Dick signed his full name as neat and proficiently as a work order. Next, an officer motioned him to remove everything from his pockets.

Dick glanced at the photo of my mother in her pram before he laid it flat on the table. Next, the photo of Irena dressed in a taffeta gown posing against an iron railing in Kraków. He put down the one of Irena reclining against him in her swimming costume, on the lakeshore in Hungary. Dick pulled off his wedding ring. He lowered his gold pocket watch, his engineering slide rule,[207] his packet of cigarettes. He looked at his life in that small pile on the table and wondered if he'd ever see it again.

An hour later, Dick lay chained to a pipe in a tiny, windowless stone-walled cell below ground. The cold chilled his bones. It was impossible to tell if it was day or night. The walls exuded dread and hopelessness. The air smelled of urine and unwashed bodies. He heard men shrieking. Screams started up from various rooms. Dick sunk his back against the unyielding stone wall.

The next morning, an officer led him into a room containing two tables. He shoved Dick into a wooden chair. At one table, a man sat writing notes. On the second, they had lined up tools in order of size; small sticks, skinny leashes of leather, whips made of rubber, electric cables of varying thickness. The officer grabbed Dick. He flung him to the floor. He hurled a whip over his shoulder and struck Dick's buttocks. The officer demanded Dick name his AK contacts.

Dick struggled to stand. He clenched his jaw. He'd vowed secrecy. His only offence was avenging Irena's death, and fighting to exist. The blood on his tongue tasted of salt.

Days later, early one evening, burly Gestapo officers hauled Dick from the basement up the stairs. They pushed him into the back of a military vehicle. They drove him 1.5 kilometres, through a set of imposing steel gates, to the prison complex on Malczewskiego Street. Comprising four buildings, the complex was surrounded by a brick wall topped with barbed wire more than three metres high and included three watchtowers.[208]

Guards threw Dick into cell number two, the one the Sonderabteilung Special Forces unit designated for the AK, Polish officers and anyone accused of sabotage. The door slammed shut behind Dick. The lock clicked.

Dick could barely make out the group of gaunt men around him. He squinted at two faces that seemed vaguely familiar. He recognised Captain Michalik – paymaster of his army regiment and fellow AK member. And Mr Lachert, a lawyer from Warsaw. An AK member named Tadeusz Barwicki murmured something to Dick. As the oldest, Barwicki had been designated as cell captain. His stocky body bore scars and bruises from interrogations.

Twenty-six men were packed like cattle into Dick's fifteen-by-three-metre cell, originally designed for six. If a man wanted to stretch his legs and walk around, the rest would shuffle alongside him. When guards returned a prisoner from interrogations, dropping him in a heap on the floor, fellow prisoners would sit him up in a corner. They would dip a rag into a bucket of water and tend to the man's wounds, trying to do whatever they could, knowing it wasn't enough.

Every evening, Barwicki reported to the guard the names of the feverish and sick, and of any who had died.[209] Twenty-six men then twisted into tangled rows on straw mattresses that during the day leaned against the 2.5 metre high wall.

When they shut off the one light in the cell at eight, Dick struggled to sleep. Exhausted and hungry, pain tore through him, his punishers' faces still vivid. Prisoners stepped over him during the night for the toilet bucket. Dick shuddered with cold. Every hour a guard would peer through the cuckoo-clock hatch at the top of the cell door. When it clanged shut, the sound reverberated through Dick's skull.

In the mornings, the prisoners swept up dead fleas and stacked the filthy mattresses. Between eight and nine they would listen for the guards. They had learned the footstep patterns of each officer – the length of his stride, the tiniest heel scrape on the stone. They could distinguish Gestapo from Polish guards. They'd matched the footsteps to specific officers and their interrogation techniques: the one who ripped out fingernails, the one who broke arms with his baton. Barwicki distracted the men. He'd lift his chin and sing – and Dick and the others would roar along with him:

Whoso to the safety shall of his Lord retire,
And in Him putteth all his trust entire,
Boldly may say, 'God be my defender,
'To no great peril shall I my soul surrender.'

When the door lock rattled, men snapped to attention and sprang into lines. A German officer shouted names in rapid-fire, including prisoners lying injured on the floor. Men helped the injured up, knowing they were only picking them up to be beaten down once more.

Three days after Dick was arrested, Alicja lay on the corner of a straw mattress in the women's cell on Radom Prison's first floor, wishing her fur coat could protect her from the stinking damp and cold. That morning, Polish policemen in navy-blue uniforms[210] had rapped on the door of the sawmill and asked to see papers.

'Come with us,' one officer had demanded. 'Let's see if you are Jewish,' he sneered to Mietek, ordering him to unbuckle his belt.

She and Mietek had spent more than four years ducking and hiding. Anger seethed in her, that fellow citizens – the Polish Granatowa policja – would be the ones to hand them over to the Nazis.

The officer had ordered that Joasia be left behind. All Alicja could do was pick up the screaming toddler for a moment before settling her into her cot. She grabbed a white teddy bear and burrowed it into my mother's cheek. A policeman snapped cuffs on Alicja and Mietek's wrists, pushing them out the door.

'Shoot us! Please shoot us!' Alicja screamed. She knew the Germans could kill her slowly while trying to find out how she'd obtained her fake papers. She'd seen the bloodied, dismembered bodies hanging from trees and poles in town squares. 'Let us go and shoot us while we're running onto the street!' she yelled. 'It will look like you shot us while we were trying to escape!'

The policemen ignored her and bundled her into a car. Now in her cell, as Alicja lurched between fear and anger, a voice in her head told her this was all Dick's fault. Her idiotic brother-in-law! He was arrogant, argumentative and cocky. He drew unnecessary attention to himself, and now, thanks to him, here she was locked up in a stinking cell, away from Joasia.

As she tossed and turned, all she could think about was an argument Dick had initiated with a fellow at the mill who'd accused Dick of being a Jew. Dick's words flew at her. Dick should never have argued with that man. His ego! His impudence!

Memories of her arrest flashed before her eyes: Joasia screaming from her cot. What would happen to the child, all alone? Alicja squeezed her eyes shut, tormented.

During the night, any time a guard switched on the cell light, Alicja saw a carpet of insects swaying on the ceiling: moths, fleas, cockroaches. She could bury her face in the straw, slap her face and arms to stop them crawling in her hair, in her ears, but sometimes they would crawl up her nose.

When I was nine years old and staying at Nana Alicja's beach house, one evening someone left the sliding door to the deck slightly ajar. Moths, mosquitoes and all manner of flying creatures swarmed and spun, circled lights, pinged and banged against the windows.

From the living room, I heard Nana screaming. She ran down the hallway towards the kitchen. A black bat winged by. Then Nana ducked under the table. Her fearful screams horrified me. I'd never heard anything that scared me so badly – and I scrambled under the table, too.

Years later, she told me moths had terrified her more than that bat. Now I understand why. Those insect-swarmed ceilings in the prison stayed with her. A glimpse of a moth decades later could send her reeling back.

In prison, Alicja roused herself from the mattress. Steel mesh covered the only window in her cell, so dense it blocked out daylight. But you could still hear sounds from the courtyard behind it, the 'Secret Yard', as the prisoners called it.

The Germans had covered the ground there in szlaka, shards of iron ore. Whenever Ferdinand Koch, head of the

Sonderabteilung overseeing Dick's cell, and Prison Director, Reinhold Rummel, ordered men to remove shoes and run on the spot, the iron slashed their feet. They forced men to lie down, then beat them with bats. To do squats, push-ups and crawl until the iron tore away their skin.

One morning, the cell of Alicja's door swung open. Alicja saw him. The Ukrainian officer's eyes were set low below his expansive forehead, spectacularly bulbous where his hairline receded, his stubby fingers taut as cigars. No-one in the cell seemed to be breathing.

'Darewicz, *Alicja!*' the officer yelled.

Alicja stepped forward. Women in line dropped their shoulders, relieved. The officer locked shackles around Alicja's ankles. It wouldn't be the last time this man would snap cuffs on my grandmother's wrists and lead her from that cell. This, I think, predicated her corrosive relationship with my mother.

'That was a terrible fellow who was beating everyone,' Alicja said decades later, of the Ukrainian officer who interrogated her. 'A very famous, very cruel man, this fellow . . . Ach! How he beat *women!*'

However, she said, 'He was like an angel with us.'

This unsettled me. Despite the fact that when she told me this, I knew nothing about the horrible order Koch and Rummel imposed: the dehumanising routines; the interrogation procedures; the torture tactics prisoners who survived later wrote about. On reflection, I doubt Alicja communicated the full picture. So I try to connect the historical accounts with her descriptions and what Dick told me about that place.

✳

Dick's interrogations continued. Most mornings an interrogator would yell Dick's name at the cell door. He'd hobble along corridors, his leg chains clinking. Then over a kilometre in the jeep to Gestapo headquarters. Dick sat for hours on the concrete floor, his arms clipped to the pipe running across the ceiling. He couldn't feel his hands. Men hung next to him, arms strung up like carcasses at a slaughterhouse. Dick waited his turn.

'So, are you still a Jew today?' an SS officer asked.

'Herr Untersturmführer, I hid my identity because I wanted to survive, to live on the Aryan side.' From his very first interrogation, Dick had repeated he was Jewish, that he knew nothing about the AK, that his papers were a charade.

'Ah – but we know you are a Russian. You are a Soviet spy! We found *this* in your room.' The officer pulled out a photo of a theatre Dick had designed for the Russians in Morszyn, Dick's notes in Russian written on the back.

'I am not a spy, I am an engineer, and this was a building I was paid to design,' Dick explained, trying to remain calm.

'You are a Soviet Communist!'

'No! I come from a capitalist family. My father owned a sanatorium in Otwock, near Warsaw.'

Seconds later, the whip hissed. The lashes cut his skin, reopening old wounds. The room spun and faded away.

I will later sit at my desk in Boston analysing Dick's 1966 restitution application and an accompanying statement from his physician: 'He continues to have nightmares during which he relives his torture by the Gestapo [. . .] There is a great deal of rage and hostility and the patient tends to ruminate about his persecution by the Nazis [. . .] he suffers from a chronic anxiety state with depressive features.'

The words unnerve me. Here they are, in black and white. Dick only alluded to me of his and Mietek's mistreatment at Radom. Mietek never spoke of torture. Dick never said a word about ongoing nightmares. Perhaps you can carry on if you don't speak the words out loud. Perhaps uttering them unleashes monsters that dominate you.

As I look through the doctor's notes, I think about Dick's black moods in Canada. I remember how he would snap whenever I incorrectly answered his Polish history questions, how his temper would cause me to cower in the basement, to find shelter from his cutting words.

Yet, remarkably, Dick was not defined by his trauma. Once, my sister asked Dick if he bore animosity towards Germans.

'No,' Dick told Jacqui. 'Germany brought many beautiful people to the world. Philosophers, musicians and other intelligentsia.' He maintained there were Russian and Polish peasants who 'had more culture in one finger than many German officers and professionals'.[211] Still, he insisted, 'not all Germans were bad'.

'Tell us a story,' the women in the cell begged Alicja.

My grandmother could send her cellmates into a starry-eyed trance. They'd huddle around her, ignoring rules that forbade them to sit, lie down or speak. When vermin scampered along the floor like spies eavesdropping for the Gestapo, Alicja could tell the women about the third-floor window she'd peer out of on Orla Street. How when she was a child, she and her brother Kuba would listen for the *clack, clack* of women's heels from the pavement, dangle dead mice over the windowsill, calculate the precise moment, wait, then let the mice fall.

She would hold out her hands before the women and stroke her long fingers, whispering of her father and his elegant gloves, how he had taken her to plays at the marble-balconied City Theatre[212] and to concerts at the Warsaw Philharmonic Hall. She would invoke the elbow-length kid-leather opera gloves embroidered with pearls and diamantes that he gave her to wear, and tell her cellmates how from her seat she'd craned her neck to see the Bechstein grand piano Artur Rubinstein played. During the interval, her father Eljasz would stand in his tail coat in the lobby with her under glittering chandeliers, where she ogled the throngs of women dressed in silk[213] and ankle-strapped heels. Dainty shoes of the kind that in years to come, after marching to slave-labour factories in her Auschwitz-issued wooden clogs, she could never again wear.

Prisoners would talk about anything out of boredom, particularly food: recipes they wanted to cook when released, their mother's and grandmother's favourite dishes. Alicja would have described the boiled hare and rich French cassoulets she'd learned to cook in Lwów. The best coq au vin she'd eaten in France. Ham and tongue antipasto from Italy. Jewish pickled herring and knishes. Anything to distract the women from prison-ration soup.

Night after night, Alicja's words fashioned vibrant scenes. She created a theatre in the round in her cell, every syllable evoking wishes, smells, colours, sounds of somewhere far away. The women asked her for travel stories, of young couples promenading on the Ponte Vecchio in Florence, the splendiferous views of the Duomo. Alicja would describe the pounding church bells and Italians pouring into squares after mass.

Alicja's spellbound audience egged her on. The cell captain, a former prostitute named Isabella, shared her mattress corner and gave Alicja some of her rationed bread. Another, Esther – who was Jewish, had been incarcerated for nearly a full year, even though the Gestapo typically shot Jewish prisoners or sent them to camps after interrogating them. They no longer interrogated Esther. Guards did not pat her down. 'They were supposed to kill her,' Alicja said, 'but they didn't say when.'

Any day now they would come for Esther. Meanwhile, Alicja's stories helped to distract Esther, to help her forget. Every day for a few moments, Alicja helped the women in her cell forget about the prison walls. You could say she helped them, however briefly, to escape.

One afternoon, Alicja stood in her cell, confused. Some women sneered at her. They had noticed when she returned from her interrogation sessions that she bore no bruises, no bloodied limbs. The women suggested Alicja was spying on them – that she was cooperating with the Ukrainian officer with the bulbous forehead.

'Nobody ever came from interrogation in one piece, they were beaten terribly,' Alicja said later. 'I don't know why he never touched me. He said to me in Polish, "Pray to God that the war will be finished and we can all go home soon." Over and over, he said it.'

'I am not a spy,' she told her fellow prisoners defiantly as they poked fingers and hissed at her.

Alicja only hoped the Nazis hadn't killed Mietek.

Throughout our interviews, Alicja maintained the Ukrainian officer hadn't touched her. Even back then, I doubted her. Dick once let it slip he'd seen people killed in the interrogation rooms. When I prodded Alicja, she insisted that because Dick and Mietek spoke perfect German, it had impressed the Ukrainian officer and exempted her from torture.

I learn that at the prison, Director Rummel was famous for his 'exercise' sessions. Jewish prisoners titillated him. He would order them to run, then smash his baton against their limbs, breaking bones as if they were twigs. Koch, meanwhile, liked to play games. He'd force Jewish prisoners to paint their faces and hair with shoe polish. Then he'd hand them a gun. He'd order them to shoot other prisoners. It was said that he alone killed between two and four Jewish prisoners every day.[214]

Perhaps the Ukrainian officer spoke in Polish, so the drag of his voice would ingratiate him to prisoners. They might perceive him less perfidious. If he could leverage their desperation, they'd surrender secrets and bargain for their lives.

Alicja's explanations never felt solid. If the Ukrainian officer spoke Polish to her, then why would speaking German impress him? Even if it did, why would that be enough to spare her? Maybe there was an ugly truth she wanted to protect me from. Maybe the effects of whatever happened in that prison – in that interrogation room – were so devastating, she'd blocked even a single word from entering her mind.

✳

Weeks passed. The stone floors in Dick's cell froze. Barwicki had been hauled away to a concentration camp, or worse. Dick had taken over Barwicki's activities, routines that helped keep the men sane. During the half hour the men were allowed to move around the yard, Dick urged them to exercise. Every morning, my Jewish grandfather led the men in Christian prayers:

Our Father, who art in Heaven . . . Forgive us our trespasses, as we forgive those who trespass against us . . .

Meanwhile, Dick's floggings continued. His captors pushed him to the brink, checking and re-checking every aspect of his claims. Dick learned they'd executed two of his Radom AK colleagues. The Nazis collected two more from Auschwitz and brought them back to Radom for 'interviewing'. It was still not clear they had tied these AK connections to him, but Dick knew if they broke him, he and the others would die. To protect the AK Home Army, he continued to assert that he was a Jew trying to hide and live on the 'Aryan side'. But when the SS shifted their focus to his false papers, the whippings intensified.

At this point, Dick did not know if Alicja and Mietek had revealed the source of their false papers. He had no idea if the Germans knew about the papers he'd procured for the partisans and Jewish people he hid in his warehouse. Dick kept thinking about how to protect as many people as he could. It was critical the SS didn't mistakenly connect these papers to Alicja and Mietek's source. Dick blamed himself for their arrests. He needed to get word to Alicja and Mietek. He needed to tell them what to say.

Communicating with prisoners or anyone on the outside was difficult, but not impossible. Certain Polish guards risked their lives passing messages, but Dick avoided using guards, since the Gestapo had caught them – Rummel ordered them killed or sent them to camps. Instead, Dick wrote to Alicja and Mietek in minuscule script on hidden cigarette paper, reporting pertinent information from his interrogations.

Dick would smuggle these notes, that the prisoners called gryps, through a young prisoner the inmates dubbed 'Stupid John'. John had been incarcerated for stealing. Because his crime was considered minor and apolitical, John could move around the building, cleaning and carrying out laundry duties. Once a week, the men in Dick's cell walked in single file to the washrooms to bathe. In the washroom, Dick would watch out for John. He'd stand at a basin and scoop water in his hands. When John slid his mop across the floor, Dick glanced around, checking for guards. From inside his clothing, he'd remove the paper he'd crumpled to the size of a pea. When John brushed past him, he slipped him the gryps. Sometimes John would pass Dick a message back from Alicja or Mietek.

Gustaw the barber also couriered news between Dick and Alicja's cell. Once a week, usually a Tuesday, Gustaw visited Dick's cell to shave the men to control lice infestations. When Gustaw discovered Dick's talent for drawing, he proposed Dick create sets of playing cards in exchange for cigarettes.

On 'Fat Thursdays', when prisoners were allowed to receive meatless food packages through a window next to the Trinity Church on Malczewskiego Street, Dick began his weekly production of cards. He used wrapping paper from bread the local

Magdalene sisters would drop off, a respite from the one-slice-per-day of woodchip-thickened prison bread. In Dick's cell, the men would first separate the barley, carrot and onion babka cakes and bread loaves, searching for small pieces of speck or kielbasa as well as gryps messages from family and others on the outside. Dick would rip a portion of the paper for his own gryps.

In the afternoons, when men assembled leather shoes for the Bata Shoe Company, Dick would sit in a corner. The men formed a barricade around him, watching out for guards who might peer through the door. Dick would take a sharp object like a piece of glass or slag from the yard and scrape at a wooden stool. He'd peel off thin shavings. He'd roll them into a tight coil, tuck them into the brown paper. He'd sketch on numbers, hearts, diamonds and clubs. He'd tear the paper into rectangles around a template he'd created. Onto one piece, he'd smear a little of the glutinous breakfast soup he'd saved especially, then press it against the second piece. Voila! A playing card. Whenever the door rattled, Dick scurried to the shoe polish box and hid the cards and materials. On Tuesdays, Dick would pass his finished cards to Gustaw, who in turn would hand Dick a packet of twenty cigarettes.

However, the Nazis forbade smoking. A prisoner could drift away sucking on tobacco; an antidote against the Reich. When you sucked a cigarette, you could smell a bar in Warsaw, you could imagine a sweetheart's red lips sipping a cocktail. Cigarettes were coveted prison currency. Four or five could buy a coat to take the edge off frigid nights. But smoking required careful planning, depending on which guards were on duty. If men heard guards talking freely, it signalled Koch may have left the building. Prisoners tapped against the walls from cell to cell in Morse code to alert others. When it was safe, men retrieved tobacco squirrelled away in hiding places.

Dick would light cigarettes with flint and an old piece of cloth he hid inside the shoe polish box. He'd suck, then pass the stub to the next man, who passed it to another, musty smoke filling the cell. The Nazis caught Dick smoking on more than one occasion. They would shunt the men to the Secret Yard. Swinging whips behind them like cowboys, they flung them across Dick's back.

A guard unlocked Alicja's cell door and lugged in a pail of breakfast soup. He swung it onto the table, then stepped back. Did Alicja feel his elbow? He bumped her again. She curled her wrist, fist slightly open. She felt him press something small into her hand.

That night, before guards turned off the light, Alicja felt in her pocket for the small piece of bread. She pulled out a rolled-up sliver of paper. 'Tell them your name is Dortheimer.'

Alicja was wild with relief. Mietek was still alive! He wrote that she should share some history of their papers with her interrogator.

The next morning, guards shoved Alicja into the car for the brief journey to Gestapo headquarters on Kościuszki Street. Perhaps she would see Mietek? In the basement, she waited in knots on the floor.

'So. You got your papers in Lwów?' the Ukrainian started in the now familiar room. Maybe Alicja fiddled in her lap at her dress. Maybe it was the gap between the officer's front teeth that made her say, 'Yes.'

'From whom?'

'There were these people. Others from Warsaw and Kraków told us where to find these people,' Alicja told him. I picture the man at the table scribbling in his notebook.

'And where did you find them, these people?' the Ukrainian asked Alicja.

Alicja stayed silent. Perhaps she lowered her eyes to the floor.

'Where did you *find* them?'

'There was a woman. She was in this small street. Outside. They told me where to find her and at what time of day. She wanted money for these papers, and so I arranged it. I bought them from her,' Alicja said.

'Where did you get the money?'

'I was selling scrap metal for the Germans. Instead of food, I bought these papers. We wanted to travel to Tarnów.'

'And the name of the street where you bought these papers?'

'I don't remember the name of this street. This place was not my home. We were just running there from Kraków,' Alicja said.

'Ah, yes. Your husband was from Kraków,' the annoying man continued.

Alicja swallowed her alarm. The officer must have already extracted information from Mietek. That must have been what she was thinking when her eyelashes caught the officer's eye.

'Well, you should pray to God that the war is finished soon, and we will all be safe. Pray that the war will finish soon and you can go back to your Kraków,' the officer droned. 'And what is your real name?'

The papers were impressive. Everything about them was authentic. They'd fooled the Nazis more than a few times. Only the names were false.

'Dortheimer. My name is Alicja Dortheimer.'

I'm sitting at a genealogist's desk at the Jewish Historical Institute in Warsaw. I want to build a tree of Alicja and Irena's lost relatives and go back a few generations to understand their roots.

'What was your grandmother's name?' the genealogist asks.

'Alicja Mizne. Married name Dortheimer.'

'No, that can't be. Alicja is not a Jewish name.'

I tell her about Alicja's false name, Darewicz. But the genealogist wants to know what Alicja's parents named her at birth.

I look puzzled.

She taps on her keyboard and points to her computer screen. 'Yes, here it is. Sara. That's her birth name.'

I am only beginning to know Alicja-in-Poland. 'Sara' startles me.

Parents sometimes give us names that don't match who we turn into. They rarely consider how names serve as fodder for bullies, or what might embarrass us at school.

'Her parents probably changed the name to a Polish name like Alicja, to assimilate,' the genealogist says. 'It was not so good back then to be a Jew.'

If my rummaging in archives has taught me anything, it is that documents help validate anecdotes and memories. But sometimes establishing truth feels like playing a guessing game. Me filling in Alicja's silences and memory gaps risks imprecision.

Alicja never told me her name was Sara. As it turns out, yes, she was Sara. I interpret her concealing this as a rejection of her identity. Alicja wanted Sara hidden. But I could be wrong about this. I could be wrong about a lot of things related to hiding one's identity.

When I retrieve my grandparents' prison records from the Radom archive, the looped capital A of Alicja and D of Darewicz look similar to Alicja's handwriting in letters she wrote to me. Dick is noted as her brother-in-law. But on the page for admitting prisoners, Alicja and Mietek are not noted as Jewish.

From my interview with Alicja, I assumed the Polish Blue Police had asked Mietek to drop his trousers after they'd arrested them, yet I see the prison registered Alicja and Mietek as Polish Roman Catholics. Memories can amalgamate. Maybe the officers toyed with Mietek knowing the Gestapo would torture him regardless, or they tried to extort him, given police briberies were routine in nearby towns now cleansed of Jews – Judenrein.[215] Maybe Dick's earlier arrest connected Mietek to the resistance, and that's why the police didn't disclose his Jewishness to the Gestapo. In 1939, the so-called Polish Underground state gave the Polish police its reluctant blessing after the occupiers re-organised the policing institution, but also urged them to protect Poland's interests.[216] Maybe the officers withheld Mietek's true identity as a form of passive resistance. They were trying to save lives.

But this is all speculation. Conjecture embellishes notions of kindness. Conjecture bypasses hate. I may have misinterpreted or conflated the snippets Alicja told me. Maybe Alicja meant Gestapo. Maybe checking Mietek had been circumcised occurred at Gestapo headquarters, *after* the police arrested her.

Nonetheless, I have been unable to connect this encounter, this memory, to cities, towns, villages other than Suchedniów. I cannot prove anything. But I do know Alicja evaded capture until that day the police knocked at her door. If you scream and beg policemen to shoot you, you would remember this.

She knew.

Back in the interrogation cell, Alicja remained handcuffed to the chair. The Ukrainian officer had left the room and she was eying the Polish note taker. Did he hate his job? Did he take notes for Mietek? Then again, if Mietek and Dick spoke to their interrogators in German, perhaps he had not even been in the room.

The door opened a crack. A voice mumbled something from the corridor. Suddenly, the note taker scraped his chair back and left.

Shortly after, the Ukrainian walked in cradling a bowl. A sweet smell rose from it. He pulled the table closer to Alicja's chair and placed the bowl in front of her. The steam dampened her nose. *What does he want? Will he beat me if I eat this?*

'I'm sorry, but there is no meat today because it's Friday,' the Ukrainian said to her.

Alicja stared in disbelief. The bowl was thick with carrots, grains, potato and cabbage, no rotting turnip smell.

'Eat. But first you should pray – pray that the war will finish soon. Soon, so we can all go home.'

'Nobody believes it when I tell them I got dinner,' she would say decades later. 'It's amazing. You never forget something like that.'

Days passed. There was a commotion in Alicja's cell. Women were gathering around Esther, some crying. Alicja was distraught. After more than a year, the guards had finally told Esther she would be shot.

In prison, everyone was equal. The peasant farm girl who'd never sat in velvet concert hall seats suffered alongside the educated woman who'd read Bolesław Leśmian's philosophical poems. A pianist? The tailor's wife? Their place in society before prison didn't matter – everyone moaned after beatings, they all drank the same watery gruel. Alicja had curled up between Esther and Isabella on a filthy mattress. Esther knew Alicja hated to be dirty. Esther had tried to calm her when moths and insects rained from the ceiling. She knew of Alicja's taste for fine things and fashionable clothing.

When Alicja was first admitted to the prison, the Germans confiscated her fur coat, but allowed her to keep her undergarments. Esther had suggested *she* should wear Alicja's corset to protect it, because the Gestapo guards had long since stopped strip-searching her.

Now Esther remembered. She ripped off her stained smock. She snatched at the undergarment and flung it at Alicja, who quickly stuffed it under her clothing. The lock in the door rattled. Guards fastened handcuffs to Esther's wrists.

Along the hallway, the guards allowed Esther to pause outside cell doors. Through the peephole, she said her goodbyes to prisoners she had come to know over her long internment. Then a loud clanging began thundering down the hallway. It pounded up the stairwell to the second floor. German guards ran back and forth, yelling, smashing batons against doors.

Hundreds of prisoners rammed metal bowls on tables: *Goodbye, Esther, goodbye!*

Back in the cell, Alicja said nothing. And she wouldn't, for years.

After Esther's captors led her away, women went crazy. I imagine them sitting in a corner humming tunes, curled up in foetal positions, rocking, Alicja trying to block out the sight of them. Occasionally, a guard arrived with a gryps message from Mietek. Alicja would unravel the paper and read his notes, then destroy them, swallowing them or tossing them in the toilet bucket.

Alicja needed to conjure reasons to live, to hope for some kind of life after the dehumanising stink of this place. If they killed Esther, they would come for her, too. They'd killed Mama, Papa, Irena, brother Henryk and women she'd trusted. They'd imprisoned her husband. What had they done to Joasia?

The plot was her idea, Alicja told me. She and Mietek shuttled gryps between their cells, scribbled with coded suggestions. If her idea did not go according to plan, at least she would see Mietek, one last time.

At Alicja's suggestion, Mietek sent word to the Ukrainian interrogator through a guard: he and Alicja had secret information, but would need to see him in person. When inmates learned of the meeting, rumours spiralled. 'You are spying on us for the Germans!' women hissed.

The day the Gestapo car jolted her along the road to headquarters, Alicja was full of purpose. In the basement, she saw Mietek for the first time in nearly two months. His clothes hung loose. His Adam's apple protruded like a stone. A guard pushed her to the floor and locked her cuffs to the pipe. She could sit close to her husband. He could take in the curve of her lips when she smiled.

Eleven years since that day on the cruise ship when she noticed spray from the ocean fleck his brow, since the sun cast amber rays on him, since the wind whipped his silk tie over his shoulder, two months since she last kissed him. Now they could crouch close in the shadows, maybe for the last time. They could ignore the intermittent wails from down the hallway, the *ting, ting, ting* of cuffs tugging at bed frames like wind slapping rope on a flagpole.[217]

Eventually, an officer unclipped them and led them into a room more office-like than the interrogation cells. The walls smelled of dried mushrooms. A light bulb hummed and flickered. The Ukrainian was there already, but the note taker was nowhere to be seen.

Mietek scanned the room for whips, butcher hooks, pokers. Arranged in front of a wooden desk stood a few empty chairs. Behind it was a larger, more comfortable chair.

The Ukrainian motioned to Alicja and Mietek.

Alicja sat by the desk, beside her husband. She rested her handcuffs on her thighs. Mietek sized up the Ukrainian officer's boomerang eyebrows, neck tucked in like a mouse, woollen uniform that in the damp, smelled of horse.

After the Ukrainian nodded to the guard to leave, Alicja pulled awkwardly at her dress. She slid her fingers to the top of her stocking and fiddled and twisted. She unravelled the fabric wrapped around her upper leg and yanked hard. She pulled the corset off.

'We want to give you something,' Mietek said.

Alicja fumbled. She kneaded slits in the fabric, and rolled her thumb and fingers. Rings and earrings tumbled out.

The diamonds were enormous. Alicja's mother's jewels – the stones Irena had sewn inside the bra she wore the day the Gestapo came to kill her. The bra my mother dragged while she crawled screaming on the floor. Dick had smuggled some of the jewels to Alicja when he sent Joasia to her. Alicja had sewn the jewels into her corset. The corset Esther slept in. Every night, earrings had embedded red welts in Esther's thigh.

Now Alicja tilted the stones. She let the facets sparkle. She lowered earrings embellished with gems onto the desk. Dazzling diamond rings.

When Alicja was a child, if her mother stroked her face with the back of her hand, Dorota's diamond ring would tickle her. The last time her family gathered for Passover only months before the bombs, Dorota, seated at her dining table, held her wine glass high, wedding ring alive on her finger, rubies like ladybirds dancing at her neck. Irena was there, too.

Now, the thirty-three-year-old Ukrainian officer stared like a teenage boy seeing a naked woman for the first time. Gum glistened between his teeth like a snail.

'When he saw those earrings, he nearly fainted,' Alicja said later of the officer. 'He said he would promise anything.'

He'd taken bribes before. 'What do you want?' the officer asked.

'We want you to promise to save our child.'

For a month, Alicja had been clinging to hope that someone had heard Joasia screaming in her cot after the police arrested her, but she did not know if the child was alive. She did not know that someone found her, and at great risk, gave the Jewish child some food. But to this day, no-one knows who.

In my hotel room, I rewind the part of our interview where Alicja described the scene with the Ukrainian officer.

'We are saying it is our child,' she repeats, impressing on me it seemed that while caring for my toddler mother after Irena died, she and Mietek treated Joasia as their daughter.

I play Alicja's voice again. I will play it in twelve months after discovering a document that will force me to question the motives of the grandmother I love. Including her claims that she always treated my mother as her daughter.

The car with beetled headlamps and bulbous wings slowed as it approached the low-slung wooden schoolhouse in Suchedniów. In the back seat, I picture a little girl clutching a dirty white teddy bear. The car turned into the driveway, alongside a small chapel and convent. It pulled to a stop by the wooden abode sheltering blonde, adolescent war orphans. A man in a woollen grey-green uniform stepped out. Nazi SS lightning bolts were stitched at his collar, eagles on his sleeves.

The officer knocked at the rear convent door. He asked to see the Mother Superior. The sister he startled summoned Serafia Adela Rosolinska.

Serafia stared at the Untersturmführer on her doorstep. A plump and slightly stooped woman in her late sixties, her hair was pinned back in a severe bun. The child the man carried was thin.

A cardigan hung loosely from her shoulders. Woollen stockings sagged around her legs. The little girl's dark eyes sank into her pallid face, black hair poking beneath her knitted bonnet. Just under two years old, one would have thought her much younger.

Serafia took the Jewish child from the officer, along with a small suitcase.

Was the Untersturmführer thinking of a daughter around the same age, her stubborn hair curl tickling his cheek, his chest crushing when she waved him goodbye?

'Don't harm a hair on her head,' the Nazi officer now commanded the Mother Superior. 'The child's name is Joasia.'

25

Not long after I arrive in Poland, Zbyszek, the Catholic magazine editor I met on the platform in Otwock, emails to tell me he has found my mother's nuns.

I knew from Dick's writings that the convent had belonged to an Ursuline order. I'd emailed more than a dozen Catholic churches near Radom, asking about convents and orphanages. But I heard nothing. At Zbyszek's request, I asked my mother to describe the habits the sisters wore. She said the nuns wore skirts and shirts, and jumpers when it was cold, and some covered their heads with scarfs – no black or white head-to-toe smocks.

Zbyszek dialled convents close to the prison and in Warsaw, and matched my mother's descriptions to the Siostry

Najświętszego Imienia Jezus, Order of the Most Holy Name of Jesus. He phoned their archivist, Sister Honorata, who confirmed the existence of one small Jewish girl kept at an orphanage run by the order during the war, in Suchedniów. Zbyszek organises a meeting for me with Sister Honorata in Warsaw.

I jump into a taxi with Iza, a friend of the woman I met in Boston who introduced me to Zbyszek. Slim, with pixie-cropped blonde hair, Iza's tanned skin highlights fine cheekbones and a broad smile. We cross the Vistula River and drive through Warsaw's suburbs.

If Zybszek is right, he's been able to connect the dots in a way I never could have on my own. If these are *not* the right sisters, then I'm back to square one. There are few people alive in Poland who might have had contact with my mother.

The taxi drops us outside a large complex of school-like buildings, brick pillars flanking an iron entrance gate. Inside, it's dark. Women's voices in hushed tones spill into the foyer. Sister Honorata comes out to greet us. She walks slowly but determinedly with a cane. Eighty-three years old, short and plump, she's the Polish grandmother archetype you want to throw your arms around and hug. She wears a polyester cream shirt, black calf-length skirt, black Birkenstock-style sandals with white socks.

She leads me into a simple but spotlessly clean living room, sparsely decorated with wooden furniture. Plain chairs surround a dining table covered with a snow-white linen cloth. A small, wiry sofa is pushed up against a wall hung with crosses.

As we settle around the table, Iza coos and pats Sister Honorata's arm as she translates. Sister Honorata smiles and pushes dishes forward piled with cakes and biscuits.

'There was only one Jewish child hidden in Suchedniów during the war,' she says in a scholarly tone. 'The sister who took care of her often asked: "What happened to my child?"'

'What was the sister's name?' My voice cracks.

'Sister Kornelia.'

Sister Honorata describes her friend as humble and prayerful. Then her voice hushes and turns hurried, as if someone is eavesdropping. 'Joasia was always on her mind. They were more like mother and child.'

Hearing her say Joasia's name makes my pulse gallop. 'M-m-m-my God,' I stammer.

Then she pulls a photo from a book. 'This is the school in Suchedniów.' Sister Honorata leans across and passes me the picture, a single-storey wooden building large enough to be a factory, set behind a picket fence. 'Before 1942 it was a trade school, teaching young people how to become shoemakers and other trades. After 1942 it became an orphanage.'

'My mother might remember it – she remembers around one hundred children.'

'There were seventy-five orphans. Most children were between eleven and seventeen years old.'

I gasp. Mum's memory fragments loom large in my mind. I had wanted validation that the pictures she'd painted of the orphanage were real, not imagined. Now I sit back in the chair. My mother was between three and four and a half years old when she left the convent – the youngest by far. All of her anecdotes of children much older than her playing in a yard – all of it was *real*. I wanted evidence. Now I have it, I worry I've doubted my mother. I'm addicted to data and details. Once I unearth them, I want more.

'Why didn't she come back, your mother?' Sister Honorata asks.

Mum visited Poland more than ten years ago, trying to find the Catholic sisters. She did not check Dick's letter where he'd noted the Suchedniów orphanage, nor had she referred to his memoir. She did not listen to Alicja's interview tapes I'd given her. She thought God would simply guide her to the right place. She had wandered streets and knocked on doors near the Przygoda Sanatorium in Otwock asking about Ursuline nuns. She had searched in the wrong town. She brought home a photograph of herself standing with two smiling nuns draped in black head-to-toe Ursuline habits. Those nuns were happy to hear she'd been saved, but they'd found no record in their convent of a Jewish Joanna, or Joasia.

'Ahhh . . . your mother was looking for *Ursuline* nuns.' Sister Honorata nods, her plump cheeks wobbling. She explains that while Ursulines had indeed once occupied the Suchedniów property, the Imienia Jezus order had purchased it from them in 1928. '*That's* why she couldn't find us!' Sister Honorata exclaims.

Sister Honorata shuffles off to find Mother Superior. Twenty minutes later, Mother Superior – in her sixties with white roller-curled hair and glasses – joins us, listens to the story and studies the black-and-white photograph of Joasia that Dick had smuggled through the camps.

Mother Superior tells us about Sister Kornelia, the woman who took care of Joasia so lovingly. I learn that Kornelia professed her vows of poverty, chastity and obedience two years before my mother arrived in Suchedniów. Sweet natured, small-framed, with light brown hair and cheekbones smooth as tumbled stone, thirty-one-year-old Kornelia[218] loved children and possessed a gift for prayer.

'But after the war, there was a fear. You could sense her fear. She was scared to talk about what happened,' Mother Superior says, frowning.

Sister Honorata nods sombrely.

'But who carried Joasia away after the war? There is no proof of who those people were,' Mother Superior asks. 'Someone *must* have had papers, or they couldn't take her.'

I phone my mother. It is 3 am in Australia.

'Hello?' Mum says, groggily.

'Mum, it's me.' I pause. 'I found the sisters! It's them! Are you awake?'

'Really?' she squeals, panting for breath, laughing hysterically. Then she breaks into sobs. I wait for her to compose herself before handing the phone to Sister Honorata.

Sister Honorata croons, 'Joasia,' gently and lovingly. I feel her words in my hand as she holds it. She talks of how Kornelia pined after my mother, worrying what happened to her, how she cried, 'Joasia, Joasia, Joasia,' until her death in 2004. 'You must come back to Poland to see us,' Sister Honorata insists. 'How old are you?'

'Sixty-nine.'

'Ahh, so you are young enough. Come soon. Hurry, so I don't die before you come!'

The next morning, Sister Honorata accompanies me in the convent's Toyota Corolla to Suchedniów. Wedged next to me is Iza, who has taken the day off. We wait in endless traffic snarls on Warsaw's outskirts. Once on the open highway, the sister driving us turns up the volume of her Catholic pop tunes and suddenly accelerates.

Sister Honorata pulls out her rosary beads. I glance at the dash. We're whizzing along at 130 km/h. Sister Le Mans, I think nervously, of the shy sister behind the wheel.

Hours later, Warsaw's flatness breaks into gentle hills and farmland. We exit the highway and I dry off my sweaty palms, certain we will slow down, but Sister Le Mans slams the gearstick back. She swings out wildly and overtakes slow vehicles as though in a video game.

Anxious, I keep my eyes peeled for a towering church steeple to match the photograph of the enormous building I saw yesterday. Finally, Sister Honorata points to a small chapel painted daffodil-yellow with white multi-paned windows, its front door flanked by Greek pillars. Not the steepled brick building I had expected.

Beside the chapel is the orphanage dormitory my mother has described. Today, plywood sheets cover windowpanes. The timber siding sags, pipes rusted amber droop from the loose planks, paint peelings dot rotted window frames like moss. Freshly mowed grass surrounding it smells like a damp facecloth.

A brick path cuts between the yellow building in front and a large house painted salmon-pink at the rear, the roof tiled green. 'That's where the Germans lived, the SS, just there beside the sisters,' Sister Honorata says. She tells me the Gestapo first commandeered the building, then the SS, who interrogated and often killed local Jewish adults there. 'They took some of them to the ghetto.'

Half a dozen sisters pop out of the yellow building and rush to the car, arms open. They hug Sister Honorata, then peck our cheeks and squeeze my hands. They lead us through the back door into a wide living room. Whooping and fussing over Sister Honorata, they fling arms around her shoulders, whispering in her ear like teenagers.

The sisters lead us to a neatly arranged table in the dining area set with white china and glasses. The women introduce us to Kornelia's former companion, Sister Zofia, a warm-hearted woman with grandmother-grey hair and large rimmed glasses. A younger, shy sister, also dressed in a white shirt, black skirt and cardigan, carries in plates of food: a hearty tomato soup, pork cutlets with white balls of mashed potato atop lettuce leaves, braised carrots and salads. 'Jeść! Jeść!' — *Eat! Eat!* the sisters all beg.

As they pile more food onto our plates, Sister Zofia tells us my mother didn't live with the children in the orphanage, but with Kornelia, in her room, upstairs above this dining room, where the sisters slept after the Germans moved into their living quarters.

'Joasia was fascinated by the boots and spurs of the German soldiers,' Sister Zofia says. 'She'd say, "Oh what interesting shoes he has!"' Zofia imitates a child's voice.

This picture troubles me. My mother's nightmares: grey uniformed men in black boots. Why did the SS in the pink building not kill my mother? I wonder if the Ukrainian officer who profited off the last vestiges of Alicja's family shared his spoils to obfuscate the bribe, since accepting one was considered a crime.[219]

The sisters presume the SS officer in charge of that building didn't know about my mother. But maybe he did. After the Ukrainian officer delivered her to the convent, he reported back to Alicja. 'He kept the promise,' Alicja told me. 'She was not allowed to be shifted. And that's how she survived.'

I didn't understand it at the time, but now I do. Alicja meant that the Ukrainian SS officer who took the jewels held power over the SS in the pink building. As far as Alicja was concerned, the diamonds – and her plan – kept Joasia alive.

According to Kornelia, the SS officer in charge of the pink building treated the sisters well. He would warn the Mother Superior which sisters were in danger of being arrested or sent off to labour camps. One day, when a German soldier barged into the convent looking for Jews and rushed to the chapel, Kornelia pushed Joasia behind the altar flowers. Miraculously, my mother kept absolutely still, not betraying her hiding spot. There was some instinct in the child, Kornelia told the others. My mother knew when it was critical to be quiet and still. To listen. She was a child who had only ever known war and danger. She knew how to survive.

I open my laptop and pull up the old photo of my mother tucked into a pram that Dick hid under his foot in Dachau. It was taken a kilometre or so down the street.

Sister Zofia adjusts her glasses, stares at the picture, then reaches into a cabinet. She pulls out a black-and-white photograph of a girl, three or four years old, with a full round face, dark glossy hair, coal-black eyes, fringe cut in a dead straight line across her forehead.

I stare, my heart drumming in my throat. 'That's my mother,' I stammer. We line up Zofia's photo next to my one of Mum as a toddler in the pram. The nose, the dark eyes, her hair, nearly identical. There is no question. The child is the same.

When the sisters hear of my mother's Christian faith, they nod and smile. They don't appear surprised. They paint a picture for me of life here in 1944, when sisters would rise early in the morning, kneel and fold their hands to pray, despite the Reich closing convents and killing thousands of priests[220] and nuns. While Kornelia prayed, Joasia slept nearby. After prayers, the sisters would wake the seventy-five children. The children would fold bedding, sweep floors and cross the courtyard to the chapel to sing songs of devotion at matins, listen to gospel readings and pray. The sisters allotted older children chores: feeding chickens and pigs, scrubbing floors, clearing weeds, plucking vegetables from the small garden. At noon, the sisters prayed to Mary. Tranquil hymns floated from the chapel.

Hitler's General Government forbade schooling the children. Most high schools were closed in an attempt to destroy Poland's language, education, economy and culture. They allowed only primary schools with a limited curriculum[221] to function. When my mother arrived at Suchedniów, academics and teachers had long been carted off to concentration and labour camps,[222] along with the orphans' parents.[223] Sister Honorata says it's likely the sisters taught the younger children to read and write in secret. But it must have been difficult to concentrate when there was so little to eat. Many days they fed Joasia only bread and water. Potatoes and cabbages harvested from the convent's garden helped fend off starvation, along with meagre allocations from relief organisation Rada Główna Opiekuńcza, the Central Welfare Council.[224] Whenever Mother Superior received word from Catholic charities of food available in some corner of the country, she'd dispatch her nuns at night. Meanwhile, the SS in the pink house ate plenty.

Sitting at the table, I wonder about my mother's time here, if this setting planted the seed of her later religious devotion, if this is why she finds such comfort in God and a church community. War and Christianity: these had been the major backdrops of her life. No wonder she chose the latter.

'Well, at least you know your mother was here,' Sister Zofia says in an affectionate tone. She nudges my elbow. 'More cake?'

26

Dick felt uneasy in the back seat of the Gestapo car. It had been weeks since he'd read Alicja's gryps message. The Ukrainian officer had apparently reordered their files, giving him protection. They had paused Dick's interrogations. Until now.

In the interrogation room, Dick sensed something askew. The SS officer fished about in his pocket. He handed Dick a cigarette. 'Go ahead. Smoke.'

The officer began writing on a document at the desk. Dick sucked at the cigarette, checking the insignia on the officer's uniform for his rank.

'Are you writing a report with the final conclusions?' he asked in his best German.

'Ja.' The officer continued to scribble.

'I know there are two possibilities for my future,' Dick said, as if negotiating a business transaction. 'Either death or confinement in a concentration camp.'

Dick did not know that of the around five hundred prisoners the Gestapo confined in the basement, only around ten would survive.[225]

'You are right,' the officer said. 'I have sentenced you to execution.'

Dick was a resourceful man, but he had nothing left to barter. Still, he had to try.

'You know, Mr Hauptsturmführer, before the war, I worked as you do now in a nice office like this.' Dick paused, thinking, *This is a nice office where they kill people.* 'Usually my boss didn't look too closely at what was on his desk for signing,' Dick said. 'He simply signed what was put in front of him.'

Tap, tap, tap. The Hauptsturmführer raised an eyebrow. Jews were not supposed to question. According to his Nazi propagandist training, Jews could not be intelligent.

'My life and the lives of my family are in your hands now,' Dick continued. 'My brother- and sister-in-law are not guilty. They were caught because of me.' Dick waited a beat. 'Why don't you write on your report that we should be sent to a concentration camp?'

The officer looked up. He put down his pen, leaned back in his chair and laughed. 'You are the first prisoner who has ever talked to me like this. And you are very astute to describe this place as an office.' The officer hesitated, deliberating. Finally, he picked up his pen. 'I will change it.' He scribbled something on the forms – a pen stroke with the power to change destinies, prevent lineages. 'The rest is up to Obersturmbannführer Fuchs.'

Fuchs! Dick's stomach reeled. Paul Fuchs was the man who oversaw the SIPO intelligence unit charged with destroying the Polish resistance. He liked to observe tortures that took place in a special room on the third floor. Dick's AK Radom unit had tried to assassinate 'The Fox from Radom'[226] three times.

The Hauptsturmführer put the pen down on the table, then stood as abruptly as if Fuchs had entered the room.

'Go back to your cell!' he ordered, his laughter long gone. He yelled for a guard.

The 'Judas window' in the women's cell door popped open. A Polish guard entered. 'Sara Dortheimer?'

Alicja froze. No-one ever called her by her Jewish birth name.

'You are free to go. Bring your things,' the guard said, motioning.

'I don't believe it,' Alicja mumbled. In Radom, 'you are free' most often meant a bullet to the skull.

The guard led Alicja into the mouth of the hallway. Prisoners clanged their metal bowls against walls as she passed by their cells. *Goodbye, Alicja, goodbye!* Downstairs, somewhere near the entrance, the guard handed her over to an SS officer. Then she saw Mietek. Dick was standing with him.

The SS officer led them all into a room. Alicja recognised her fur coat on a table, alongside envelopes. Dick's photos and Mietek's coat lay on the table, too. The officer removed something from one envelope and passed it to her. She looked at her wedding ring in disbelief, then risked a glance at Mietek. Thinner than when she'd last seen him in the Ukrainian's office, his face was a shade of white.

Five SS officers entered the room. Dick recognised one – it was the Hauptsturmführer who'd given him a cigarette.

22 March 1944. 14.10: the release time they noted on Alicja's record.

Alicja, Mietek and Dick walked through the prison gates, accompanied by five SS Officers. The Hauptsturmführer led the way. To see a Jew walking on the Aryan side at this time was unheard of. Most had been rounded up and killed or taken to camps.[227] Those remaining worked in two camps: Szkolna and Kolejowa 18, the SS and Gestapo supply depot.

'Are we being led to our execution?' Mietek whispered to Dick.

'No, I don't think so. I think they are taking us to the camp close to the Łucznik Mauser rifle factory, near the railway.'

Dick was weak, yet there was a lightness to his step. A day later he would faint from hunger, but in this moment hope kept him moving.

Two kilometres more and Alicja glimpsed the camp entrance. It was difficult to envision what awaited them. Her regimented days in the prison had been predictable. She knew her cellmates, their quirks and foibles.

'Forget you are a lawyer,' Alicja heard Dick whisper to Mietek. 'From now on you are a Bautechniker, a building technician. Maybe you will live a little longer.'

Through the gate, they saw what remained of the Radom ghetto. Jewish prisoners stared, their faces bleak, streaked with dirt. Two of the SS officers walked away. The other three SS escorted them to the barracks.

A man stepped out of a small building and saluted. The SS Hauptsturmführer who'd interrogated Dick shook the camp Kommandant's hand. 'I bring you a top-notch engineer today,' he said, pointing to Dick. 'Use him for construction work.' Then the Hauptsturmführer turned to Dick. 'Are you happy now?'

'Yes, I am. Under the circumstances, I must thank you,' said Dick.

The Hauptsturmführer stretched out his hand. Dick regarded what was in the Nazi's palm incredulously. At last, he took back his engineering slide rule.

'The slide rule you can have,' the Hauptsturmführer said. 'Your gold watch is going to the Third Reich.'

'Jews were not allowed to wear fur in Radom,' Alicja explained to me decades later. 'So it was a great sensation when we came there to the camp, because they didn't think we were Jews. They thought we must be spies for the Germans. Also, the fellow who brought us, the SS man, told the other one in charge of the camp: "These prisoners should be treated well. She should work in the kitchen. These two are architects."'

This lines up exactly with Dick's description of the Hauptsturmführer's orders, except Alicja never mentioned him. If she knew nothing of Dick's AK activities, it's likely she didn't know about that day he'd negotiated for her life.

'And I really got a job in the kitchen,' Alicja continued, 'because they were afraid of SS. Not that they *liked* us. They were terribly afraid of us for a long time. So, I could feed them – my men – from the kitchen.'

Alicja explained that the three of them lived there until the Germans evacuated the camp, then forced them and around three thousand prisoners to walk more than 100 kilometres to Tomaszów Mazowiecki, where they separated men and women and loaded them into cattle cars headed for Auschwitz. The march took eight days.[228]

'People couldn't walk such a distance. If you stopped you were shot. They shot older people. If you got a sore leg they shot you. If you wanted to sit for a moment and have a rest, or if someone looked at their feet, they were shot immediately. You had to walk in certain order, and if you wanted to change that row, you were shot, because they thought you were going to run away.'

A Gestapo officer let Alicja move up the column to the front, so she could walk with Dick and Mietek. The officer had been friendly with Dick and Mietek from their work in Radom. 'Because they could speak German, he talked to them there. He was not *so* bad – I mean he was *Gestapo*, but you *could* talk to him.' The Gestapo fellow kept his eye on them.

'Dick had this idea to escape,' Alicja said sullenly.

He had recounted a plan to crawl through latrine ditches one night of the walk, away from the SS sitting around bonfires. He mentioned Lola Ksieski, a woman Alicja befriended, who would stick by Alicja's side in the months to come. It was Lola's brother who volunteered to crawl first. Not long after, a shot rang out. Dick presumed Lola's brother was dead, but hours later, after the guards were asleep, Lola's brother came back. Dick later learned that three prisoners escaped. They'd dug a hole, covered themselves with dirt and grass and breathed through glass bottles. The next morning, after Alicja and Dick's column left, those prisoners ran into the forest and joined the partisans.

Alicja sounded sceptical of Dick's idea to flee and hide with his Polish friends. As far as she was concerned, Dick was arrogant and dangerous, and his friends were not to be trusted. But, much later, I would read testimony about two brothers on that march.[229] They protected their eyes with paper from the dirt that family had piled on top of them, and sucked air through a glass bottle.

The 'death march' as these forced walks were later called, was just the start. The camp they were taking Alicja to inflicted atrocities so horrible, she could never have foreseen them.

When the cattle car arrived at Auschwitz, music serenaded her. 'So you thought it was paradise,' Alicja explained. 'Can you believe that? The orchestra was playing so beautifully you think it's a holiday camp!

'The gardens were pretty and all made up,' she continued. 'You didn't see the crematorium from there. We thought we are going to camp to work . . . that's what we thought it would be.'

Alicja received a note from Mietek, passed to her in a blanket by the Gestapo man from the march who'd talked to Mietek and Dick in German. The note said Mietek and Dick were travelling further, by train, that he hoped they would be reunited someday. That was all.

Meanwhile, the SS on the platform divided those who had survived the train journey to the left and to the right. 'We knew something was going on, but not exactly what,' Alicja explained. 'But the Jewish people who were working there, they were telling us quietly, that is good if you are on that side, and bad if you are on the other. The older people, sick people . . . they were going to the bad side. And if you had children. You could leave the child and save yourself. But no mother wanted to do that.

'You had to strip naked,' she said with a cough. 'Completely naked, all the women. And the SS *look* at you again as you are standing there. Oh, that's terrible. If you had any jewellery, you had to give it to them.'

Not wanting to part with her wedding ring, Alicja gave it to a girl she had befriended in Radom, one who had a crush on Dick. Later, with Alicja's permission, she traded it for a slice of bread. Alicja never got her ring back.

'There was a shower, but you never knew what was true, if it was a real shower. We suspected they would gas us, yes, all the time. They shaved our hair off. I had at this time very nice hair, but I looked *terrible* shaved. There were no mirrors, but some women had them. And we got these terrible clothes, you know, and they didn't have shoes, only those wooden things from Holland, clogs which were never good for you because they were not your size. I got terrible feet after that.

'In a few days they gave us the numbers in Birkenau. Yes, they tattooed us, because there was no names any more. After we survived, a German doctor when I was trying to get restitution said to me, "Why do you have this tattoo? Why don't you remove it?" Never! Why should I remove that?

'They sorted people to different barracks,' Alicja said, her voice turning mechanical. 'Well, we had to sleep in those bunks . . . Of course, there were too many people squeezed in . . . Every morning there was an assembly and they took some to the gas chambers. Dr Mengele, he was coming in his white gloves, *beautifully* dressed with a whip in his hand. You had to stand in this parade naked. They didn't care if it was winter or summer. You never knew. If you had a pimple on your skin, he could take you.

'They were afraid of sickness and also they are saying we are dirty, but there were no facilities to wash. It was hard to keep clean. In the morning we had cup of coffee,' she said of the bitter drink made from a grain-based substitute.[230] 'It was dark water and I used this for washing, not drinking. Did others? Yes, some did.

'To eat? Oh well, there was some soup-like water to eat, and one slice of bread a day, if you were lucky. Of course we lost weight. There was a woman with a teenage daughter. She was [sleeping] next to me. I could hear the daughter stealing bread from her mother. The mother accused her, "You took my bread!" The daughter told her, "Well, you are old and you don't need any bread any more, and I have to live." Things like that aren't normal, is it? But because of the war, that came up. Just the only thing was for us to survive.'

Alicja described the houses just outside the camp, in occupied Poland. Polish and German people who lived there knew what was going on, she said. How could they not? 'The wives came to visit,' she said, referring to the likes of Hedwig Höss, the wife of Auschwitz's Kommandant, Rudolf Höss, who lived in a villa beyond the wall with their three young children who would play with the family Dalmations in Hedwig's 'pleasure garden', one resplendent with strawberry plants, a pond, a swing, climbing roses and vegetable gardens tended by prisoners who fertilised them with human ash and excrement.[231] 'Yes, they were bringing their children, and they were so good to them,' Alicja said.

She was lucky she never fell ill. To get sick meant entering the infirmary, the waiting room for the crematorium, as the prisoners called it, where Dr Mengele and others performed medical experiments.

'At the end, you know, the Russians were not far and you could hear bombs. They still had trains to take us away, all the prisoners.'

Alicja didn't know it yet, but the train they loaded her onto was headed to Germany.

27

Sixty-eight years after my grandmother's cattle car crossed the German border, I walk from Lichterfelde Ost railway station in Berlin's outer suburbs, past boxy postwar apartment buildings to the Bundesarchiv. A plaque at the entrance reads: 'During the Third Reich here was the barracks of Adolf Hitler's SS Leibstandarte,' Hitler's personal bodyguard unit.

'I'm here to find an SS officer,' I say in German to the uniformed man peering through the archive's sentry window. 'The man saved my mother.' I smile apologetically.

The guard hands me a visitor pass and a white plastic bag emblazoned with the German coat of arms – a black eagle with red talons – and directs me to a red-brick building across a parade ground where thousands of SS officers once lined up.

After registering, I explain to a librarian with shoulder-length blonde hair that I'm looking for an SS officer who saved my mother. 'I know some details about him,' I say, trying to sound confident, 'but I don't know his name.'

Why do I need to imply this Nazi might be a 'good' Nazi? Who am I trying to protect?

'No. We can't help you,' the librarian says, scowling. 'You can't find the names of these men without the permission of the families.'

When asking strangers about this period of time, I've learned my black hair and dark eyes can make people skittish. 'Perhaps you can help me find a list of men who served in Radom Prison in 1944, and we can start there?' I ask, smiling. Patience is my goal here, although that virtue only comes out on special occasions. I have been on the road for twenty-one days. I've combed through too many prison and camp records. I miss my husband, my dog. I am exhausted.

The truth is, I have little to go on. I know from Alicja he was an officer of Ukrainian background with a reputation for torturing women, but I figure that last titbit won't get me very far. If I can find a list, I can narrow officers down by filtering for Ukrainian names, those ending with '-chko', '-enko', '-ovich', or '-iuk'.

'It will take us at least six weeks to find that kind of information,' the librarian says. 'You can't just show up. You should have emailed us.'

I did email, I explain, and was told their researchers couldn't help with this kind of search, but if I wanted to visit, I could look through reference books on my own. I show her a printed copy of the exchange. She reads it and frowns. Then she leaves her desk and walks out of the room.

It is unnerving to wait among the ghosts of Hitler's body-guards. I fidget with Alicja's filigree gold chain at my neck; a chain I will later find in pictures of her near Dachau, after the war. I scan rows of tables lined with computer screens, where dozens of men in their seventies and eighties sit along-side younger academic types. Are these people looking for Nazis, too? Trying to understand how a father or grandfather took part in Hitler's grand plan? Then again, perhaps they're researching something as ordinary as property records.

I think about the woman I sat next to on my flight from Warsaw. In a German accent crossed with nasal Australian, she asked why I was travelling to Berlin. I couldn't tell her about the Nazi, because some tourism guides still warn not to mention the war. But my jaw dropped when she told me she'd emigrated to Australia and was here interviewing children and grandchil-dren of German Nazi party members, including war criminals, for her PhD thesis on the transgenerational impacts of war.

Years later I will realise how I glossed over this term. Because I did not experience the dehumanisation, the violence, the loss of a parent – or an entire family – I find it difficult to apply the word 'trauma' to me: invincible, stubborn, opinionated. I will realise my family's traumas live inside of me, that my search for answers is in part to understand how the war, and orders to exterminate Alicja's parents and sister, has impacted me. My attempt to come to terms with it.

In the archive, I remember something my father said on the

phone a few months earlier: 'I think you want to find the Nazi more than your mother does. You're obsessed!'

I reflect on how Alicja trusted me with her stories. How I've been laying out her fragments, trying to solve her puzzle. Yes, her pain, Mietek's and my mother's *have* shaped me. So has Irena's death. Because Alicja is the grandmother I love, I must interrogate her burden, a burden that is my mother's, and now mine. Sometimes I wish it would just leave me alone.

The librarian marches through a door up the back. She holds a manila folder that includes my printed email – the one I'd sent requesting a list of SS officers. She adds a few more notes to the file and asks again what I am looking for. 'A list of Gestapo and SS officers who were stationed in Radom Prison in Poland in 1944,' I repeat.

I take the black book she hands me containing lists of reference numbers and archived descriptions. I sit at a table. The librarian logs me onto a computer, then leaves me to it.

When I open the book, it lands on an arbitrary page: Kommandeur der Sipo und SD für den Distrikt Radom. My stomach lurches. 'Vot voz his name?' I hear Alicja: 'You remember everything,' she told me. 'You might forget the names, but you don't forget what happened.'

Hunched close to the computer screen, I key in reference numbers and scour dozens of documents with titles like 'Criminal proceedings against polish citizens', (the lower case 'p' appears often, a deliberate slur against Polish people).

I tell the librarian I'd been unable to find anything meaningful besides what I hand to her on a piece of paper, a few numbers with descriptions in German.

'Maybe my colleague can help you,' she says, curtly. She wanders over to a man with a shock of neat black hair and a thick moustache like pine needles. He glances back and looks me over. After hearing my conundrum, he tells me in a polite tone to come back the next day at 2 pm. He'll have documents for me to look at. I thank both of them and leave.

The next day at 2 pm sharp I am at the reception desk. The anticipation of a discovery is killing me. I look around for the librarian with the moustache. He dips his head in my direction, but scuttles across the room away from me in an awful rush. Much later, he directs me to sit at a table.

I wait. An hour passes. Still no sign of any documents. I rifle through books on shelves close by: Aktion . . . Konzentrationslager . . . Juden . . . Groß-Rosen . . . I text my husband: 'I'm in Berlin archives looking for a murderer . . . looking at Nazi files describing arrests and killings. Not sure why I'm doing this?'

His message back is tonic: 'Because it is important. Because in some way it will make a difference, even if you don't know what that is yet. All of this is taking you somewhere you need to go. Be patient. Stay passionate.'

It's true the Nazi saved my mother, but I am the beneficiary. There is little chance this man is alive still, but I feel some irrational responsibility to thank his children. It has nothing to do with forgiveness, not after what the Reich did to my family. I wonder how a man who whipped and disfigured women would treat his own children. Knowing about his kind act might help them bear a past that was not their choosing.

Just as I am about to give up, the librarian places two reference books in front of me. He returns with a piece of paper and pencil and pulls up a chair. I retrieve the prison files I'd paid Radom archives to mail me from my plastic archive bag. I point to Alicja's prisoner number at the top of a page, hopeful he can match it to an officer.

The librarian asks questions. He scribbles notes. Then his face turns grim. 'This is very complicated. It will be very difficult,' he says.

'But the man I am looking for is of Ukrainian descent,' I tell him. 'There can't have been too many Ukrainian SS and Gestapo serving in Radom Prison.'

'Yes, that's a good clue. Let me ask a colleague.'

While I wait, I study Alicja's prison file. I turn the cover page. I scan the section titled Distinguishing Features: 6. Face. 7. Forehead. 8. Eyes. 15. Hands. 21. Special markings.

No-one seems to have recorded the enormous angry mark on Alicja's neck. I tap at her gold chain tickling mine. If Alicja's captors were so meticulous, how could they have missed her scar? In a few years I will see it noted on her Australian immigration permit, but now I think about Dr Mengele's experiments at Auschwitz and the chemicals doctors injected into their victims at Ravensbrück. I wonder if those atrocities are catalogued in the books stacked behind me.

I am obsessing about this. It's entirely possible the blemish *was* a birthmark. Purple has long captivated me. As a child I would stare at my bedroom walls papered with lipstick-purple swirls until the veins of colour pulsed, twirled, turned to tentacles and swayed like a monstrous sea anemone. The room would spin. I would sink into a kind of vortex. I wanted to be like the boy in *Willy Wonka* who fell into the chocolate river and disappeared.

The librarian slides back into the chair. He whispers, 'But there were *many* Ukrainians working in Radom Prison. I will try, but I don't hold much hope. You see, it's impossible to search by prisoner number. The records are kept under the name of the officers.'

Even if they recorded interrogations under officers' names, I want him to do a reverse search. He can see when Alicja and Mietek entered and left the prison. There must be records somewhere. Out the back, maybe? What did they *do* with all that information?

Of course, I realise with a thud: in 1944 and 1945, the Gestapo and SS tossed hundreds of thousands of files into fires as the Allies and Russians approached, to eliminate evidence of atrocities. For a second, I want to give up. But I can't. I've lurked in online forums, throwing names of Radom SS men at war buffs and collectors of Nazi memorabilia. I've pestered historians across the US, Israel, Poland and Germany. I've travelled through Poland and now Berlin. Above all, I've promised Alicja I would tell her story.

'We should never forget what happened,' she said all those years ago in her thick Polish accent that takes me back to all that accompanied it: borscht, Chopin concerts, oil paintings, trips to the beach, her gold necklace, the yoke of memory I now wear around my neck.

'People are so bad for each other, you know. They hate and kill,' she said after I'd asked what she'd like to see change in the world. 'But I don't think it's possible to change that. Everybody's got something inside them that's bad, and when the opportunity comes up, like during the war . . . it happens.

Yes, there is some evil thing in us. I think everyone must have that evil thing.'

The Ukrainian officer could have taken the jewels and killed Alicja. Other Nazis had no qualms about accepting bribes then breaking their promises. By all accounts, that officer should have killed my mother, too. Whatever his motivations, he saved their lives.

'It will be difficult, if not impossible,' I hear the librarian whispering, me too sour to notice he is trying to help.

'We don't know what we would do if we were alive at that time in those circumstances,' I say in an evangelical tone. 'This man deserves to be remembered for a good deed, despite his bad ones.'

'Ja,' the man nods, his lips turning upwards a little.

As I walk back towards the railway station, I think about what Alicja told me: 'There are certain things I was doing during the war which you, or other people who didn't go through the war, wouldn't approve of. But to me that was a normal thing to do.'

This haunts me. I will never know the full truth of what the Ukrainian took from her. I read of officers who coerced women in exchange for food, in order to defer executions,[232] to save a husband, a mother, a son, a daughter.

In this moment, Alicja's courage overwhelms me. She'd stared death in the eye. She'd utilised a source of leverage – the jewels – but instead of using them to save herself, she used them to save her sister's child. Even if I never uncover the identity of that officer, Alicja's bravery is what saved my mother. Alicja's actions catalysed my existence. If Alicja had not decided in that moment to protect – no, to *love* my mother – I would not be writing this story.

28

When the train slowed 95 kilometres north of Berlin, Alicja heard German men yelling. Dogs snarled and ran alongside her cattle car. The train jolted to a stop.

Someone outside slid the door open. Light streamed in. Women covered their eyes. After days of lying and standing in the dark and cold, the light blinded them. 'Raus! Raus!' — *Out! Out!* A German officer close to the door was yelling orders, but some women near Alicja were too sick to raise their heads. The dead lay in piles around her, stinking and rotting after the 650-kilometre journey from Birkenau.

Surrounded by thick forest, the Ravensbrück camp lay across a shimmering lake from the town of Fürstenburg. In November

1944 Alicja did not know that with the Soviet Army advancing across Eastern Europe, deportations from camps and death marches were accelerating as Hitler manoeuvred to eliminate evidence of the Third Reich's depravity. Thousands were forced to march towards Ravensbrück from Hungary, more than a third perishing along the way. Thousands, like Alicja, were hauled there by trains.

Stronger women helped the weak to exit the cattle cars. Female SS guards whipped them into a line then poked whips into ribs and buttocks. They motioned the weaker ones to step forward, and herded Alicja and others towards a tent. German Shepherd dogs strained at leashes, snarling and snapping at heels if you moved too slowly.

To cope with the overwhelming number of prisoners, Ravensbrück's Kommandant had erected a tent to process and house women. By the time Alicja arrived, a second tent had been set up; about 20 metres wide and 50 long, more than three metres high at the sides, with a twin-peaked roof, but no natural light.[233] The tent leaked. Women sloshed in a permanent puddle the size of a large classroom, fighting for space. At night, Alicja and the prisoners listened to high-pitched screams from women giving birth to babies that would soon die from starvation.[234] Earlier, there'd been straw or blankets to sleep on. Now Alicja lay with women on cold, wet, cement blocks. Behind the tent they emptied lavatory buckets into overflowing pits. Pneumonia, gangrene and typhus swept through the camp.

'You were so used to people around you dying,' Alicja would later recall. 'That was your future.'

Throughout December, the tents overflowed as yet more women arrived. Dead bodies mingled with the living. Perhaps this is where Alicja developed her habit of staring right through people. She blocked out the deafening din, the sick and starving,[235] as if they didn't exist at all.

One morning, at 3 am, the siren wailed.[236] Alicja and the women lined up in rows on the Appellplatz. Frigid winds from the Schwedtsee lake cut through thin rags of clothing. Alicja stood shivering in snow next to Lola Ksieski, the friend who'd been with her since Radom. It would take hours to count the women, who numbered about forty-five thousand. The Meisters – representatives from aircraft manufacturer Heinkel, Daimler-Benz, and munitions manufacturers – scrutinised Alicja's row. Doctors trailing them ordered women to stretch out hands, open mouths. Alicja raised her smock. The doctors inspected legs for boils and sores. The Meisters yanked the least blemished and starved from the line. Prisoners waited for eleven hours or more without food or water for their turn; those selected would last longest. Some would endure the factory slave labour, the twelve-hour day-and-night shifts, the unbearable quotas, the exhausting marches to and from the camp four times a day, and the low-calorie watered-down soup rations that smelled of horses' hooves standing in fouled straw for too long.

'Schnell! Schnell!' — *Quick! Quick!* The SS drove the screaming mob towards the train tracks. Exhausted, Alicja's legs dragged. They pushed Alicja into a cattle car. Inside, the air was thick with fear and frozen sweat.

The train hauled Alicja 80 kilometres north to a Ravensbrück sub-camp. Malchow comprised ten wind-rattled wooden barracks designed to house one thousand but overflowed with five times that.[237]

The SS chief, Reichsführer Heinrich Himmler's, new orders to accelerate exterminations included an additional gas chamber for Ravensbrück. Rudolf Höss, the formidable Auschwitz Kommandant out of a job after gas chambers there had shut down, arrived with his extermination plant overseer around the same time as Alicja. Her work at a nearby armaments factory would save her life.

Hours before dawn, Alicja would roll from her shared bunk-plank and slide onto the damp floor. She'd push bare, swollen feet into her Auschwitz-issued wooden clogs and draw her baggy smock tight.

'Zum arbeiten!' — *To work!* a guard screamed. One group of women marched to town to dig canals and clean buildings. Alicja's ragged troupe would trudge in a faltering line in a different direction – through town, past the Plauer See lake, to a clearing with artificial trees covered with netting, through a door set in a sandy hill leading to a honeycomb of underground workrooms[238] – to the Dynamit Aktien Gesellschaft (DAG) armaments factory, originally established primarily to manufacture pentaerythritol tetranitrate, a powerful explosive.

'We were going like dead people,' Alicja said, of her gruelling daily march. The 'coat-hanger' women, as they called themselves, staggered through town day after day, forbidden to utter a word at the risk of being shot. Locals watched them move through the streets. Years later, Alicja would grow irate at the suggestion that Germans didn't know what was happening. 'They could see us walking, and they were saying they didn't know!'

For hours each day, Alicja sat at a long table with twenty to thirty women, her fingers stiff and frozen. She pushed gunpowder into capsules nestled into assembly boards filled with around two dozen small holes. Alicja compressed the top half of the waffle-iron-like board against the bottom half, melding the capsules into bullets. An SS woman would glare from the end of each table, yelling at prisoners who were too slow. That year, Alicja and the enslaved women pushed out 3125 tons of explosives.[239]

But Alicja purposely misaligned the boards. The bullets still melded, but with a slight defect.[240] After hearing rumours of the Soviet advance, Alicja and the women grew bolder. They did what they could to produce bullets that would pass inspection but wouldn't fire. 'No-one would know,' Alicja said matter-of-factly. 'But if they find you out, you were shot.'

Prisoners at Malchow were expected to work to their deaths.[241] Conditions in the munition factories were harsher than the Siemens plant at Ravensbrück. Besides dying from starvation, exhaustion, madness and increasing SS cruelties, the women had to suffer the daily march to and from the factory, treacherous given the lack of food and adequate clothing. Prisoners collapsed and lay motionless. Many died while marching back and forth. Stick-thin prisoners froze standing in the snow on the Appellplatz. They fell down dead while waiting to be counted. 'We were standing there on the Platz and they were counting if everybody came back from work. If you were punished, they left you standing – everyone there for one person, standing in the snow for the whole night.'

One morning, dizzy with hunger, Alicja staggered off to work slipping and sliding on snow and ice, no match for her 'clappers', as the women who'd come from Auschwitz called their wooden clogs.[242] Each step, her toes thrust forward against wet wood. Her navicular bone smashed against the roof of the clog. Her feet chafed and bled. Any slight incline, and her heels slammed back against wood that bit and pounded her bare feet. Lola and a second woman drew closer to Alicja. The women touched her arm. She felt herself dropping, leaning her reedy body onto them. Lola propped her up with her arm.

Alicja wanted to quit that day. She wanted to lie down on the road. She said so to her friends.

'You can't do that!' they hissed. 'They'll shoot you!'

'I don't care,' Alicja said.

By the middle of January, temperatures had dropped to -30°C.[243] Ravensbrück gassings escalated. Gassing provided space for new arrivals. It also helped stretch meagre food supplies and minimised the number of prisoners who might fall into enemy hands.

Although at this point, prisoners in most camps knew about the gassings, the duping of Ravensbrück's staff and prisoners was so effective, Alicja, like many others, believed the main gas chamber no longer functioned. To avoid mass hysteria, Ravensbrück's Kommandant had spread rumours of a sanatorium with good conditions.[244] The rumours took root perhaps because Alicja and the prisoners were so desperate for hope. Meanwhile, those selected for the special sanatorium were moved out of view, behind a fence at the rear of the compound, then marched a kilometre to the youth camp.[245]

There, mostly in the early evening, the Chief Guard would brandish her silver-handled whip and order women to line up in the snow and strip naked. A dark-haired woman in a white coat would then write numbers on prisoners' forearms and chests.[246] Hours later, the SS would help load the women into trucks and deliver them back to the main camp, to a chamber by the south wall, where around two hundred women at a time could be gassed.[247] By mid-February 1945, around 1500 women had been gassed.[248] That wasn't enough. Soon, they began pushing women into a converted train wagon and buses with green painted windows.[249] The SS threw in tin cans of gas.[250]

Early in 1945, SS Obersturmführer Schwarzhuber, newly arrived from Auschwitz, issued a starvation order. Alicja's meagre calories were slashed.[251] Women ate grass and tree bark.[252] Some prisoners were locked up at the main camp without food or water. To keep Alicja alive, her friend Lola occasionally shared an extra mouthful of her soup.

Sometime before April, the SS stopped marching Alicja to the DAG factory. There was barely anything to eat. Someone had smuggled in a radio, so there was some news. 'Knowing the Russians were coming, it helped,' Alicja said. 'It was the only thing that kept me going.'

By late April, the SS in the camp were on edge, food supplies waning still. The Red Cross delivered parcels for prisoners, but the SS stole them for themselves. By this point, Alicja had faded into starvation delirium. Her bones bulged from her skin, her legs and arms unrecognisable. She thought only of food and the Russians.

One day, a guard entered Alicja's barrack. 'Raus!' — *Leave!* he commanded.

Women sobbed. After all Alicja had endured, now it was her turn to die. When the SS led her outside, Alicja made out two white buses with Red Cross signs. She was certain it was a trick. 'It was typical of the Germans to put on some signs, and you thought you'd be safe, but then they are gassing you.'

On board, Alicja noted the driver, a Black person. Surely, this meant he was American. She allowed herself to breathe. For the first time in an eternity, she felt hope. Perhaps after enduring thirteen months of prison and camps, she would live. Perhaps she would tell the world what happened to her.

Alicja had no way of knowing at the time, but the Swedes had devised a plan. They'd send in a convoy of buses to rescue all Scandinavian prisoners under the flag of the Swedish Red Cross. Count Folke Bernadotte, Red Cross vice-president and grandson of King Oscar II of Norway and Sweden, had the pedigree and track record to negotiate the deal. He'd already secured the release of captured allied airmen.[253]

Bernadotte had negotiated with Himmler to collect imprisoned Scandinavians,[254] even though Hitler had expressly forbidden such releases. It was suggested Himmler wanted to position himself strategically as a rational man the Allies could work with once Hitler was gone.[255] Still, he forbade Bernadotte to take any prisoners from Ravensbrück.

Jewish organisations, as well as the French and others, had pressured the Swedes to expand prisoner release requests to non-Scandinavians, including Jews.[256] Bernadotte was therefore shocked when, at their fourth meeting, a tired and agitated

Himmler did an about-face and told him he could send his White Buses to collect *all* remaining Ravensbrück prisoners, Jews and non-Jews alike. Himmler said the camp was about to be evacuated. With Berlin now bombed to rubble, he was manoeuvring to disassociate himself from crimes against a future Germany.[257] He no longer cared about those White Buses.

On 25 April, twenty buses arrived in Ravensbrück. Dodging bombs and craters, the buses carried the women through the ghostly German landscape – bombed-out buildings, trucks turned over like beetles on their backs – to the Danish border, and onto Sweden by ship. Alicja, finally, was free.

When Alicja arrived in Sweden, she was 1.67 metres tall and weighed about 27 kilograms. On the train carrying her to safety there, the Red Cross handed out milk and sandwiches. The ham and meat were glorious, the sandwiches dazzling. But Alicja warned the women next to her not to drink the milk, to eat only the bread, aware their bodies could not handle the rich food. 'Everyone got diarrhoea. I didn't drink. I knew I'd get sick . . . because I still had my brain.'

The train pulled into a station somewhere between Germany and Sweden. People on the platform stared at the women with strangely hollowed-out faces. Someone pressed sweets into their claw-like hands. Mothers and fathers lifted children high to see the living skeletons from Hitler's camps. 'They probably will remember that for the rest of their lives,' Alicja said.

She was awake when someone came aboard and coaxed them

to disembark. Staff carried the sick and dying off on stretchers. Stronger women in prison smocks placed arms around the weaker ones.

Alicja found herself outside a monastery. Women with sunken eyes and open sores shuffled behind nuns who led them into a large hall lined with chairs and tables laden with more food. 'There were basins, like in a bathroom, and water and towels,' Alicja recounted. 'This was so stupid because we were so dirty. They said to wash our hands before we eat. We thought they were *crazy*, these people! We were supposed to sit around the table. No-one ate. We just stared.'

Alicja had been thrust into a scene that would have been unremarkable a few years before, but for women who'd been turned into animals in the camps, the normalcy bewildered them. The neatly arranged tables, the chairs, the nuns praying on the floor, the idea of sitting down to a meal after washing: it was too much. The women found the aroma of soap and paprika, the plates of food intolerable. Finally, someone took a sandwich and put it in her pocket. 'Then we all did the same. They thought we were crazy.'

That evening, Alicja lay on a thick, clean straw mattress that smelled of a barn. Around her was a sea of mattresses. Many of the women were too weak to raise their heads. Eventually, the prostrate nuns stood and slipped from the room.

In the dark, someone reached into a pocket and pulled out a sandwich. Another followed. Another. In the dark, the women began to eat.

29

In April 1945 when the Allies approached Dachau concentration camp 666 kilometres from Ravensbrück, SS officers chased Dick through Dachau's gates and onto a train. A month earlier, Dick and Mietek had been pushed into a cattle car at the Vaihingen Enz camp near Stuttgart. Now, for the first time in a year, Dick and Mietek had been separated. Mietek lay shivering with typhus fever back in Dachau's infirmary. Dick did not expect him to live.

Inside Dick's train, Dick and the prisoners feared the SS might toss in a gas canister any minute. People heard machine sounds outside and grew convinced an allied bomb would blast the cars. The uncertainty exhausted them.

They screeched to a halt somewhere near the Austrian

border and the Tyrol mountains. The SS ordered Dick and the matchstick-thin men to line up. The men slogged towards the border in a long column. High-altitude cold and wind whipped through Dick's baggy prison clothing. Up ahead, someone fell to the ground. Dick passed the crumpled pile. Behind him, an officer aimed his gun. He heard the shot echo along the valley.

Shortly before the column reached the border checkpoint, the SS halted them. Dick stood waiting. Officials on the Austrian side denied permission to march across their border, given Austria had abandoned allegiance to Hitler. Dick heard the SS order the column to turn around. He and the men doubled back.

Snow had been falling all day. Dick sat shivering on the bank of a small mountain river cut into a narrow valley. Men wiped flakes from wet heads. Dick clawed at the snow with numb fingers and stuffed small handfuls of ice into his mouth.

The SS officers guarding him seemed restless. They'd lit fires and were rubbing their hands close to the flames. Dick watched as they tossed boxes of files carried from Dachau into the fires. In one of those boxes, Dick knew, was a list typed with his name. If the Nazis were obliterating evidence of his imprisonment, he suspected they would shoot him and the others.

That night, Dick nudged the men closest to him while the SS officers slept. 'Let's go,' Dick whispered to men in the shadows. 'If we don't leave now, tomorrow may be too late.'

The men were reluctant. Dick listened to the rush of river water tumbling over the rocks. 'We will try to reach the Americans,' he said. 'The front line is close.'

An hour later, Dick crept along the highway, followed by

around forty Hungarian and Polish Jews. Five kilometres from the river encampment, just as Dick allowed himself to believe they had escaped, he heard the sound of boots. He froze.

A young SS officer sprang from the shadows and shone a torch into Dick's face. 'Are there Jews in your group?' the officer barked, his machine gun pressed in Dick's ribs.

'No, only Poles and Hungarians,' Dick replied quickly. They'd all torn the yellow triangle indicating 'Jew' from their uniforms.

'Where are you marching?'

Dick explained his rag-tag group of men were prisoners from a Dachau concentration camp transport and had been ordered to march to the American lines. The SS officer looked at him dubiously before letting him and the others go.

The men marched for kilometres; more a slow, steady shuffle, the former prisoners too weak and emaciated to stand straight, their faces filthy and unshaven. 'We were an apparition that emerged from another world, walking skeletons dressed in clownish prison garb with wooden clogs on our feet and strange numbers on our chests, a glint of fire and determination in our eyes,' Dick said.

The men negotiated their way through German roadblocks. One German Army major gave them food and directed them to a farmhouse to shelter. They crawled through tall grass beside highways. Now and then, the ground would shudder; US artillery in the distance bombarding German positions, Wehrmacht trucks thundering by towards the fight.

One day, as the men crawled along the highway towards the American lines, a rumbling sound drifted closer: an American tank. Hope filled Dick. An American soldier's head popped up from the hatch. A minute later, the soldier began tossing out candy and cigarettes at the prisoners.

'God bless America!' Dick shouted.

Tears streamed grime down the men's faces. They collected the bounty before staggering forward.

Up ahead, Dick saw American soldiers marching towards them, singing:

'Glory, glory, hallelujah!
Glory, glory, hallelujah!'

30

On 6 May at the liberated Dachau concentration camp, a slate clapboard snapped shut.[258] A camera rolled, then it zoomed in on Mietek.

'Why are you here as a prisoner?' an American interviewer asked.

'Because I am a Jew,' Mietek said, his voice robotic.

Earlier, filmmakers John Ford and George Stevens had filmed the US Rabbi David Max Eichhorn leading a service.[259] They'd introduced Mietek as 'leader of the Jewish community'. The filmmakers had already captured the US Army 45th Division barrelling through Dachau's gates, the grizzly spectacle of human carcasses piled high.[260] Now they wanted to hear how prisoners had survived.

This is the video interview that propelled me to Poland to sift through my family's stories. Decades later, this man would become the grandfather who played with me and pulled silly faces. Later still, he would sit in his chair staring at the wall, his face as blank as a corpse.

Now I know how my family survived a war, I need to know how they could live with what they'd endured. I watch Mietek's interview over and over, looking for clues. You would never know that weeks beforehand, he'd been carried to the camp's infirmary burning with typhus fever.

'Have you family?' the American interviewer asks.

Mietek cocks his head and stammers, 'I . . . my father, he was in Warsaw. He was killed by the Germans. My sisters are now safe overseas. They escaped.' He doesn't mention Alicja. Perhaps he presumes her dead.

Hundreds of curious people surround him. Some wear striped prison uniforms. Others wear caps, plain shirts and pants. Suddenly, shots explode behind them. Only one man blinks. Mietek remains still. He wears that blank expression I remember. War taught him to block out emotions, too. This had helped him focus on hope that he'd survive, that allied troops would eventually free him. 'If we hadn't that hope, we would kill ourselves,' Mietek says into the camera.

I wonder how he will shelve six years of brutality in order to start over and raise a family. It's possible grief struck him every minute of every day, and as a child I did not see it. I presumed the mysteries in our house were normal.

'Have you had many friends go to the crematorium?' the interviewer asks.

'No one of my friends is left. All of them are in the crematorium.' A corner of Mietek's mouth twitches. 'The crematorium,
that was the nice death which killed our friends and our families.'
He emphasises nice. 'They tortured us in other ways much worse.
You were hanged. You were beaten to death, one hundred fifty,
two hundred times with whips.'

I think about Radom Prison: the electrical cables, the leather
whips and rubber lashings.

'They had also in Auschwitz a special kind of treatment.
They put a piece of wood behind your neck, and with their foot
they break your neck.' Mietek cups his hands behind his neck to
demonstrate. Maybe he thinks Alicja died like this. In his mind,
maybe this is kinder than gas.

'You were telling me your feelings about the future?' the interviewer gently prods.

'Our future is a question we cannot picture now.' Mietek tells
the American about the millions killed in the gas chambers of
Auschwitz, Treblinka and other death camps. 'We are more
than sure that no-one is alive from our families. We are without
homes – we have been put out from our homes in Poland. Then
we have been put out from the ghettos and taken to concentration camps. Now the problem is that every other nation can go
home. They know their addresses, they know someone will be
waiting for them; their families, their wives, their children. We
don't know what will be with us. We have no place to go back.
We are like beggars without homes, without anything . . .'

Dachau's liberated Jewish prisoners elected my thirty-four-
year-old grandfather as their leader, even though he was an
atheist. A lawyer fluent in English, Polish, German, French

and Russian, at night in the barracks he'd urged them to recite SS officers' names along with specifics of their most insidious crimes. He had been cataloguing lists of them in his head for more than a year.

'We are of different nations and we were destroyed here,' Mietek says to the interviewer. 'But now we come together. From today we will unite and hope it will improve with us.'

Putting the SS on trial for war crimes. Seeing them hang. This will be Mietek's revenge.

Meanwhile, days earlier in Malmö, Sweden, Alicja and other women were carried off a ferry on stretchers.[261] Outside a series of tents, men in white coats who knew nothing of Auschwitz asked women to step inside and strip so they could be sprayed with disinfectant, and then asked them to stand under showers. Nurses swooned at the shrunken bodies and fell to the floor.

Thirty-year-old Alicja swirled in delirium. 'What is your name?' one nurse asked her.

'I don't know,' she whispered, her only proof of identity – 2 4 5 3 3 5 – printed on her arm.

Survivors were dying all around her. The thought of telling the world about what the Nazis were inflicting on people had kept her going; dreaming of freedom had kept her alive. But now, that freedom was undamming the grief and hopelessness that Alicja and other prisoners had repressed for years. The Red Cross and Jewish organisations nursing them despaired. Eventually, doctors realised the starved women could not digest food, so they eliminated dairy and meat from their diets. Alicja's health began to improve along with her appetite. 'We-want-bread! We-want-bread!' she and other women shouted. They yelled for potatoes, too.

The war was over. Countries and families had been split into shards and scattered throughout Europe. Alicja was alive, but the war had stolen everything. Her mother, father, her sister Irena, her brother Henryk, all dead. She had no idea if Mietek or her brother Kuba were alive. And what of Joasia?

The Red Cross and Jewish organisations typed up lists of names and set up files to help survivors search for missing family. Months after Alicja regained strength, the Red Cross asked who she wanted to contact. She listed Mietek as missing.

'I didn't know if he survived,' Alicja said.

It was at this point that Alicja changed her birth year from 1915 to 1920. I suspect it was her way of trying to cope after losing more than five years of her life, time she would never recover. Alicja also listed her new name as 'Alice'. She left her old name behind, in the camps.

'It was a different world, suddenly. It was difficult,' Alicja told me. 'I didn't cry a lot,' she added.

That was Alicja. So full of grit she needed to clarify this, for the record.

After receiving the Red Cross communication records from the US Holocaust Museum, I phone my mother. 'You were the first person Nana wanted to contact. First on her list!'

'Really?' Mum says.

'Do you think that's a sign she loved you?' I ask, too enthusiastically.

'I suppose it is.'

This puzzles me. That my mother can be all hugs and kisses when she cannot remember receiving love.

Alicja's brother, Kuba, found her on a Red Cross list. He'd escaped Gestapo arrest by hiding in a convent and was living in Brussels. By this point, Alicja and a small group of women moved from the refugee camp in the Swedish town of Lund to work in a hospital on TB wards.

'Kuba got mad at me because he thought I would get sick working there,' Alicja said half a century later. The hospitals needed refugees like her to translate. 'We couldn't speak Swedish, just a little bit of English. I pretended I had a Red Cross Diploma from Poland.'

Pretending helps you move forward. Alicja dressed in a white apron, mopped floors, cajoled patients and emptied chamber pots. Even months after she arrived in Sweden, she continued to watch women die. 'You can't imagine. People who were still walking, who thought they were alright, once they were free they couldn't walk any more. It was the end.'

But working in the hospital had benefits. 'We had a bath,' Alicja almost purred. 'It was *wonderful* for us to have a bath.' After years of having to dip her sleeve into watered down coffee and soup to wash herself, Alicja was clean again.

She and her friends preferred the night shift. In between napping and walking around the wards to check on patients,

Alicja's access to refrigerators was unfettered. After years of thinking about food, now it was everywhere. And she had recovered enough physically that she could relish rich food rather than fear it. 'We ate cream and fruit and milk. I got so fat I thought I couldn't walk on the stairs!' Alicja laughed. 'I had short breath and palpitations. The doctor told me I gained too much weight too quickly.'

Somehow, she found the will to build herself up again when everyone she loved was gone. Although she'd listed Mietek as missing with the Red Cross and tried not to think about him, it was impossible.

One day, someone at the hospital found her on a ward and told her to come to the office. After years of blending into a sea of grimy, nameless faces, it must have felt strange to hear someone call her by her name. In the office, Alicja nervously picked up the phone. The woman on the other end introduced herself. 'Do you have a chair? Sit down. Are you sitting?'

'Yes, I'm sitting,' said Alicja.

'I heard on the radio, they were talking about people who survived Dachau,' the woman said.

I picture Alicja's left hand tugging the cord.

'I heard your husband's name,' said the voice.

31

Mietek, of course, did not know Alicja was alive. Two months after the Allies liberated him, he and other Dachau inmates were busy drawing up lists of survivors. A representative from the Jewish Committee for Relief Abroad visited the camp and reported that: 'Dachau has a well-organised Jewish Information office whose chief representative is Dr Dortheimer, a capable Polish Jew.'[262]

At this point, two thousand Jews remained in the camp. Jewish Poles had refused to be transferred to a different camp set up for Polish nationals. 'Non-Jewish Poles are still actively anti-Semitic,' Mietek wrote in a report. This, despite that for the past three years, Polish people had watched the SS line up their fellow citizens for crematoriums. A year after Mietek wrote his report, some Polish citizens would act on the same racist premise. A conspiracy theory would spread in Kielce that Jewish survivors had kidnapped a child and were planning to sacrifice him. Polish citizens and police would beat Jewish Poles with steel rods and clubs.[263] They would shoot them, stab them with bayonets and kill forty-two. Conspiracies have a way of splitting nations. Tens of thousands of Jewish Poles, including those who returned from the Soviet Union,[264] would then race towards Poland's borders, most headed, of all places, to Germany.

But now, most Dachau prisoners were still wearing concentration camp uniforms, and there was a marked shortage of underwear. Mietek requested English dictionaries and literature in Yiddish, Hebrew, German, Polish, French, Hungarian and Romanian, to help survivors re-engage with a world outside the fences.[265] 'Large numbers of Jewish women were said to have been evacuated to Sweden from Ravensbrück, women formerly in Auschwitz,' Mietek's report said. 'Garmisch is supposed to have about a thousand Jews who were evacuated from Dachau.'

It isn't clear if Mietek knew Dick marched there, or if he hoped Alicja was among the former Auschwitz women. What is clear is that Mietek was on the hunt.

Mietek wasn't searching for long. Three weeks later, more than 100 kilometres from Dachau, in Garmisch, Mietek squeezed Dick's hands. Dick lay in a hospital where a doctor determined his severe stomach pains were due not only to malnutrition but also to a duodenal peptic ulcer.

'Dear dearest Mr Meyer!' Mietek typed in German to the American Jewish Joint Distribution Committee's Swiss representative. 'I am most saddened at the condition of my brother-in-law.'[266]

Mietek had found Dick. As for his family, Mietek knew only that his two sisters were alive, in Australia. Both men told Mr Meyer they yearned to go there. Poland was a cemetery. Nine out of ten Jewish Poles had perished. Nothing could bring back more than three million dead Jews. In total, Poland had lost nearly five million of its citizens.[267]

Dick had been searching, too. 'The first person I attempted to contact at the end of the war was my brother-in-law, Mietek,' Dick would write years later. The bond between the two men was stronger than that with his own daughter. 'I was all the time with Mietek, we stuck together,' Dick said.

The two men set up the Jewish Information Office in Garmisch to register survivors. They networked for food and supplies. Dick commandeered German council trucks to pick up bread from the SS barracks in Dachau to feed survivors. The men wrote letters to officials and old family connections. 'Our Jews are waiting for help!' they entreated Mr Meyer.

The connection Mietek and Dick forged during the war and in its aftermath would bond them for life. Years later, as a girl, I watched 'Uncle' Dick embrace Papa Mietek. Their first time seeing one another in over thirty years, it sounded like dogs whimpering. They squeezed their eyes shut as they sobbed.

By August, Mietek was working for the Americans in Dachau as administrative director of the War Crimes Branch. He had complete access to the SS compound and bunker to solicit information and to oversee high-ranking Nazis awaiting trial.

A photo taken at this time disturbs me. Mietek in a suit and tie stands outside in the compound, next to Field-Marshal Erhard Milch who oversaw the development of the Luftwaffe, and a shirtless, thin-chested Nazi general. The two German prisoners wear shorts. Mietek and the men casually smoke cigarettes and appear to be conversing.

'They looked no different from scores of people you might see in any city street,' Mietek would tell a journalist years later in Australia.[268] 'This deceived the Americans – who had no experience of Nazi dual personalities – into leniency on many occasions.' At trials, SS members blamed others for the killings, some insisting they'd been forced to join the Nazi party. Others believed the Protocols of Zion conspiracy theory (that flourishes still today) that a cabal of Jewish elites wanted to take over the world, and were responsible for Germany's economic ills.[269]

'There was one guard we nicknamed The Bonecrusher,' Mietek continued. 'He used to put the fingers of prisoners in the crack of a door and shut it. He was a married man and had a house near the compound. In the dusk of the evening we used to see him strolling along the road with his wife, singing lullabies to a baby in his arms.'

This duality comes across in that photograph. Three men standing, two of them Nazi criminals, one a Jew – but in that moment, for one moment of time, they appear to be men in light conversation, as if standing around a backyard barbecue.

When I think about Papa Mietek now, I think about his chair nestled under a window against a bookshelf in his Burwood lounge room – the velvet a blue so deep you thought of the ocean, so plump my bottom would disappear, my legs swinging off the floor. When Papa sat there, he'd cross one leg over his thigh, perch glasses on his nose and stare at a book or newspaper. We all knew it was Papa's chair. I never remember Nana in it. She always sat far away from the scary books about Auschwitz. I never remember her dusting the bookshelf or placing flowers underneath the window. But she'd often carry in a plate of cake for Papa. And a cup and saucer for his tea.

32

When the war in Europe ended in May 1945, my mother was days shy of three years old. Months earlier, Poland had been cut off when the Red Army swept into a Warsaw that was a wasteland of rubble. Himmler had ordered the city be razed after Warsaw's citizens rose up to oust the Germans. Demolition experts had methodically dynamited houses and other structures across neighbourhoods. The destruction surpassed Hiroshima and Nagasaki combined.[270]

Later that summer in Germany, Dick pleaded with a woman on a repatriate transport headed for Poland to inquire in Otwock as to whether his mother, Helena, was alive. Dick received Helena's letter later that year. He learned she had served as a nurse in the AK resistance during the Warsaw Uprising, that the Germans had arrested her, and that she had escaped a camp through a latrine.

With transportation and postal services still in disarray, Dick got word to his mother as to where the SS officer had driven Joasia. Helena set off for the convent. But when Helena showed up in Suchedniów, Joasia was gone.

My mother recalls moving between three houses after the convent. She was told to call the women mama, and men who did 'bad things' to her, ojciec, or father.

'What kind of bad things?' I ask her.

My mother's eyes glaze over. She begins to cry. This is warning enough I should not push her. It seems my desire for truth trumps her wellbeing. I'm a daughter who has morphed into interrogator. I am torn between not asking questions and asking her more. If I don't push, when it comes to her faith in Dick's version of events and her conviction that Alicja didn't love her – how can I piece together whom she should believe? I wish I had let Mum stick to whatever version she needed.

'Fetch and carry, fetch and carry,' my mother remembers of long days in the third house. 'I worked like a slave.' She was between three and four years old. A dirt-streaked smock hung loosely from her body, space enough for warm, groping fingers.

Some Polish people took in Jewish children out of empathy and compassion.[271] Although the Suchedniów sisters treated my mother kindly, more common was to treat them as cheap labour.[272] I read an account of one seven year old who washed nappies, cleaned the house and carried water from the cellar. Her 'rescuers' beat her unconscious.[273] It's difficult to interpret how a child compartmentalises traumas, how my mother designated sexual ones a period in time, a specific place. In my research, I read that children as young as two remember events. And babies as young as eleven months accurately recall incidents.[274] This hits me hard. My mother was eleven months old when her mother was shot.

It was Dick's former bookkeeper who'd convinced the nuns in the Suchedniów convent that he was connected to my mother's family. He was the one who'd whisked my mother away from the convent. Helena showed up in Katowice to collect Joasia from the bookkeeper early in 1946. She paid him for taking good care of Joasia, Dick wrote.

But Alicja's view of events contravened Dick's. 'They thought they would get a lot of money for her if her family is alive,' she said of the bookkeeper and his family. 'Because it was like that. When someone found a child hidden somewhere, you had to pay for them.'

It saddens me that it was common for people to demand payment to release Jewish children.[275] And that when Jewish survivors began trickling back into Poland, those who'd left homes and valuables with neighbours were not always welcomed.[276] Sometimes, people who'd taken over Jewish mills and small businesses killed the returning owners.

'Mietek paid my ransom,' my mother says, on one of those rare occasions she agrees with Alicja. Given Mietek was earning a US Army salary, Dick asked Mietek to send Helena the money.

❀

In Warsaw, Helena ushered Joasia into a room on Lekarska Street, inside one of the few townhouses still standing. It smelled of curdled milk, soot and wet plaster. Nearly 90 per cent of the city had been bombed to ash. Less than 6 per cent of the prewar population, 174,000 people, remained in the city, including approximately 11,500 Jewish Poles[277] and thousands more starting to trickle back into Poland from the Soviet Union.[278] People turned over bricks looking for books and photos in the dust. They moved into basements of blown-up buildings. They plundered furniture from abandoned tenements. They stripped wood from ceilings and door frames and burned it to cook food with water lugged from the Vistula River. Over time, the Communists set up a ration card system, but if you had money, you could buy food on the black market from 'stalkers' who carried baskets of vegetables down streets, or from farmers who'd smuggle pieces of meat under their jackets and in milk cans, and then chop them up on dirty tree stumps or on piles of bricks.

I picture my nearly four-year-old mother looking out a window on Lekarska Street, sliding her finger along the sill, pushing and dragging the little swirl of black grit. Dirt, dust and grime will obsess her for the rest of her life. Decades into the future, she will pack cloths, sponges and yellow vinyl gloves in her suitcase when she visits me in Boston. She will mop, scour and scrub to put things in order. Things she can control.

'The child was locked up the whole day in her room,' Alicja said. 'That was her grandmother looking after her with hardly anything to eat. She had this soldier who was doing everything for your mother. That soldier was giving her some food.'

Alicja certainly had her own theories, but I can never be certain exactly what happened in that room. Memory is a slippery creature. Fragments from Mum's childhood bore no timestamps. Maybe bad things happened back in Katowice under the supervision of Dick's bookkeeper, maybe it happened here on Lekarska Street. She was a child without a father, too young to know a man's gaze.

'Dick's mother married a Russian officer.' Alicja's eyes narrowed to slits, her way of explaining the junior soldier in my mother's room. 'Did Dick tell you about that? It was very convenient,' she said, her voice skewered with spite. I think she wanted to say: *That woman was a whore. Just like Dick.*

Alicja didn't tell me that Helena's new husband was a Holocaust survivor, a Jewish doctor like Dick's father, that Warsaw was uninhabitable, that the Soviet secret police were hunting down AK members like Helena.[279] A husband with a military pass gave Helena access to food and one of the few intact buildings in the former German-only sector of the city.[280]

How ironic that Alicja judged Dick's mother after Helena had surmounted starvation, after she'd crawled through sewers waiting for the toss of a German hand grenade, after she'd nursed limbless men and women blown up fighting the Germans during two uprisings. Alicja herself told me how the war had altered her. 'Certain things which for you are terrible, I don't have a problem,' she said – what was illegal, or what we might consider wrong in peacetime, hadn't mattered back then. She wouldn't give me examples. 'I had to step out of the boundaries to survive,' she said.

❋

I always believed the reason Dick gave my mother away was because Mietek offered to take her to Australia. In Dick's first bombshell letter to my mother, he explained how Alicja and Mietek had made that offer on one condition: he allow them to adopt her as their daughter. I believed he agreed because he wanted to protect her and enable her future. The war was over, he wrote in his letter, but he had no money; he had lost everything. Sending Joasia to Australia was his only choice. Far from the horrors of war.

At some point, adoption papers had been drawn up for my mother. My assumption was that Alicja and Mietek requested this, because they would be raising her. Apparently, they asked Dick to sign papers declaring he would never contact her.

It turns out my assumptions are wrong – about this, and a lot of things. Including why Dick gave up his daughter.

Here is where the story turns. In February 1946, Dick was living downstairs in a room on Riffelstrasse, in a chalet on the edge of the alpine town of Garmisch. Remember this: the waterfall's icicle fronds, snow-covered fields, a frozen lake. The nearby Polish officers' camp had given Dick clothing and food and issued him a US Army permit to travel by car. This enabled Dick to visit his brother-in-law, Kuba, in Brussels.

In Brussels, Dick stepped into an office. He signed adoption papers. He paid 180 Belgian francs to legalise his signature. The paper reads as follows:

I the undersigned Przygoda Zdzisław, engineer–architect, born on 25.2.1913 in Warsaw, Poland, declare herewith that I agree without reservation that my daughter JOANNA PRZYGODA born on 17.VI.1942 in Warsaw, daughter of Irena Mizne, be adopted by my brother–in–law Mr Dortheimer Mieczysław and my sister–in–law Mrs Alicja Dortheimer–Mizne, sister of my wife, so she can depart with them to Australia. My wife, Irena Mizne, was shot by the Germans in Poland in 1943.

Bruxelles, 6 February 1946

When it comes to events and facts Dick has told me about, and written down and published, almost everything checks out. Everything except his account of how he came to give up my mother. The first clue: there is no signature from Alicja or Mietek on the so-called adoption papers. The second: the February 1946 date on the Brussels document. In February, Dick's three-and-a-half-year-old daughter was barricaded in a room in Warsaw. When Dick signed this document, he had not laid eyes on her for two years. Before being reunited with his daughter, how could a father decide to give her away?

33

Five months after the 'adoption' papers were legalised, Polish soldiers arrived at Helena's door. The Belgian embassy had sent them. Helena had received word and was waiting. When the soldiers tugged four-year-old Joasia from Helena, she screamed, but Helena let her go. She knew the child would soon receive what she lacked: medical attention, milk and meat.

One of the soldiers tucked my mother into a metal seat at the back of an enormous military aircraft. She remembers the plane: ropes hanging, a ceiling of steel curved around her like a tunnel, a smell of men and sweat. When the plane shrieked and lurched forward, she clenched her jaw. As her stomach plummeted during lift-off, she clung to the ropes. She could not afford to let go.

I think about my mother alone on that plane hurtling towards Brussels, and the father who would be invisible to her.

When the US military plane from Brussels touched down near Dachau, my mother and Mietek emerged through a side door. Mietek had explained to the Americans that Joasia was a child of some witnesses, referring to the Nuremberg and Dachau trials. But after the plane landed, he told the Americans that Joasia was *his* child.

Word must have buzzed around that a child was arriving from Poland. Cameras flashed at the scrawny girl with knobby knees and thick ankles who dug her fingernails into her palms. A Polish officer guarding the SS at the Dachau camp passed her an orange. Another held out chocolate. My mother had never seen fruit or chocolates. She cried and asked for cabbage and potatoes.

In Dick's version of my mother's rescue, Helena had written from Poland begging him to collect Joasia. Dick had leaned on a former leading Belgian government official, Arthur Haulot,[281] who'd lain in a bunk alongside Mietek and him, who organised to send my mother to Brussels on the understanding she was a Belgian repatriate.

But Dick's version clashes with Alicja's. Alicja claimed that her brother, Kuba, helped remove my mother from Poland, through the Red Cross. 'Kuba knew everybody,' she insisted.

These two different versions perturb my mother. She prefers Dick's. 'She wasn't even there!' my mother says, angry at Alicja. 'She made up her version!'

My mother wants Dick to be the one who lobbied officials, Dick to be the one who leveraged his connections, Dick to be the one who rescued her. She wants to believe in her father's love.

After the plane landed in Dachau, Alicja was the one who led four-year-old Joasia to the camp barracks. Alicja watched as US Army medics pinched my mother's swollen legs and wrists, poked her ribs and flashed lights in her eyes. Alicja listened as doctors diagnosed malnutrition and rickets.

A lack of Vitamin D had retarded my mother's growth, the doctors said. It had weakened muscles and softened her bones.[282] Her skin had rarely absorbed sunlight while hiding inside.[283] Alicja watched as doctors injected my mother with calcium.

My mother moved with Alicja and Mietek to a villa on Schillerstrasse in Dachau formerly occupied by an SS general, where refugee families each had a room. Alicja boiled and mashed vegetables for my mother and fed her apple sauce from jars. Alicja knew little about rickets, but a lot about malnutrition. Months passed before she would allow my mother to chew and swallow solid food.

Only then would my mother wolf down tiny pieces of meat and cheese. Always small portions. She thought about food constantly, the feeling of beef rolling on her tongue, the smoky, fat aroma. She was so hungry that one day she knelt on the floor next to a bowl filled for Bonke, Alicja's Jack Russell-Chihuahua cross. My mother scooped up dog food by the fistful, then retched. Alicja was the one who rushed her to the doctors at the army base.

When I was a child, Mum wouldn't allow me to leave the table until I'd finished every scrap of food – even liver. I remember sitting alone staring at the rubbery meat that even fried onions cannot mask. My mother owns a drawer full of Tupperware but cannot bear putting leftovers in the fridge. So, we eat everything. I still pick at my sister's and brothers' plates. My husband says he's never seen appetites so enormous. People visiting for dinner hold up their hands and protest my mother ladling seconds and thirds. But not my sister or brothers. The only thing for my mother is to make sure we never go hungry.

In a photo taken outside the three-storey Dachau villa, my mother stands near a pine tree, her hair in a ponytail, braids tucked into her neck. Dressed like a toy sailor in a pleated frock, striped sleeves and collar, she clenches her fists, holding in fear, damming up anger.

Living near the former concentration camp, Alicja suppressed anger, too. 'I had a terrible time in Dachau, for a long, long time. I was terrified. I couldn't stand those Germans, the voice and the language.'

Every day, five or six former German commandoes would arrive at the villa, with Polish guards to monitor them. 'Which of you has the highest rank?' Alicja would ask the prisoners. She ordered them to clean the toilets and scrub floors. At first, my mother would watch crouched in her spot under the table, clinging to her doll.

'I was the boss standing there telling them what to do,' Alicja said. If the men didn't clean the toilet to her satisfaction, she ordered them to clean it again. 'I felt it was my revenge. Yes, it made me feel better.'

Alicja would visit the former concentration camp to prey on the interned SS men and women officers. In the SS bunker, she would gaze into cells through wire grates and chutes in locked doors and say nothing. 'They stood there quietly, like I was some officer,' she said. She would walk through Munich with the air of a conquerer. 'They were hungry and cities were ruined completely. It was a nice feeling to see no house standing. It was revenge, as it should be,' she told me.

Mietek's revenge played out at the Dachau and Nuremberg trials, where transcripts of his perpetrator interviews aided prosecutors. His job also gave Alicja access to the US Army supply store. For the first time in years, Alicja shopped. She ate lavishly in the army canteen. Maybe she thought about her wedding ring, how she'd traded it in Auschwitz for a small piece of bread. It must have been a strange sight, the Polish Jew dressed in a US Army uniform, his tall wife piling a plate high with cakes and cream.

34

Alicja had been right about Dick. Seven months before he legalised the 'adoption' document, when Alicja was still recovering in Sweden, Dick pivoted away from Irena.

Picture the large chalet in Garmisch fronting a babbling brook on Rathaus Street, the Polish Information Office where Dick is the secretary. Standing at the counter is a woman named Margrit. Dick, who is thirty-two, makes her out to be in her twenties. She smiles at him, her lips red and firm, like strawberries. Margrit wants to know about her in-laws, Polish Jews. They live south of Lwów. He notices her lips flatten. Her eyelashes flutter. He ushers her into his small office.

Now Dick is all business. 'Your family is most likely dead,' he tells Margrit. 'Few Jews in that area survived.' See Margrit's hand shake when she raises it, when she wipes a gloved finger under her eye. As she weeps, Dick listens. It is strange for him to feel emotions after all he's been through. He notes down particulars. He will ask the Red Cross to inquire further. 'Come back,' says Dick. 'Come back to see if there's news.'

This is how it began. They were young. They had both lost something. For years, Dick had lined up next to men who looked like cadavers, who smelled of death, who felt dead inside. Every time Dick saw Margrit, he noticed his breathing. In a photo, Margrit's hair is wild and alive – untamed, not the severe, pulled-back bun you'd expect a German woman to wear at that time. Blonde tousles you want to fling to the side of a pillow.

The two discussed travel, philosophy, books. Mark Twain's *Following the Equator* riveted them. Dick compared Margrit to a philosopher Twain met in India: 'An incarnation so pure, the holy man can walk naked on the street.'

At night, Dick thrashed his arms. In nightmares, he flinched at Gestapo whips tearing at his skin. He awoke in a sweat, his heart galloping. I see Margrit running fingers down his chest. If Dick was to learn how to live again, to love, Margrit would teach him. She encouraged him to plan for the future, Dick told me. To undertake a doctorate in engineering. To plot a path for his new life. Maybe she'd already told him her husband was missing, and that like Dick, her husband was Jewish, and that he once owned a factory in Munich. But maybe she waited to tell him this.

Margrit invited Dick to her Riffelstrasse chalet – remember the chalet I told you about? You could hear church bells toll from

Margrit's patio, cows lowing in the fields. The sound of water whooshed from falls near the lake. Margrit introduced Dick to her Viennese mother. A German firm offered Dick a position as a regional engineer, but he did not want to work for Germans. Margit offered Dick a room downstairs. He filled his room with papers and a drawing board, and took a job working for the US Third Army to design their winter sports centre and oversee its construction.

Margrit would write to Dick that, 'we are two souls wandering different roads but in harmony with each other, each developing in their own way'.

'He wanted to marry her,' Alicja would tell me decades later, her shoulders slumped. 'She said, "never with a child!"'

The thing about clues is that you don't always pay them the attention they deserve. Now I know that Dick set up the adoption document while my mother was still in Poland, I think I missed the turning point in my mother's whole story. I missed what Alicja meant: Dick had fallen in love with Margrit, and that's why he gave my mother away. And the fact that Margrit shunned Joasia – it hurt. Alicja didn't want Irena's memory to be erased, as though her sister had never existed. She felt wounded on Irena's behalf – and on my mother's behalf as well. And she bristled with anger towards Dick.

35

At the villa close to the Dachau camp, Alicja touched her gravid belly. Beneath jagged hills dotted with spruce, fir and pine, she watched Joasia play with Bonke the dog on the lawn. Joasia knelt next to the small dog in her dungarees. Mietek snapped a photograph, wanting to capture the sweet moment, but my mother screwed up her face.

To placate Joasia's angry moods, Mietek had constructed a train set on a table in the lounge room. At a carnival in Hamburg mingling with thousands of revellers, he hoisted her on his hip, then watched her spin on a roundabout pony. She fed donkeys and watched polar bears on a trip to the zoo. Slowly, Joasia was making progress. At the army base, the doctors gave her candy.

She had grown less scared of the soldiers; the Americans sang her ditties as they knelt beside her. Her health had improved, but she still had issues. Unruly. Aggressive towards adults and children for no apparent reason.[284]

Alicja did not know about the emotional and mental health conditions of the estranged Jewish children who'd survived. Alicja didn't know how she would take care of this angry child when, seventeen months after arriving on a stretcher in Sweden, she was expecting a child of her own. After the camps, it had taken six months for her period to return. She feared the Germans had done something to her. Maybe her baby would have brain damage or be missing organs as a result of the starvation and traumas of the camps. Irena had eaten so little during her pregnancy – and look how Joasia turned out. Alicja sealed off her fears. Like many survivors, she built a wall.

Months passed. Mietek carried in a Christmas tree and set it up in the lounge room. Joasia ran her fingers through the tinsel. Soon after, Alicja rocked her new baby Antony in a chair. Alicja's feeling at this time must have been relief. Her baby signified a new start. Maybe she saw her mother in Antony's eyes, and her father's ears. Alicja would always remember Eljasz and Dorota. But maybe Antony would help her forget, too.

The nanny Alicja hired wore a white cap and apron and pushed Antony in an enormous rattan pram while Joasia walked alongside them. The Americans had issued nannies with health certificates and vetted them for Nazi party connections.[285] 'Sometimes she wouldn't let me hold him,' Alicja said of one. 'But I had to have a nanny. I had no mother; I didn't know what you do with a child.'

The nanny, however, was stern. She threw away the threadbare doll my mother slept with, the doll she'd carried from Poland, the doll she rarely let go.

'Poor child,' Alicja remembered, tenderly. 'She cried and cried.'

Decades later, Alicja would realise how the nanny discarding my mother's one comfort object had haunted her. 'I thought maybe that's why she was always so stubborn. Always very stubborn and angry,' Alicja said about Joasia.

After the camps, like many survivors, Alicja shut down when she saw people crying. Repressing empathy was a way to survive. She was able to recognise Joasia's difficulties later, but not in the moment.

In the end, Alicja fired the nanny for overfeeding Antony. She had seen people die from rapid weight gain. 'He was so *fat*,' she said of her baby boy.

Shortly after my mother arrived in Germany, and before Antony was born, Mietek drove her and Alicja to the Nuremberg trials in a BMW 327 sports coupé. My mother remembers the journey, but not watching Albert Speer, Hitler's minister for armaments and war production, skirting prosecutors' questions, denying he knew about plans to exterminate Jews. She was unaware that the BMW Mietek drove had supposedly been built for Speer. It may even have been requisitioned from Speer's wife.

Outings in the BMW remain stamped in my mother's memories. Mietek would drive my mother to Brussels with Alicja to visit Kuba. The weekend they drove to the German alpine village of Garmisch to visit her 'Uncle', Mietek peeled back the sunroof. The BMW raced along winding roads below the Zugspitze mountain. The trees blurred. Wind tore at my mother's hair.

The first time my mother had visited her 'uncle', Dick lay sick in bed in an infirmary. Even today, she remembers the smile stretched across Dick's face, the most enormous smile she'd ever seen. Sometimes Dick would sing to her in a deep baritone. They would natter in Polish, and then she'd repeat to him German phrases she'd recently learned.

On this particular day, American soldiers walked with her and Dick along a path on the outskirts of Garmisch. The burly men helped her pluck white-petalled, fuzzy edelweiss flowers, split the stems and fashion them into a crown. Edelweiss is said to hold mystical powers: roots tunnel deep to anchor it from extreme winds, furry bracts store moisture to withstand the hottest sun. When the Americans placed clusters of edelweiss in my mother's hair, she twirled and danced. She tossed her head back and laughed. The sound of her laughing surprised her. Dick snapped a photo of her smiling.

While Dick was watching, if he had thought about it, he might have noticed his daughter's anger changing to delight at the posy the soldiers put in her hair. He might have noted how teaching a child to laugh again could help him heal.

Back in Dachau, before bed, my mother removed the flowers. In the morning, she put the crown in her hair. Much later, when the flowers wilted and died, she wore them, still. Not wanting them gone, ever.

'He didn't have time for her. He was busy with other things,' Alicja said about Dick and my mother.

It's interesting that Mietek was the one who drove my mother to see Dick in Garmisch. I did not know this when I interviewed Alicja, but I will later find in a box containing Dick's personal documents a photo of Margrit, presumably in Garmisch, draped in a fur coat sitting at the wheel of a car.

'He *never* did anything for his daughter,' Alicja told me. 'Absolutely nothing! Just left like that!' she said, clasping her palms, pressing her forefingers together. 'The father should have gone and picked her up in Brussels. Not *us*.' Alicja's face reddened. 'Because he *could* pick her up. He was free. He *could* travel.'

'Did you argue about it?' I asked Alicja.

'No, no. I don't think so,' she said calmly.

'So, you offered to adopt her?'

'I offered to take her to Australia, because we knew we wanted to go there.'

'What did Dick say?'

'He agreed with that. Didn't even worry for a minute,' snapped Alicja.

It was less socially acceptable then for a single man to raise a child,[286] and it's possible Dick believed my mother would be safer far away from Europe. But now I know Alicja's offer to take her occurred *after* my mother arrived in Brussels, I understand better the anger she and my mother both bear.

Dick lived with Margrit until around the time Alicja, Mietek, Joasia and Antony boarded the *Napoli* in 1948 to sail to Australia.

Until the day the husband who Margrit thought was dead walked up her path on Riffelstrasse and knocked on her door.

I wonder if Dick letting himself love another woman after the Nazis had killed his wife may have been him trying to prove to himself that Germany lost the war, like Mietek driving Speer's supposed BMW. I see Dick's falling in love with Margrit as a sort of revenge. Revenge again when he took up with a Polish woman after losing Margrit, and moving with her to Israel, before emigrating to Canada. And when they later divorced and Dick fell in love yet again and married another woman he'd met while living in Germany, I see grief mixed in, too. Or maybe this is how you survive a regime that aspired to kill you – by constantly moving and loving and striving to start over and asserting your right to exist.

Dick had lived through something terrible. But so had Alicja and my mother. People deal with calamity differently; they grieve differently. The camp survivors were now physically free, but every day they had to push away thoughts of lost loved ones. Whenever they saw a man with his arm around a woman's waist, a child tossing a ball or skipping rope, a grandfather bouncing a granddaughter on his knee, their thoughts hurtled back in time. Back to Dachau and Auschwitz. Days when they wanted to die.

36

In October 1948, my six-year-old mother and her family settled into a granny flat behind Mietek's sister's house on Riversdale Road, Camberwell, in Melbourne. Two small rooms, a kitchen, an outside laundry. My mother's two new cousins lived with her Aunt Giza in the rambling Edwardian out the front. Through the window, my mother would listen to trams rumbling along the busy road, *ker-clickety-clunk, ker-clickety-clunk*. In the evenings, the wheels screeched when they came to a stop to let off men in suits carrying briefcases. The scraping sound of cattle car doors closing on a train.

Alicja had to ride the tram to town to shop. When conductors in buttoned jackets and leather pouches approached to sell

her a ticket, she had to fight off rising panic. At night, sometimes police or fire sirens wailed outside. My mother would
wake shaking. She saw visions of aircraft flying at her through
the window. She heard uniformed men in boots yelling orders.
She'd leap from her bed and crouch under the table. But Alicja
was often already there, shivering, balled up on the floor.

Three years after arriving in Melbourne, Mietek purchased the
brick three-bedder I would later think of as a palace. There was
a backyard for my mother and Antony, enough room for poodles
and for hosting barbecues.

Auntie Berta, and Jewish refugees Mietek and Alicja knew
from the camps, lived mostly in the inner-city suburb of
Caulfield, and by the bay in St Kilda. Mietek would drive Joasia
to cafés along Acland Street, where she'd gape at windows
brimming with cakes, salami, gefilte fish, dill-pickled cucumbers
and kabanosy. She'd watch old men hunkered on benches telling
stories, waving arms, arguing in Polish, Hungarian and Yiddish.

But gefilte fish and yarmulkes reminded Alicja of Poland.
When she and Mietek had applied for International Refugee
Organization assistance in Germany, they did not mark the line
noting 'Jew'. After visiting a man in a long robe who'd touched
my mother's forehead with water, they wrote in the Protestant
line: 'Evangelical'.

In Melbourne, Alicja preferred staying close to her neighbourhood of Burwood, where people accepted her but were not overly
curious about the numbers on her arm. Occasionally, neighbours
and parents at school would ask Alicja if she'd been in a camp.
She'd simply reply yes. Then they'd turn and look away: *Crikey,
look over there! See that pretty dress Mrs Brown is wearing?*

Some weekends, Alicja would pack rye-bread sandwiches in a picnic basket before Mietek drove them to Wattle Park. Alicja would sit with her children under ghostly eucalypts, dodging gumnuts like bullets that parrots dropped from the branches above them. Kookaburras laughed in the background. Joasia clambered atop logs with Antony. She launched herself into the air, falling into Mietek's arms. She crouched inside an old tram in the park and played hide-and-seek. Mietek crept through the door: 'Boo!'

Life looked so perfect out there, hiding in the suburbs. Away from all the ruins.

Meanwhile in Canada, Dick ignored a landing permit for Australia that Mietek had sent him. He would not make a single attempt to contact his daughter, until years later when he fell in love with a woman a few years younger than my mother. A woman with two children and a husband who'd abandoned them. She would rail at Dick, incensed that he had a daughter who did not know she had a father. She would eventually talk Dick into writing. She would lick stamps and paste them onto an envelope. She would push it through the slot of a postbox. Thirty-six years after my mother waved goodbye to Europe, Dick's letter would arrive in Australia.

PART THREE

37

I'm walking on a trail near Boston. Butter-yellow daisies bend in the breeze and the trees seem greener than last year. But no matter how many kilometres I walk, how many balls I toss to my dog, my visit to Auschwitz still plays in my head in black, white and dull grey: the mountains of leather shoes piled behind glass; the rows of wooden bunks stacked three-high where Nana Alicja slept. Birkenau's smell of rot, dust and death remains lodged in my throat.

That night I phone Mum in Australia. Since I returned from Poland, we talk at least once a week.

'I want to go back to the convent. I want to see the sisters,' Mum says. 'But I need your help to convince your father that I should go.'

After seeing the SS outbuilding at the orphanage and watching films of bombed-out Warsaw, I am beginning to understand the stubborn, optimistic side of my mother. She endured violence, grief and hunger, yet whenever I share discoveries from my research, she can't hide her excitement, and any new information seems to triumph over the trauma. 'Amaaazing!' she almost sings. I only wish these developments that solve pieces of her puzzle could alter how she perceives Alicja.

It's true Alicja saved my mother, but Alicja then unwittingly transposed her own pain onto a scarred child. Sometimes we hurt those we love because they are closest. Perhaps my search for Alicja's history may not be what this quest is about. What I ultimately want is to heal my mother's pain. Perhaps her pain is imprinted in me. If I can open Mum's eyes to what Alicja lived through, maybe she will understand that despite Alicja's coldness, she risked her life for her, over and over. 'She never caressed me,' Mum would tell me over and over. 'She was an ogre towards me.'

But this conflicts with a film Mietek took behind their picket fence in Dachau: Alicja holds Joasia's hand and smiles as she performs for the camera.

Looking back, I should have listened more to my mother. I thought I could fix the situation. Solve it for her, as though she were a problem. I thought I was helping, but it was short-sighted and arrogant to view her this way.

The more I learn about what happened to my mother and Alicja in Europe, the more I think I understand Mum's need. She's looking for hard proof I doubt even exists, such as a letter from Alicja saying 'I love you' – like letters Alicja would send me in Canada: *We miss you, darling. We love you very much xxx.* When Mum mentions Alicja, it's always negative: how Alicja talked badly to her; how she and Mietek treated her brother Antony differently; how they beat her.

'I was always told I was to blame,' I once heard Mum say in a packed church auditorium. She was smiling, as she usually does when discussing painful points. 'I thought I deserved all the wrong things done to me.'

My mother speaks at Christian seminars and in evangelical churches about her journey from the ashes of Poland to a fulfilled life in Christ. You can hear a pin drop when she talks. In a professional but gentle tone she explains that despite what her adopted parents did, she has learned to forgive them. She inspires women to grab life by the horns, to forgive those who hurt them. They weep into their tissues, kneel before God and pray to be born again.

The first time Mum remembers her parents beating her was in Dachau, when she was five. After she'd danced for some American soldiers, Alicja or Mietek, she says, had belted her for 'showing off'. When I asked a psychologist about the abuse, she told me I needed to take Mum's accusations seriously given she had shared her experiences with my father and her close friends over years.

'I remember one day, Mietek was so frustrated he punched a bread tin, and caved in its middle,' Mum tells me. 'He kicked me down the corridor. If I got up, he would kick me.' She was ten years old at the time.

This is not the Papa Mietek I remember. My Papa folded his newspaper to kiss me when I slid into the banquette in Nana

Alicja's kitchen for breakfast. My Papa smiled when I twisted my serrated-edged spoon into a grapefruit and accidentally flung a wet slice *smack* against the wall. My Papa snatched it up and grinned at me before my grandmother noticed anything amiss.

Mum says that shortly before Mietek died, he phoned her. 'He told me he loved me. I told him I never would have guessed it.'

This Mietek I recognise. He began phoning Mum when Alicja wasn't home. After Mietek had passed away, Mum confronted Alicja about the beatings. She denied it.

I regret not questioning Alicja about them, not drilling deeper when I interviewed her. Because she had been mostly silent about her war experience, I was scared she'd stop talking if I probed too much. I find it difficult to accept that Alicja and Mietek beat my mother. Then again, she was an angry child raised by parents struggling to re-enter a world without gas chambers and gun-wielding Nazis. Perhaps it is naive to assume that grandparents who were wonderful to me could not abuse my mother. Disbelieving is easier. I wonder if this is what guilt feels like – because I knew their love and my mother didn't.

On the phone, Mum says goodbye to me and passes me over to my father. I hear her shoes click on the kitchen tiles and fade away.

'I don't want her to go to Poland,' Dad whispers.

'But she wants to go, Dad,' I say. 'What is it that worries you?'

'She thinks *you* want her to go.'

Even though I've been careful not to push Mum, Dad might be right. He fears she will be altered if she confronts her past in Poland, that she will return to him emotionally broken. He sees the cracks already. They argue and bicker more. 'She won't listen to me,' Dad says. 'She would jump on a plane tomorrow if I let her.'

Are these changes my fault? Should I stop searching for bits and pieces about her past? It may be too late. Her history is like a steam train tearing down tracks at a speed I cannot control.

'I want to go to Poland, but it's not to please you,' Mum assures me days later. 'I need closure.'

But I worry. I worry that after a long trip from Australia, I will drag her backwards, to a place that took years to escape. She needs to remember, she tells me. She wants to thank those who cared for her.

So, I slide the jigsaw puzzle pieces of her life closer together. I nudge them towards the other bits, turn them and snug the ends into the beginnings.

Once, on the outskirts of Milanówek in Grodzisk Mazowiecki near Warsaw, there was a small girl whose grandmother forbade her to play in a corner of her garden, not to pick mushrooms there, sorrel, or even flowers.

'That is where they killed Jewish women,' Iwona's grandmother, Maria, explained. 'They buried them under the fence.'

I find Iwona's story in an article online. Embedded in the text I see a photograph shot in early evening light. A large boulder rests against a wooden picket fence, two votive candles glow on top beside a pot of yellow flowers. Hardened wax droops from a tall, black candelabra. A few years ago, Iwona moved the boulder to where the women were buried. On All Souls Day she lights the candles, bows her head and prays.

'Not many people know what happened here,' Iwona writes in her article. 'I don't know what to put on this stone.'

In the 1970s, she recounts, a man from Canada showed up and exhumed the remains of his wife. A man from Canada? This must be Dick! And the remains must be my grandmother, my mother's mother: Irena.

I push back my chair, then trip over the rug. I grab Dick's memoir from my bookshelf to check a name mentioned in the article, the surname of a woman killed with Irena. I flick through the pages, my hands shaking. I grip the book and stare. The name matches.

What do I do now? Should I keep it to myself? Or should I tell my mother I've found the house where she hid? The house where they killed her mother.

Two days after her thirty-hour trip, Mum lounges in a chair in my living room outside Boston. She is seventy now. The dark spots that dot her hands from the intense Australian sun are like jewellery on her, and there is barely a wrinkle on her olive skin. I pour tea from a pot through a strainer and pass her the cup, together with a hardback book: *The Jews of Otwock*. I hope it will help prepare her for our visit, given she knows little about Dick's town.

Mum flicks through pages of photos showing starving and dead Jews in the ghetto and testimonies from the few survivors, some who knew Dick. She puts the book down next to her teacup. She removes her glasses. 'It's too much looking backward,' she sighs. 'Enough of the horror stories – these people need to look forward.'

I worry this trip is a colossal mistake. If she is always looking forward, I can't tell her about the story I found online. I can't tell her what I know about her mother's murder.

Two months back, after discovering Iwona's story, I'd emailed the website's administrator and sent a few details from Dick's account about the house outside Milanówek. 'I am 90 per cent sure the author is talking about my grandmother, Irena Przygoda,' I wrote. That night I couldn't sleep. In the morning, I saw a message on my computer from Iwona. After her parents divorced, her grandmother, Maria Kaczyńska, had raised her – in the same house where my mother had sheltered with Dick and Irena for ten months after escaping the ghetto.

Maybe a higher power wants the mystery of my mother's past solved. I think of all the serendipitous collisions since I embarked on this quest: my book-group friend introducing me to her Polish friend who by chance attended school in Otwock, who connected me to Zbyszek there, who because of his connections with various Catholic church orders, found my mother's nuns. And then coming across Iwona's story about Irena. My trek for the truth is like a line of black dominoes. One leans forward, taps the next one, until they all topple and fall in a line.

For a month, I exchanged emails with Iwona nearly daily. On waking, I rushed to my computer, adrenaline pumping. If there was no message, a weakness swept through me. Iwona's information and descriptions filled some kind of void. It was like drawing a curtain back. Seeing for the first time in colour what Dick had been unable to say or write beyond the barest of facts. I had lived with Irena in my head for so long, but she was one-dimensional. A ghost. I knew from Dick some details about how Irena's life ended, but little of how she lived. So I soaked up Iwona's descriptions. How, for example, when my mother lived in the house the women were on kitchen duty. How mostly everyone (including Dick and Irena) would eat together at the dining table. How in the winter, they smoked cherry leaves and fried potato pancakes on a griddle.

These everyday details fleshed out Irena. Now I can picture her peeling potatoes. I can see her flicking the skins into a bowl. I can see her kneading and rolling out pastry, pinching the squares she'd cut into pierogi, just like her sister Alicja – my grandmother – did when I was a child.

Iwona knew little about the couple who'd rented a room in her grandmother, Maria Kaczyńska's, house. Maria had said nothing to her about a baby. Maria knew that by harbouring Jewish people, she would have faced the death penalty if caught.[287] Gestapo officers used to zip along a nearby railway line on motorbikes to visit the house, the commander having taken a liking to the old Bechstein piano in the living room. 'He played beautifully,' Maria told Iwona. 'But I left so the bastard wouldn't have an audience,' she continued.

On that fateful spring day in 1943, the one that would splinter my family, they did not come to play the piano. 'The Germans just appeared,' Maria told Iwona. 'They came with purpose, and an interpreter. Someone must have told them there were Jewish ladies hidden here. They made us leave the house and took us to the corner of the garden.'

This detail puzzled me. My mother always told me they shot Irena inside the house, not in the garden. In Mum's version, Dick found her crawling among women and children's dead bodies *inside*. Even today, Mum says the children were killed because when the Gestapo began shooting, the mothers clutched their babies to their chests. She says she survived only because Irena threw her on the floor.

After booking my flights to Poland, I'd planned to take a train from Warsaw to visit Iwona. We set a date. But I told Iwona I'd visit her alone.

Now in my living room I swallow a last sip of tea and put down my cup. I avert my eyes from my mother. Maybe I'll wait until we arrive in Poland to tell her about Iwona. But maybe I won't tell her at all.

38

We're standing at a counter stacked with mountains of sweet, sticky cakes. My mother points to her favourite, a Polish dough-nut filled with jam and sweet cheese, pronounced 'paawnsh-kee'. 'Poproszę jednego pączka,' — *One doughnut, please*, Mum asks, stretching up on her toes. She orders me a slice of chocolate sernik cheesecake.

In Warsaw, Mum's Polish comes back easily – the long, lazy z's, the Slavic 'tss-k', her words rising and falling naturally. Women chatting in the café next to us sound to me like birds chirping. Hearing Mum speak Polish reminds me of Nana Alicja, her babka yeast cake marbled with poppy seeds and dark chocolate. I blame them both for my sweet tooth.

When Mum first arrived in Australia as a refugee, all she wanted was to eat meat pies, sausage rolls and fish and chips. Like many immigrants, she wanted desperately to fit in. First days at school can be scary, but for my seven-year-old mother who had never attended one, the prospect overwhelmed her. The little English she spoke was so poor, teachers placed her in a class with children years younger. Her classmates pointed fingers, picked on her thick Bavarian accent and Germanic-sounding name. They screwed up their noses and called her a Nazi.

'I'm Polish! *Polish!*' my mother pleaded. When that didn't work, she'd shout in German. The children laughed at her woollen stockings and short dresses Alicja had brought in a small suitcase all the way from Dachau. After school, my mother would beg Alicja to buy her the regulated uniform worn by her classmates, the calf-length pleated skirts, pull-up socks and brown shoes.

'What's wrong with what you have?' Alicja answered in a fury. 'Why should I pay more for this?'

'Because we don't live in Europe. We live here now!'

Alicja told me that one evening the headmaster phoned her. 'Your daughter is shouting at children in German,' he said. 'She's causing problems for herself. You should encourage her to pay more attention to learning English.'

Refugees and immigrants often renamed themselves to make it easier for English speakers to pronounce. My mother was now Joan. But Alicja, or Alice, as Australians called her, was having trouble understanding Australian English too.

'G'day luv, whot-can-we-getcha today?' burly blond butchers with tanned arms would ask her while my mother stared at cow carcasses hanging on hooks behind the counter, numbers inked on white, waxy rumps of fat. 'Wouldya loike a jelly bean, Joan? Howbout a yella one?'

In my mother's schoolyard, tanned and freckled children unwrapped their sandwiches of thin, snow-white bread slices spread with Vegemite. They would squeeze the bread until black paste oozed from the sides. My mother screwed her nose up at the bitter, yeasty paste, but in the evenings, she implored Alicja to spread Vegemite on her bread. If the children saw her eating Vegemite, they might sit next to her in class. Instead, Alicja packed her lunchbox with dark rye bread, cheese, cured meats and pickles. The vinegar smell sent her classmates running. My mother would carry her sandwiches to the toilet block. She'd perch on a toilet in a cubicle and nibble her bread behind a closed door.

The children jeered at my mother, called her 'Stinky' and refused to sit next to her. In class, my mother would frequently raise her hand for a toilet pass. Teachers who struggled with foreign names would make her wait until recess. My mother knew nothing then about the repercussions of war trauma and malnutrition.[288] She would count to one hundred. Grasping her desk, she would tense her thighs. Soon, the familiar damp would spread through her stockings. When the bell sounded, she would rage out the door.

Months passed. Still she had no friends. She would sneak coins from Alicja's purse and walk to the milk bar on the street corner. She'd stand on tippy-toes and point at the chocolate frogs. Surely, the children at school would be kind to her if she gave them frogs.

✳

I find it difficult to picture my mother without friends. When I was a child, during school holidays we would drive to a caravan park on Phillip Island for a month where aluminium trailers lined narrow lanes, kids played cricket and men sat under canvas awnings in folding chairs sipping from tinnies. Sometimes at sunset, a koala would waddle by, slowly claw itself up a gumtree, and stare down at us.

After we'd unloaded the car, my mother's first priority was to wander around and say hello to everyone she'd met last year. And everyone she hadn't. Mum doesn't bottle things up like Alicja did. Her way of solving problems has always been to talk them out. She'd disappear for hours. I'd slap on sunscreen, grab a book, throw a towel over my shoulder and head for the beach. On the way, I'd spot Mum in a chair next to a Mrs Beasley, a Mrs Ogilvy or three or four other Missuses. I rarely saw Mum on the sand. Even today, at the end of any social function Mum will begin what my father calls her 'goodbye tour'. She flits around for a final chat and farewell with everyone in the room. Dad jokes this can last longer than the function itself.

Mum and I finish our cake, leave the café and walk around Warsaw. 'It looks less grey than it did when I was here twelve years ago,' Mum says, her voice lilting, as if she is still speaking Polish. 'People seem happier.'

I point at the steep rooftops as we wander the reconstructed old city. 'Nana crawled across roof tiles like those, when she snuck into the ghetto to visit her parents,' I say.

Mum stops. She covers her open mouth with her hand, her

fuchsia-pink nails sparkling. She turns to me, astonished Alicja never told her this.

I suggest we walk to Orla Street, to where she was born.

'What's the point of going back?' she asks, sullen.

For me, the great lure is walking these paths to make sense of the mysteries that pervaded my youth. I can poke and probe without it affecting me because my life has been easy. Mum, on the other hand, doesn't have this luxury. She needs to stay happy – or, at least, try. When she argues with my father and frustration spews out of her, she retreats to her study, reads scripture and prays. Hours later you wouldn't know anything had happened.

I try to think of something positive. 'How about we go to the Chopin school, where Nana studied piano?'

Mum plants her feet on the footpath. At this rate, I wonder how long it will take us to walk anywhere. '*What?*' Mum nudges my arm. 'She played *piano*? All those years she stood over me and made me practise every day. She never said a word!' Mum can't recall Alicja or Mietek discussing much about prewar life.

A couple of hours later, we exit the Chopin Museum. We meander on a path behind the Warsaw University Conservatory. Rounding the corner, we hear piano, bassoon and flute arpeggios. Sonatas float through the windows. 'Shh!' says Mum.

While we listen, I think about what we just learned at the museum. A historian told us Alicja's piano lessons took place at the Warsaw Philharmonic Hall, which had been modelled on the Paris Opera House and was destroyed by German bombs

'Music is in our roots,' Mum says.

She is thinking about the music room at Auntie Stella Uncle Paul's modest fibro farmhouse in Springvale South,

in Melbourne. Besides a piano, violins and stands spread with sheet music, rugs and furniture from Poland and Budapest lined the floors. Mum would often stay over and listen to Stella and her daughter Mary play violin while portraits of Beethoven, Schubert and Mozart stared at her from the walls. Paul would lead her down a path to rows of more than forty chicken sheds, the farm where Mietek had first worked after they arrived off the ship. My mother would squat next to newly hatched chicks and ask questions, Paul kneeling alongside her to explain.

Stella and Paul would listen to my mother's questions about problems at school, about changes she was feeling in her body, about Alicja and Mietek's Polish quirks and mannerisms. But sometimes, my mother was so sad and angry, there were no answers.

She wondered why Alicja yelled at her. 'You need to know how Poles and Germans killed Jews!' Alicja would scream, trailing her from room to room. 'They shot them! They threw them from buildings. They gassed them! They killed babies and children!'

Sometimes Mietek would ask Alicja to stop. Sometimes he would leave the room. My mother would cover her ears with her hands. 'Stop, please stop!'

Alicja would prise her hands away. 'You have to know this. You have to remember. The world can't forget what happened. They hated Jews. They killed us because we were Jews! They arrested us. Just because we are Jews!'

At night, my mother would dream of shootings, burning buildings, dead Jews piled high. Stella tried to explain Alicja's behaviour to my mother. 'Be patient,' Stella entreated.

Outside the Warsaw Conservatory I close my eyes, lost in a violin's mournful tune. I think about violins playing at Auschwitz's entry gates, how it killed any music inside Alicja. I realise why she stopped playing.

I turn to my mother. 'Yes,' I nod. 'Music *is* in our roots.'

The route back from the Chopin Museum takes us up Foksal, a street lined with nightclubs. Mum and I laugh, picturing Dick dressed in his army uniform, tumbling from one of these doorways after a cabaret show, his cheeks flushed from drinking, a pretty girl with rouged lips and red fingernails hanging on his arm.

I think about Alicja's lifelong anger towards Dick. 'She couldn't see anything good in him,' Mum says. 'When I came back from his funeral, I told her about the two Jewish men I met whom Dick hid in the factory warehouse. They said they owed their lives to him. She said: "Dick never did that! He couldn't do anything good."'

Now I know Dick abandoned my mother for Margrit, I can better understand Alicja's resentment. I haven't yet told my mother this, though. It would shatter her good opinion of him. It's clear I have underestimated my mother's resilience, but I worry I might unravel one of the threads that holds her together.

The letter Dick sent dredged up scenes Alicja had fought for years to unsee. Dick cracked her steel facade. Alicja blamed him for her arrest in Suchedniów. She probably also blamed him for her death march to Auschwitz, for choking on the stench in the cattle cars, for Dr Mengele's eyes passing her over on the

Appellplatz. She needed someone to blame. This fits theories I've read suggesting that anger and revenge helped fuel the will of some camp inmates to survive.[289]

Alicja's anger became her crutch to get through days of trying to blend in in Australia when she'd roll bowls across manicured grass with women in starched white dresses who'd never heard the sound of men rupturing babies' skulls. If Alicja let go of her anger, she'd have to remember. She'd have to acknowledge that Dick acquired false papers for her father, that her father pushed them away, that her father chose death over escaping to be with her.

Alicja kept Dick at a remove, insisting she 'didn't know him much' during our interview, but this obviously wasn't true. Dick slept in her tiny room in Lwów for around a month. Dick falsified her papers. Dick hid her in his apartment behind a cupboard. He then later helped her escape Tarnów. In a film Mietek took in Garmisch after the war, Alicja in sunglasses, laughing, picnics with Dick by a ski trail, then trudges through the snow with him. Still, when Dick broke his word and finally wrote to my mother, he belittled her courage and goodwill.

Alicja needed walls. In Australia, she didn't talk to the Polish people who moved into their street.

'She called them peasants,' Mum tells me in a small café on the way back to our hotel. 'She'd cross the road to avoid them. She had a Polish housekeeper who was pregnant and she made her scrub the floors. She was very class oriented.'

If Alicja disapproved of someone, she would look right past them as if they didn't exist. I remember once when I dropped by to see her with my younger brother, Alex.

'What's *he* doing here?' Alicja sneered.

As I remember it, Alex was standing right behind me on her portico. Alex was born after Benjamin, my Uncle Tony's son, who through no fault of his own, my brothers nicknamed 'Golden Boy'. When my mother or I visited Alicja, she would show us the latest photos of Benjamin and my fashionably dressed cousins. She would report their latest news. She would never ask about my brothers.

'I think she adopted me out of spite,' Mum says about Alicja, sipping her coffee. 'She didn't want Dick to have me.'

Mum's logic implies Alicja had coerced Dick into signing the so-called adoption papers. I don't tell Mum I believe it was the other way around. I don't lie to her. I don't say anything at all.

While Alicja had a tendency to look down on people, Dick was all about building up his image from fragments of his past. He filled his memoir with the famous people he'd associated with. He showed me all the medals he'd received for defending Poland and for fighting in the AK Home Army. Some medals, I will learn later, he applied for himself, but the details he included in his applications were all true. In my mind, he deserved more than a medal. I think about the dark oil painting hanging on the wall in my lounge of Dick in his navy blazer pinned with a rack of medals. Maybe when black thoughts surged through him, the medals helped him to fight on. He also crowed about a noble title, a patent handed down through his mother. He wore a gold signet ring stamped with its coat of arms.

Hoping to learn more about the title, I leave Mum at the hotel and head to the Jewish Historical Institute.

'Żaba?' The genealogist eyes me over her glasses. 'Better his mother didn't use the title.'

I tip my head, puzzled. I had not checked a translation.

'Żaba is a *frog*!'

The genealogist searches for the noble line that Dick said the last king of Poland gave Helena's grandfather. The title provided Dick the status he desired. It helped him to integrate. Maybe it sparked connections. Maybe it helped him to survive.

We huddle in front of her screen. Suddenly she's scrolling through a tapestry of family connections. She does not find the title. Instead, she finds the man Dick's Aunt Gustawa married, and the Art-Deco style Hotel Śródborowianka they built together in Otwock. The one I'd parked outside a few months back, wondering if my family had been there.

Two days later, Mum leans on my arm and shuffles up Hotel Śródborowianka's slippery walkway. Snow has lacquered Otwock's pines powder-white, so Mum's smooth-soled boots are completely unsuitable.

Inside, I stare up at the soaring ceilings. I picture the cavernous space lit up for dances and an orchestra, Dick watching women laugh under chandeliers.

Sitting around a plain table with the hotel's director, I pull out the family tree the genealogist sketched for me. It turns out Dick's uncle sold the hotel in the 1960s. Only a few surviving Jews returned here after the war, including Dick's mother, Helena, to help manage the orphanage set up here for traumatised Jewish children.

The hotel is now a Jewish cultural centre. College-age girls wearing fuzzy slippers wander by carrying steaming mugs of tea. 'Shalom!' says one. She's just returned from Irena Sendler's house, the former head of Żegota, an underground resistance organisation. Sendler smuggled 2500 Jewish children, like my mother, out of the Warsaw ghetto.

The girl tells me her grandfather was sent to Siberia and had no desire to return to Poland. She, on the other hand, is curious about her history. 'My grandfather said, "You can't forget, but you must forgive."' She asks why we are here.

Mum dips her chin. 'I have learned a lot about forgiveness,' she says, her eyes widening. 'And I can teach others how to forgive.'

I remember once when I was ten, a girl at school pushed me to the bitumen. I'd cowered on my back like a flipped-over beetle.

'Spoiled brat! Rich kid!' the girl had hissed, jealous I'd flown on a plane to Canada.

Afterwards, Mum told me I should forgive the girl. 'Sticks and stones will break your bones but names will never hurt you,' Mum almost sang.

But the girl's words hurt. I wanted to be like other kids with Aussie parents and fit in. I felt sorry for myself. I didn't know at the time how children at my mother's school had taunted her and called her a Nazi.

That evening at a restaurant back in Warsaw, as Mum and I tuck into our pierogi dinner, I think about how she has always stressed the importance of forgiveness. I ask her to elaborate on what she'd said to the girl in Otwock.

'I had to forgive. I had to forgive the Nazis for taking away my childhood, for killing my mother and stealing my adoptive mother's youth. The first years of Alicja's marriage should have been the happiest.'

I sip my Riesling. All my research has poisoned my view of forgiveness. I cannot exonerate those who killed my family. I have no compassion for men who blasted their way through my mother's childhood.

'I also forgave my teachers in primary school for not understanding or supporting me, a confused and scared immigrant child. And I had to forgive Alicja and Mietek.'

Years later, I will read Mum's sermon notes:

I had no peace. My behaviour was turbulent, aggressive, loud, at war with the world and myself, because I would not forgive. Jews who lived through war now live in torture chambers because they will not forgive.

But Mum's ability to forgive is not clear-cut. During Alicja's last days, she lay semi-conscious in a hospital bed, her heart and kidneys scarcely pumping. Mum sat by her bed. She held Alicja's hand. She thanked Alicja for her sacrifices. She told her she forgave her, but then she began listing her grievances: the beatings, the favouritism, the cutting words, the absence of demonstrative love. Alicja squirmed, thrashing her legs. Mum told her it was okay, that she forgave her everything. 'She had to listen to me,' Mum later said. 'She couldn't get away this time.'

For years I have struggled with this picture of Alicja's death and my powerlessness to protect her. Mum framed it as forgiveness, but she had unloaded on Alicja in a way that seemed cruel. I don't want to acknowledge this side of my mother. I want the selfless mother who always cooks my favourite foods when I visit. The vision of my grandmother lying helpless in that hospital bed struck me as terrible, but how could I be so arrogant as to judge my mother?

Perhaps I envy Mum's ability to forgive and to find peace. She walked out of the hospital room that day a new person. Unburdened. Freed.

Mum swirls a pierogi into the cream sauce. 'I had to forgive my father, too,' she says. 'Because he abandoned me. He gave me up. I understood why when I met him.'

In one of those slow and unfurling moments of insight, I decide I will never tell Mum that my research points to Dick abandoning her for Margrit. I always presumed Alicja's bitterness towards Dick for writing to Mum clouded everything. I had not yet read Dick's letters to my mother where he wrote: 'I had no financial means and no wife to take care of you, so I agreed to Mietek's proposal.' I had not seen the adoption papers Dick organised *before* my mother left Poland. When I think about it, Dick writing to Mum and saying 'I've always loved you' rings hollow.

I had been curious about Margrit. When helping Dick with his memoir, I'd asked if I could contact her to learn more about their relationship. Dick had refused to elaborate on Irena, but had no issue sending me Margrit's address. He dedicated his memoir to 'Grit', as he liked to call her, who 'helped me to come back to normal life after the horrors of the war'.

'You are the only person who knows of my love for Margrit,' Dick wrote to me later, telling me she'd financed his second trip to Australia, and had sent him the equivalent of AU$5000 for his birthday. 'DO NOT TELL ANY ONE THIS,' Dick instructed me.

Why didn't Dick want my mother to know? In his second ever letter Dick sent my mother, he disclosed his two failed marriages after Irena, his girlfriend close to my mother's age with two children, and his earlier relationship with Margrit, mentioning the fact she had declined to marry him. But Dick never told my mother *why* not – that Margrit refused to accept her, his child.

I decide I will let Mum cling to her version of the past she can tolerate, a narrative she has built on hope and fantasy that has made her resilient, one that enables her to forgive. Who am I to dictate truth? From now on, I will share only facts that won't blow her house of cards down. I wonder if this is lying. But maybe we all lie to protect those we love.

39

A few days later, we're eating dinner in our hotel room. While Mum and I spread cheese on bread, we discuss the events leading to Dick's tucking her into a backpack to leave the ghetto.

'I'm telling you, he smuggled me out of the ghetto and then back in,' Mum insists, annoyed.

She's repeated this version of her story for years[290] even though it doesn't line up with Dick's letter to her, what Dick wrote in his memoir, or what he told my siblings and me. Mum inherited Dick's sharp mind and recall abilities. She's tough to beat at Scrabble and other word games. When she listens to a news item on the radio, she can replay it word for word, but trauma can cause the unconscious brain to choose and reshape parts of the past safest to remember.

'Mum, that's impossible,' I reason slowly. 'Your grandmother was taken to Treblinka in August or September of 1942. Just after you were smuggled out of the ghetto. You were hiding near Milanówek then with Irena. Why would Dick want to smuggle you back in if the Treblinka deportations were in full force? Where did you stay if you think he smuggled you back in?'

'I stayed with my grandparents! My father told me my grandparents fed me goat's milk after my mother was killed.'

'Mum . . .' I take a breath. 'Your mother was shot on 22 May 1943.' I pause. I'm talking about her mother's murder like an anchor on the six o'clock news. 'The Warsaw ghetto uprising occurred in April 1943. So when your mother died, your grandfather had either already been killed in the uprising as Dick believed, or he was taken to Treblinka, or Majdanek as Alicja thought was the case. It's impossible your father smuggled you back in after your mother's death.'

'But that's what he told me.'

I sigh heavily.

'He put me in a bicycle bag and gave me ether to keep me quiet.'

Could she be mixing up the story of Dick visiting her grandfather and escaping afterwards by bicycle taxi?

My mother thinks I'm not taking her seriously, that with my laptop and fancy research, I know better. Yet she was *there*. I should stop trying to present her the facts. Now I feel as though I'm stealing her memory, her narrative. Pieces she's sewn together into a protective blanket. Do these details really matter? Isn't it worse if she thinks I doubt her? I should respect my mother's stories.

'Could he have smuggled you into a different ghetto after your mother was shot? Perhaps your Aunt Justyna in Wawer was inside a ghetto. Maybe Dick took you there that evening in May?'

'Yes, I was eleven months old then. Maybe it was with my aunt?'

'Or, Dick smuggled goat's milk into the Warsaw ghetto just after you were born. Maybe you weren't drinking your mother's milk because of her stress.'

'Yes. I guess that's possible, too,' Mum says, her voice flat.

I am still not respecting her. Proposing logical alternatives will not soothe her knotted pain.

40

I hear Mum's voice trill in the back of the silver Honda Accord. She and Sister Honorata – two cuddly 'Polish mamas' – share a joke in Polish I can't understand. I twist and see Sister laugh, too, her cheeks wobbling. Only a few hours ago in Warsaw, Mum met Sister Honorata for the first time. Now they both carry on as if they've known each other for years. Perhaps she reminds my mother of Kornelia, the sister who raised her.

Five months after I hugged the Catholic sisters goodbye in Suchedniów, I am headed back, this time with my mother in tow. Iza, the woman who translated for me when I first met the sisters, has organised everything: the logistics, the transportation – and the tissues. She's roped in her friend, Dominika, to drive us.

We pull into the convent's gravel driveway. My mother steps out of the car. Her eyes lock onto the long building, its window-panes boarded up, paint flaking off the weatherboard. The former orphanage is nestled in weeds like a wrecked ship. Mum presses her fingers to her chin. She stares at the panelled red entrance doors, three metres or so tall, that dominate the facade like a nose warning of dangerous odours. No need to open them yet. No need to go in.

'Do you remember something, Mum?' I ask in a too high pitch.

'Yes, I think so,' she murmurs. Her eyes linger on the doors. Then she spins around, something compelling her to turn away.

I'm struck by her pained look. She narrows her eyes, frowning. Her lips and cheeks sag. For the first time, I notice my mother's age.

Behind a wire fence at the bottom of the property, lush fields of grass roll towards low hills dotted with trees. 'Look at the mountains!' I say pointing to landscape she described to me from her childhood memories.

'Ha ha! They're only hills!' Mum laughs. She whirls back to being my happy mother, but I see her lips tremble, her usual cheer slipping.

Mum has been thinking about this day for months, wonder-ing what memories will return. When she first arrived at the convent, she'd clutched a white teddy bear, the one Alicja had pushed into her arms before the police arrested her. The sisters took my mother's bear away, maybe to appease other children who had no toys, causing Mum to sob night after night. After I'd found the sisters on my previous trip and phoned Mum, she would wake from nightmares weeping for her teddy. She would seek solace in scripture. She prayed and forgave the sisters for inflicting such a wound.

By bringing her back to Suchedniów, I fear I have pushed her too far. But now Iza, not me, stands right behind her and reaches her arms around Mum in a drawn-out hug. Sister Honorata approaches. She pulls my mother in close like a grandmother. She soothes Mum with words in a soft, encouraging Polish.

Mum says something in Polish I don't understand. She stares at the red doors again. Tears creep down her cheeks. 'I'm happy,' she says to all of us. 'These are tears of happiness,' she says. I wonder if she is trying to convince herself. I sense a fog coursing through her, too.

Grey-haired Sister Zofia walks from the pink building at the rear of the property with her arms open wide. But my mother's mind is still on the red doors. She shakes her head. Sister Zofia takes her hand and points at the doors. 'Do you remember that?'

Mum nods. 'Dom,' she says, Polish for 'house'.

'That?' Zofia asks, pointing at the yellow building, once the sisters' living quarters, where my mother lived.

'Not sure.' My mother swivels her head, side to side.

'That?' Sister Zofia points at the oldest building, next to what was once a vegetable garden. 'Do you want to go inside the orphanage building?'

'No, not yet.' Mum frowns at the door. She hesitates, then approaches the entrance. 'I remember these,' she says, gesturing at the steps. She remembers sitting here, observing other children playing on the quadrangle. She could see the 'mountains' from here, and the SS coming and going from the pink building, a hundred metres or so behind her.

Over a lunch of barley soup, fried eggs and mashed potatoes sprinkled with dill, Mum tells the sisters about the Messianic Jewish congregation she now attends along with her Pentecostal church.

'Is it evangelical?' the sisters ask. I hold my breath, not wanting to offend them, worrying Mum might interject with a 'praise the Lord!'

It pains Mum that I left the church. I'd rejected her views of agency, that God controls our destiny. I defied 'thy will be done'. I chose career over children. Or, if you will, I found meaning in career. In Poland, I find meaning pursuing people who influenced destinies. My mother's destiny. Mine.

'We believe Jesus was the Messiah,' Mum says to the sisters. 'We have Palestinians, Iranians and Indians. We welcome Muslims, Jews and Christians.'

My shoulder muscles slacken. Relief and pride rise inside me. This is my first time hearing Mum speaking about refugees who attend her congregation, some who have fled war, like her, who'd watched others drown while they clung to the sides of small boats tossing on the Indian Ocean between Indonesia and Australia.

'Yes, it is the God of Abraham,' Sister Honorata says, beaming. 'They all have their way to find God, and God will find his way to them. We are one family.'

My mother glances at me. 'I like to think of it as a tree of faith,' she says, her voice confident. 'The roots of the tree are Jewish, and the branches are what grow from the Jewish roots.'

In this moment, Mum surprises me. She is not interested in converting the sisters to what used to be her absolute way of thinking; that we are either good or evil, that if you believe in

Jesus you'll go to heaven, and hell if you don't. I see her respecting a Catholic sister in her eighties who studied and taught history, who lived through war and who was a friend to Kornelia, the sister who raised her. I realise that since leaving the church, my tendency has been to dismiss it. Perhaps I am the one who thinks in black-and-white, binary terms.

'We are your family,' Sister Zofia says to my mother. 'We are pleased you have come back to us, that you did not turn your back on God, given what happened.'

Yes, I think. That's it. Kornelia and the sisters replaced the two mothers who'd abandoned Mum. First Irena, then Alicja when the police arrested her down the road from here. I sink into my chair, holding back tears that burn hot as pepper in my eyes.

Although Mum does not recall this room, she will later write in her diary that she feels at home here. I wonder if her determination germinated here. Her faith. This is where the sisters tried to protect her from the war raging at their door. After she lost the two women who'd comforted her, maybe this is where my mother felt safest.

After lunch, Mum bounds outside. Turning left in front of the chapel, she heads down the path. We can hardly keep up with her. 'Yes, I remember this,' she points. 'This big building.'

A sister opens the tall doors with an old-fashioned steel key. The 30-or-so-metre-long hallway smells musty, the walls chipped and flaking. Painted doors leading to classrooms flank the hallway. White graffiti sprayed on daffodil-yellow wainscotting disturbs me: two Stars of David and '666'.

A troupe of nuns follows my mother inside, laughing and hugging her, the sound singing and bouncing off ceilings soaring six or so metres above. Sister Honorata shuffles on her walking stick. She reels off dates and names and answers my endless questions.

My mother heads for a door and opens it. She peeks into a room. 'Nope,' she says. She pushes the door closed. 'I remember sitting on benches, but not here.' She wanders to the next door.

In each classroom she enters, light streams through tall windows. Iron radiators line walls where paint peels off in long sheets. We wipe away thick cobwebs in one room where the ceiling is speckled black. We press palms over our mouths to block the mould smell.

'It's different now,' Mum says. 'It's empty and there are no children. I remember children. I remember benches. Rows of black benches,' she says, then heads off into the hallway.

Iza's friend, Dominika, lags behind her, then turns to me. 'Thank you,' she says.

'For what?' I respond, surprised. 'I have to thank *you* for bringing us here today.'

'You hear these stories in Poland, people being saved during the war and coming back. You know, Jews. But I have never been in contact with one. It's so different from seeing it on TV.'

It's funny, because I feel like I'm watching my mother in a movie, moving through time in an episode of *This is Your Life*: Mum as she pops in and out of rooms, opens and closes doors, Sister Zofia holding her hand. It's all I can do to keep up with her. 'Tutaj!' — *Here they are!* I hear Mum yell.

In the very last room, Mum points at rows of black benches stacked against a wall. These are not desks; more like pews with sloped ledges, meant for a Bible or prayer book.

'Ławki! Ławki!' — *Benches! Benches! I remember these!* She is beaming, clasping her hands together.

'But these were in the chapel in 1944,' the sisters tell us. 'They were moved here after the chapel was renovated.'

I think about my mother in that chapel more than sixty years ago. I see a child patter up the aisle. She hoists one leg onto the plank of the black pew, contorts her body, scoots her bottom over to where Kornelia sits, hums a hymn. She swings her legs like a clock.

Now, in the schoolroom, my mother strokes the ledges. Her fingers hover for a second, as if she's worried the blackened timber will break.

Later that afternoon, I follow Mum and a few sisters into the chapel, more a large room lined with yellowed oak pews. Mum slides into one. Sunlight through the window casts an eerie light on her. She looks something like an icon painting, as if gold leaf glitters her tired eyes and drawn face. Sisters file in for afternoon prayers. Their giggles drop to whispers when they see my mother. Younger sisters in their twenties stare at her and hold their fingers over open mouths.

Mum's face switches between smiling and frowning. I watch her vasilate between past and present. She reminds me of the painted babushka, or Matryoshka wooden nesting doll I played with as a child at Nana's. When you pull it open, inside is a smaller doll, and inside a smaller one, and another. And when you're done playing, you start putting away the smallest. You twist the larger dolls together until babushka is whole again.

Sister Zofia strikes up a tune on a digital organ. The sisters sing hymns of Mary and pray for us. Their presence warms me like a coat.

My mother sits alone on her bench.

Later, a sister and friend of Kornelia will tell me a story, of how in 1945, my nearly four-year-old mother sat on a bench in this chapel while Kornelia prayed. My mother's legs were less bony than when she first arrived, her jet-black hair shinier, her eyes more alive. Curious and bright, she'd delighted and amused the sisters. Her parents had raised her well, the sisters decided. An obedient, well-mannered and joyful child, my mother had treasured the small gifts the sisters gave her; a flower from the garden, maybe a toy sewn from cloth scraps. 'I got it from a little angel,' she'd say. But her parents remained a mystery. Some sisters speculated the Nazi who'd delivered her to Mother Superior was her father. Or, he'd accepted a significant bribe to hide a Jewish child.

Sister Kornelia knelt close to where my mother was sitting on the bench. 'Look, Joasia,' Kornelia whispered and pointed to the front of the chapel. 'That is where God lives,' she said, indicating a small, wooden chest holding the holy sacrament and chalice. 'He lives *there*, in the tabernacle.'

My mother apparently stared at the tabernacle and scowled. She turned to Kornelia. She asked, 'But why is your God so small?'

More than sixty years after leaving the sisters and the Suchedniów convent, my mother still cannot fathom a small God. Her God is enormous. Omniscient. A loving father. Her favourite hymn is the one she would bellow next to me at our Baptist church when I was little: 'How Great Thou Art'. Mum sees only greatness in her God, the same way she sees the best in people, despite what happened to her.

'You only have to decide to forgive, and God will give you the enabling,' she wrote once in her diary.

Growing up, she'd cuddle me, sign me up for whatever interested me, driving me to piano lessons and to horse shows. For my twenty-first birthday, she indulged my love of fine food and dining by cooking a three-course formal dinner from scratch for more than forty guests. Mum wanted to be the mother she says Alicja never was.

Despite Mum's emotional scars from war, she reaches out to others. She's always planning kind acts. She intuits when people are hurting. She drinks coffee with single mothers from her church. She lends a sympathetic ear, delivers them casseroles and picks up their children from school. Whenever I arrive from the US, she lays out gifts on the bedspread: chocolate Tim Tam biscuits, my favourite Australian food magazines, and Vegemite. She throws herself into church activities focused on helping others because she knows fear. She knows what it means to feel unloved. She knows hunger.

Six years from now, when she says swallowing feels like breathing water, her muscles will shrivel, her speech will fade. She will whisper, 'Death does not scare me, Jesus is waiting.' One day, she will decide: no more water, no food, yet her body will remember. It will thrum with hunger. Her body will reject hunger for an astonishing twenty-four days. Every morning I will dab her lips, blush her cheeks. On her eyelids tinged blue, I will shadow rose. Only then the thought will occur to me: my mother looks like a concentration camp survivor.

But now, I watch my mother sitting in a pew in central Poland. She's listening to the sisters chanting, their rhythm low, repetitious, soothing, like someone rubbing oil into your stiff muscles; mantras she heard here, morning, midday and night. Outside, the world spins in chaos; inside, there is a routine. One that anchors you when you're the wrecked ship. You sit, kneel, rise, knowing that in a few hours you will kneel. And, you will rise again.

On my side of the aisle, a wave of exhaustion sweeps through me, aching through my ribs. I'd searched for the sisters for months. I'd rummaged in archives and museums. I'd convinced my father to let my mother fly 47,000 kilometres to reassemble and reconcile memories that have haunted her for years. And here I am with her. I know Mum is at home here. For the first time, I know who she is.

41

I run along the platform gripping a bouquet of pink flowers and a large box of pastries and thrust my hand between the train's closing doors.

'Are we on the right train?' my mother puffs as I lead her to a seat.

I'd dragged her up and down stairs, through the underbelly of Warsaw Centralna station's network of tunnels, a sub-city smelling of fried dough and sugar, bustling with thousands of people popping in and out of shops that line the underground walkways, buying flowers, bread, meat and groceries. As we arrange our bags, Mum and I sit giggling, amazed we managed to find our way here. We are headed for Grodzisk Mazowiecki, on the the same rail line Dick travelled carrying false papers to his engineering job in Warsaw.

Just before leaving Boston, I'd told my mother how I stumbled across Iwona's article. I hadn't expected she'd want to see the place where Dick hid her, where Irena had been buried. Thinking about this, I realise my tendency to envisage Mum as still the vulnerable child. It's clear I underestimate her courage.

'I want to go,' she'd said, her eyes targeting me like a hawk.

This is my mother. Scared of nothing and willing to take risks. Always looking for ways to turn things around for the better.

The train pulls away from the platform. Mum doesn't seem the slightest bit nervous. Eventually, city buildings give way to fields, plots of trees and neat vegetable gardens.

We alight at Brzózki-Grodzisk. We're the only ones to get off at this way stop in the woods. At the end of a small platform, sixty-six-year-old Iwona waits with her partner and a large, gangly dog on a lead. There's nothing to do now but face the harrowing details she has shared with me. Slim and petite, with bobbed, burgundy hair and a blunt fringe, Iwona stretches out her arms and embraces my mother, as if she were family.

We walk across the train tracks towards Iwona's home. A gentle wind flutters in the trees. We kick and shuffle in a carpet of leaves. Iwona holds my mother's arm to stop her from slipping. A bitter taste sticks to my tongue. There is something intolerable about this place.

Where the field ends, two houses on large plots of land sit behind fences bordering the street. Opposite is an unkempt forest. The house where my mother lived once stood there. A few years ago, the land was sold, Iwona told me in her emails.

New owners tore down the old house, replacing it with a modern one. On the remaining land parcel, Iwona built a modest wooden cottage.

A little further along the narrow dirt road, I recognise the fence from Iwona's article. My stomach tightens. Iwona opens the gate. The dog whips past us.

I take Mum's hand. In my peripheral vision, I glimpse the grey mass of the stone in the yard's corner. Mum's hand turns clammy. 'Do you want to go inside first, or do you want to go to the place, now?' I whisper.

She stops. 'Now,' she says. Her voice is firm, but her fingernails dig into my palm.

I lead her to the boulder, nestled in grass. Worn into the ground behind it is a path from Iwona's dog running along the fence to bark at outsiders. A tall, black candlestick stands next to it, the candle sombre and lonely, wax twisted in long fronds.

Mum shudders, then begins to weep. Sobs wrack her body. I sense her mourning for a mother she can't remember, for the love she craved during her growing years, for the chasm between her and Alicja. She's told me she's forgiven the Nazis who stole her mother, but forgiveness cannot dull the pain I feel pulsing through her arm. In Suchedniów, threads of memories tugged at her. But here there is a void filled with violence and death.

A few metres away, Iwona observes us, arms stiff at her sides. For years she has guarded this part of the garden. Protected it when they divided the land. Memorialised it with the stone and the candle. Atop the rock, she has placed a handful of small, heart-shaped pebbles. I pick them up. I hold each of them in my hand, turn, and finger their rounded edges. I glance at Iwona and smile.

A few days after I discovered Iwona online, I told her how Dick had organised the exhumation of Irena's remains from under the ground where I'm now standing. I told her that Irena lay in the Milanówek cemetery with another woman living in the house who was killed with Irena in 1943. After I told her all this, Iwona visited Irena's grave. She cleaned the headstone. She laid fresh flowers, making sure the pebbles I'd left in a heart formation remained in place. Now I realise she must have returned here, to her garden, and after learning about the Jewish tradition, she'd found pebbles of her own to place on Irena's stone.

Mum and I stand in the wind. We stare at a corner of a garden that few people know about. A place of little significance except to us, where blood spilled into the earth. My mother notices the pebbles. She slips her hand into the pocket of her jacket. She removes a heart-shaped, grey, polished stone, a few centimetres long. I'd given it to her before leaving for Poland. A psychologist in my book group had proposed it as a calming aid for Mum if she felt overwhelmed. It could be her signal to me she was not coping. If she pulled it out and showed it to me, it would be her sign the situation is too painful, and that I should extract her from it. A few days before we'd flown out, my psychologist friend showed up with a gift for me and asked me to open it after she'd left. When I unwrapped the small box, nestled in tissue paper I found a small, handcrafted glass heart circled in delicate red candy-like threads. After we arrived in Warsaw, I'd opened the box and showed it to Mum.

Now Mum takes a few steps towards Irena's stone, where the Gestapo had forced villagers to dig a grave for her mother. She cannot touch it. She leans forward and places her heart-pebble next to Iwona's. I rummage in my bag for my friend's gift. I place my heart next to Mum's. Hearts lie on Irena's stone now. Three hearts joined through blood.

Inside her house, Iwona's cats curl up in a basket beneath a cast-iron stove. Timber-lined ceilings, bookshelves and heavy beams evoke a Swiss farm chalet. A wooden eagle hangs on one wall. Weathered and as faded as driftwood on a beach, it is what's left of a Polish coat of arms once affixed to the old villa where my mother lived, before it was torn down.

Iwona heats water for tea then removes a woman's portrait from the wall. 'I want you to have this,' she says, passing it to my mother. 'This picture is of the patron Saint Teresa. It was hanging upstairs on the first floor.' When my mother lived at the villa, the portrait had looked down the central staircase from the top of the stair landing.

'I wonder if Saint Teresa protected my life?' my mother muses.

We talk about the two other women who found shelter in Maria's house. Neither Iwona nor I know for sure if they identified as Jewish or Catholic. 'Everyone who needed help got it,' Iwona says in a raspy smoker's voice. 'My grandmother's home was her castle.'

While we sip tea, Iwona pulls out a family tree. She seems drawn to the women in her family, all strong-willed and patriotic like her grandmother who risked death by allowing Jewish people to live in her house.[291] She passes a black-and-white photo of her mother, with Sofia Loren cheekbones and long, slender legs. 'Once, on a train, a dashing Gestapo officer offered to carry her suitcase. It was heavy with jam jars and underground newspapers,' Iwona says. After asking if he could see her again, Iwona's mother thanked him and politely declined.

Iwona's Aunt Zosia, the woman who'd sung my mother lullabies, was also active in the Underground. Some of Zosia's AK colleagues hid in a cupboard near the kitchen. 'Members of the AK had to swear that no-one would know,' Iwona says as she pours more tea. 'But I'm sure my grandma knew about Zosia's work. After the war, the communists chased Zosia down – can you imagine?' Iwona says, raising her voice.

Stories like these unnerve me. I want this kind of courage. Thousands of resistance accounts exist throughout Poland, along with others that will never be told. After the war, the Stalin-influenced communist government brutally prosecuted[292] those with Underground and AK connections,[293] like Roman Talikowski who'd smuggled food into the ghetto for my mother's family. They were accused of loyalty to the Polish government in exile and some called for their extermination.[294]

'My grandmother didn't care about danger. Perhaps it was her mistake, and that is why this happened, I don't know,' Iwona says morosely of the day the Gestapo killed Irena.

'Was she shot inside the house?' my mother asks out of the blue, as if the answer will help her plug something inside her.

Iwona pauses. 'There was a young boy who witnessed it. He told my brother the story. He was watching outside, lying hidden in the grass. He said that my grandmother yelled and screamed at the German officer.'

'What did she say?'

'I don't know. I can only imagine. If it was the German who came to play the Bechstein piano, she would have challenged him, saying something like, "So is this the German culture? The nation of Schiller and Goethe?"'

'Why didn't the Gestapo shoot your grandmother?' Mum asks.

'Perhaps it was because she shouted at the officer in German? Perhaps they'd had enough blood.'

'So the boy was outside?' Mum persists.

'Yes. He heard the yelling outside. But maybe it was when the villagers were burying the women.'

I have tried contacting the young boy from Iwona's account, now an old man. I want to visit him, but he does not want to talk. Iwona believes he knows who sent the Gestapo to the house that day. Possibly someone in his family.

'I want to know if she was shot in the house,' Mum says. 'I was told I survived because my mother threw me on the ground. She didn't hold me to her chest like the other women held their children. The other children were shot with their mothers.'

I put down my tea. This is the story Mum has told me many times, supposedly as Dick described it to her. Except Dick didn't mention children to me, nor in his letter to my mother, nor in his memoir.

Iwona tilts her head. 'My grandmother didn't give particulars about this,' she says, leaning towards my mother. 'Now, I am not so sure. Perhaps it did happen in the house?'

The echoes of the dead. Grandparents often favour stories that strengthen children, withholding what is true. 'If she had told me it happened inside, I could not have lived in that house,' says Iwona.

'Dick told me he came home and I was crawling around the bodies holding my mother's bra,' Mum says.

I consider the possibility that Irena could have removed her bra and dropped it *before* they led her out.

'That's what Dick told me,' Mum says. But she doesn't mean her words for me.

Irena was exhumed and reburied a few months after Dick sent the letter to my mother. A Toronto newspaper apparently printed a story about Dick finding his wife's execution place. Someone sent the clipping to Alicja's brother, Kuba, who mailed it to Alicja. In a photo of the graveside service, a priest with a face almost as long as his robes says mass. Behind him, an older, thin man in a white gown holds up a wooden crucifix. More than sixteen people are in attendance, including a few official-looking men in crisp suits and polished shoes. A woman wearing a headscarf stands at the rear.

Alicja was furious about Irena's funeral, that a priest officiated instead of a rabbi. But a rabbi would have been impossible at the time. During a 1968 anti-Jewish campaign, the communist government stripped around half of Poland's remaining Jews of citizenship and expelled them.[295]

Alicja's anger feels unwarranted, given she wasn't religious. Years later, she visited the cemetery, laid five blood-red gerberas on Irena's slab and saw to it that the grave was in good condition. She spent some money on it, according to Dick. I wonder if she felt a loss of control over Irena's death narrative. She needed people to know her family were killed because they were Jews. As always, her anger needed a culprit. As always, she blamed Dick.

After Kuba sent Alicja the clipping, my mother tried to quell her fury. She told Alicja, 'A husband has more right than a sister to determine what should happen in these matters.'

Iwona and I leave Mum with her tea, pull on our warm coats and walk through the thick forest. The villa where Irena and my mother hid stood three to four hundred metres from the property line of Iwona's current home. Three regal pillars of crumbling concrete mark the former entry way. A fourth lies smashed on the ground. A tree collapsed across the path makes it difficult for anyone curious enough to enter. Leaves cover the long driveway, now tangled with undergrowth.

Iwona smiles as she tells me about the butterflies she chased in the woods here as a child. She points to where she picked wild strawberries in the spring, under the birch trees bordering fields of rye.

We walk back to the house and duck under an old, gnarled apple tree. The air tastes of vanilla and ants. Iwona entreats us to stay for dinner, so soon we find ourselves sitting around a warm fire eating fried potato cakes, the smell of cooking oil wafting in from the kitchen. In my mind, it travels from across the yard, from behind the fallen gates in the woods, where Iwona's grand-mother once cooked the same recipe with Irena.

That night, I cannot sleep. If I close my eyes, I see Irena's stone looming in the garden. When I jolt awake in the dark, my head jerks back so as not to smash my face against it. I turn on the light and open a book. It's the first book Dick ever gave me, titled *Żegota*, about the underground Polish council to aid Jews.[296]

I re-read a section where Dick was interviewed: 'The baby was found alone, playing on the floor beside the dead women . . .'

I stare at the words before comprehension dawns. I want to jump out of bed and wake my mother. Instead, I turn on my laptop. I find the transcript of Alicja's interview and scroll through the pages. 'She had the baby in her arms and she threw her down,' Alicja said. 'That's my sister.'

I think about what would have happened if Irena had clung to her child. But she didn't. She let her daughter go. And despite the grief swirling in my mother and all she has endured, she has raised four children she loves. I wonder if, all along, Dick wanted my mother to be secure and safe, far away from Europe. I wonder if his decision had nothing to do with Margrit. I wonder if he let my mother go, too.

42

On our last day in Poland, we lunch on cakes at our favourite café, then walk through Warsaw's old town. I point to a restaurant sign in a market square and ask Mum if she wants to dine at 'U Fuk-iera'. People stare as we bend over, shrieking with laughter at the naughty word.

Over dinner, I ask Mum if she's achieved everything she wanted on this trip. She nods thoughtfully. 'My reunion with the sisters was the most important.'

In the dim light of the restaurant, her dark brown eyes are brilliant. She looks beautiful. We've grown closer while travelling, me guiding her; her teaching me how she came to be. She knows more now of the horrors Alicja experienced in Lwów, in the ghetto and in the camps. I think Mum has come closer to understanding that Alicja did in fact love her, even though she could not comprehend this when Alicja was alive.

'She never hugged me,' Mum used to say of Alicja.

'She was not affectionate as a child,' Alicja used to say of Mum.

I have learned that emotional numbness can often follow trauma, that victims avoid touch and gestures of affection.[297]

To prepare my mother for getting through this trip, I'd encouraged her to seek out a therapist specialising in childhood trauma. When I called her one morning, she'd howled into the phone. 'I can't stop crying,' she said. She was waiting in a room for her follow-up appointment with a 'prayer counsellor'.

Scorn had reared up in me. I'd looked up the counsellor. No tertiary degrees, only church courses in counselling. Without clinical expertise in how the brain processes trauma, I worried the counsellor could damage my mother.

But it turned out that Mum experienced a breakthrough. The counsellor had prayed with her in a spiritual language laced with scripture. She discussed the 'five love languages'[298] and helped Mum see that Alicja provided love in the form of a safe home, an education, gifts of stockings and trinkets she left on her bed.

While my mother had craved hugs and explicit 'I love you' statements from Alicja, now she comprehends that Alicja expressed love through acts of devotion. Alicja had nursed her back to health in Dachau; she'd risked her life to negotiate with an SS officer in Radom Prison to save her.

'I understand now. She *did* love me,' Mum says in the restaurant. She clasps her fingers together and twirls her thumbs. She rolls them over and over.

I understand more now, too. I know that while Alicja tried to shut away what happened to her in Poland and Germany, she unintentionally passed her pain onto her children. Alicja, like other Jewish people liberated from the camps, survived by putting up walls. They pretended not to see things. Some hated themselves for the anger boiling inside them, for the night-mares they couldn't tell anyone about. When Alicja arrived in Australia, there had been no therapists to help her cope. No books or resources to help her process what she had endured, to teach her how to re-enter a world where people were civil. Alicja just focused on getting through each day. But Joasia was not the kind of child Alicja could project her hopes onto. Alicja could see her own pain, her anger. She could see her own sorrow in my mother's eyes.

And children like my mother constructed stories to blot out and explain their parents' vanishing. They pretended everything was rosy. When that myth shattered, they could not hold in their rage. They too survived by raising children. My mother lived the childhood she'd lost – and her dreams – through my siblings and me.

But what happens when your child begins to study the war you want to escape?

Mum and people who know me think of me as indomitable. But researching this story has turned me fragile. My husband wakes me from nightmares. He worries about me. The more I dig, the less I sleep.

43

Six months after flying back from Europe, I endure the thirty-two-hour trip to Australia. Mum seems unsettled and weepy since Poland. She cries often. She gave an interview on a Christian radio station and told the host that Alicja and Mietek beat her, that a man burned a Nazi swastika in their yard on Riversdale Road. Her cousin heard the interview and sends me an email filled with invectives shouted in CAPITAL letters. Mum, it turns out, has mixed up the dates of the swastika incident. Plus, her accusations about Alicja infuriate him. It isn't possible that Alicja beat her, he says, because *he* witnessed no abuse.

I'm sitting alone in a trendy Italian restaurant waiting for Mum's brother. I wonder if he'll notice the petticoats of filigree chain my neck. Alicja is gone, but wearing her necklace makes her feel present in my life. It preserves her legacy. Her story.

When Uncle Tony arrives, it stings to see him. I notice the grey streaks in his hair. I stand to hug him, but nerves ripple in my stomach. I haven't seen him for ten years.

When I was a child, I'd track down Uncle Tony at Polish Circus parties. I loved his Australian accent, his wicked sense of humour. Over the years, I valued his advice on boys I dated, on my career, on whether I should trek in Nepal or safari in Africa. But after Alicja died, Tony, the executor of Alicja's will, didn't share it with Mum. Mum hadn't expected Alicja to leave her anything, despite visiting Alicja often, bringing her cakes and spoiling the poodle. Mum didn't seem to care about not seeing the will. I, on the other hand, was furious. Tony, of course, knew none of this.

Over drinks, Tony laughs. He describes how he'd hidden in cupboards and toilets at primary school, nibbling rye-bread sandwiches, how he'd craved Vegemite, desperate to jettison anything Polish, how he lay in bed sobbing when Alicja and Mietek went out dancing and left him alone, and when they screamed at each other, smashing mirrors and plates.

As a child, I found it odd that Alicja and Mietek slept in separate beds. Mum told me how she'd listened from her bed to their yelling. 'The war was very successful as far as the Germans were concerned,' she said.

Survivor mothers with limited emotional capacity to parent often battled so-called death guilt.[299] Alicja felt guilty for 'abandoning' her parents in the ghetto. And then Alicja's parents abandoned *her*, in a sense, by dying. Yet she left her own children at home, scared and alone.

'Why didn't you call out to your sister, or climb into her bed?' I ask my uncle now.

Tony says he and Mum weren't close growing up. He chuckles. 'They say children of Holocaust survivors have more issues than the survivors.'

My mother is both, I want to remind him, but don't. And I don't say: 'I am a child of a survivor, too.' Maybe it's why growing up I was a loner. Why I felt alienated. My parents, grandparents and the Polish Circus spoke differently. We *were* different: rye-bread sandwiches, classical music, taboos you didn't talk about – like my mother screaming and stomping around the house like a Heffalump.

I read about behavioural patterns observed in some children of survivors, describing 'a high need for control, obsession with the Holocaust, a need to repair the world, for parents and grand-parents, for themselves, albeit often unconsciously',[300] and how, often, there's one child or grandchild who fixates more on the Holocaust. One child who carries the family's trauma.

What I did not see when I first set out to Poland that I can see now – I am that child. I inherited my family's grief and pain. The need to carry the torch for my mother and for Alicja and her dead has metastasised in me. As if I am burning candles for them all, memorialising and honouring them in a way Alicja couldn't. I now bear Alicja's fear that demonising people, censorship and conspiracy theories can crumble democracies and lead to genocide.

In the restaurant, Tony entertains me with stories of his wild days and nights while studying medicine: the fast cars, the motorbikes, the surfing, how he made dozens of blond, tanned

Australian friends who carried no concentration-camp baggage. Like my mother, Tony rarely dwells on negatives. Predictably, his children call him 'Mr Happy'. A successful cardiologist, he fills every spare minute with fun, tending his rose garden, tossing back beers with his mates at the footy, travelling to India, Bhutan and Spain. Born in Germany amid displaced persons camps, Tony's 'untameable, getting-kicks-out-of-life' way of living is typical for some children of survivors. Their way of escaping their parents' daunting expectations, the yokes of obligation to the perished. In my mother's case, anger would sometimes burst out of her. Tony's pleasure-seeking is a distorted form of damming anger in.[301]

The waiter places our orders on the table. The dishes reek of garlic. I sip my water, then gulp.

'Did you ever witness Mum being beaten?' I ask my uncle, fingers trembling.

'No.' Tony pokes his fork at an olive.

'Why does she remember being kicked then?'

Tony shakes his head.

If he was twenty months old when he arrived in Australia, it's unlikely he witnessed Alicja or Mietek hitting my mother in Dachau. And if they beat her until she was twelve, Tony would have only been seven. Sometimes, distance makes you remember differently. Maybe all the yelling and fighting Tony remembers blended together. Maybe if you block out events, you can protect yourself. Or as in many families, you learn to pretend the abuse doesn't exist.

'I think it was the religion,' Tony says, suggesting this was what pushed Mum and Alicja apart. 'But I'm so glad she has religion. Otherwise, she would have gone crazy.'

I remember what Alicja said after I'd asked if the war had changed her atheist views: 'No,' she said. 'Where was God when this was all happening?' Yet she admired those who believe in God. 'Because life is much easier if you really believe in something, isn't it?'

The woman at the Victorian Archives Centre smiles as she passes me a package across the sleek white counter. 'There ya go,' she says with the nasal Aussie twang I notice more now my accent has changed into long American vowels and soft consonants. I thank her and find a seat at a long desk.

I lied to my father this morning when he dropped me off here. I told him I wanted to visit the archive to find information relating to Mum's immigration, to learn about her ship – the *Napoli* – with its supply of potatoes and onions below deck that fed hundreds of refugees for over a month. Alicja told me the onion stench seeped into clothes and hair, that refugees wept from the fumes, joking that they'd survived Nazi gassings but the ship's onions would kill them.

Now I stare at the manila folder on the table. Maybe there's a note inside. Some kind of explanation. But then again, maybe it stinks.

I turn back the cover. On top is Alicja's Certificate Of Death. Line three in the section noting 'Children' does not include my mother's name. A knot forms in my throat.

On all Alicja and Mietek's identification documents (their registrations in Dachau, their immigration applications and naturalisation papers), they'd consistently noted my mother as their daughter. In conversation with friends and strangers, Alicja would refer to Mum as her daughter. In our interview, Alicja discussed treating both her children equally.

'We didn't want her to know she's not our daughter,' Alicja told me. 'There were situations when I wanted to tell her, like before she got married. But then she was so happy and I thought – why should I upset her now?'

At that time, my mother had grown suspicious when Mietek insisted he should be the one to procure her birth certificate for her marriage. The only document proving my mother's birth is the 1946 Brussels document listing Irena and Dick as her parents.

I read through Alicja's will and testament. I weigh every word. It is dated months after I interviewed her, six and a half years before she died, more than twenty years after Dick sent the letter to my mother. Alicja's mind had been as clear as her signature.

She willed all her financial estate to her son. She bequeathed some of her personal belongings and jewellery to my mother, according to wishes she'd already conveyed.

I scratch at Alicja's gold necklace with my thumbnail, like at a rash. My mother gave it to me because, she said, it didn't sit well on her neck. Now I stare at one line in Alicja's testament that does not sit well with me.

In 1948, Mietek and Alicja arrived in Melbourne with little more than the few bags they carried. They couldn't afford to rent a house. Many refugees escaping war hold degrees in medicine and law, but who they were does not match their destination's requirements, so they end up pumping petrol or driving taxis. Mietek took care of chickens on a farm, then worked his way up in a clothing factory. Bosses who ignored his productivity ideas drove him to start his own business on the side. He asked a contact in Germany to send boxes of cards adorned with Christmas trees and children pulling wooden sleds. He cut deals with newsagents all over Melbourne. Before long, he was importing oil paints and brushes. For extra income, Mietek-the-lawyer sold cars. He hired his friend Marion from the Dachau concentration camp as a mechanic and built a repair business.

Mietek did well over the years. He was not a tycoon by any means, but he built a nest egg. He even saved enough to buy a beach house at Wye River on the Great Ocean Road, surrounded by two vacant land blocks that Mum told me were for her and Tony.

After Mietek died, Alicja sold the beach house.

In Alicja's will, there is only one line where she references my mother, a reference most would not even recognise. Regarding her jewellery, Alicja notes Mum as her niece.

Maybe because this is a legal document, and because the 1946 'adoption' document was not exactly official, Alicja might have felt it was reasonable to call her a niece. My mother doesn't care about money. But to be expunged from Alicja's will, to be alluded to in such a minor way – it reveals Alicja.

In a final clause, Alicja instructs that if her estate cannot be distributed to her son, or to her grandson, all money and assets should be held in trust for charities. My mother does not merit even third place.

I once asked Alicja if I could borrow a needle and thread to repair a hole in my jacket.

'Why would I have this in my house?' my grandmother said. 'I've never sewn anything in my life.'

But this wasn't true. She told me she'd sewed her mother's jewels into her corset. She told me that in Auschwitz she'd stitched scraps of fabric together to make a nightdress. She told me this.

When I think about Alicja now, I like thinking about my childhood nana, how she doted on me, how she kept her silver bowl on her mahogany buffet filled with lollies and chocolates. Jacqui and I would tear past it as we thumped through Nana's dining room like an earthquake, dashing in and out of her kitchen, where she cooked me delicious treats. She'd yell when our stomping rattled the glass doors and shelves of her display cabinet, when her crystal poodles and trinkets clinked and clattered. But I remember how I'd kneel on the floor staring at those untouchable glass poodles, their noses and tails erect, manicured heads held high. For years those poodles stood impassive while we stomped by. As if we didn't exist.

Had Alicja included me in her will – older than her grandson, but female – would she have referred to me as the child of her 'niece'? When I took her to symphonies or over dinner, maybe she looked across the table thinking: Irena's granddaughter – she belongs to Dick. Maybe she detached *after* I interviewed her, after I'd forced her to relive and regurgitate her past.

But maybe family is less about a name on a paper. It's more about moments of joy, shared experiences imprinted on our memories. Moments we look back on over and over. Flashes of colour with smell and taste that help us conjure the family we *want* to remember, not the family we inherit. I like to think back to my nana squatting with me on rocks by the sea. I'd squelch in amber carpets of seaweed with her, peer into deep pools rounded like teacups searching for starfish, the *pop-pop-pop* of beads bursting under my toes.

I wish I could hold onto my childhood version of Alicja and keep my later knowledge at bay. But I know now I never really knew her. I love her, but love is no straight arrow. Alicja risked her life for my mother, but in death she disowned her. I will never understand completely why. History is not a box you tie a pretty ribbon around. There are no neat bows to finish things off.

44

A week after visiting the archives, I drag my mother to a doctor. I'm worried about a weakness I noticed while travelling in Poland, when she'd stumbled down stairs.

The doctor is an immigrant, like Mum, but from Russia. She pokes and prods Mum's ankles and knees with needles. She asks Mum if 'this hurts', or 'that'. Mum answers cheerfully. The doctor shakes her head and frowns. She glances at me across the room. She suspects Mum is not telling the truth.

When I was eight, I lay writhing next to a large cactus bush my father planted under the pergola near a door to our house.

As I remember it, Jacqui shoved me there after I'd accused her of stealing my chocolates. My arm, leg, hip and my bum stung as if an army of nurses had stabbed me with needles, cactus spines lodged in my palms.

'I hate her!' I sobbed inside, draped, bum-up, over Mum's knee, wet patches from my tears blotching her stockings.

'Ha ha ha!' Mum chuckled like the kookaburras in the gum trees outside her back window: *koo-koo-ka-ka*! 'No. You don't really,' Mum said. She was tweezering cactus spines through my white underpants stained with red dots of blood. 'There's *no* such word as hate.'

Mum was strict on the hate word. No toy guns in our house. No pointing at each other with sticks, either.

'Two wrongs don't make a right,' Mum rattled off one of her many slogans, then told me I should forgive my sister. When she dabbed the raised cactus bumps on my arms with a pad soaked in Dettol, I screamed. I wanted my mother to realise how mad I was, how quoting the Bible and sweeping everything under the carpet didn't make anger or lies disappear, or bring my chocolates back.

But back then, I did not know that forgiveness is Mum's superpower.

The doctor stretches both of Mum's hands out. She examines her fingers. She turns her hands over so Mum's fingertips curl. She runs her fingers across Mum's wrists, towards the crook of her elbow joint, back up to the wrist again.

'What are these lines?' the doctor asks, referring to raised, threadlike pink scars.

My throat seizes.

'Oh *that*,' Mum swipes the air, as if the marks are mosquito bites. 'That's from when I tried to kill myself, when I was a teenager.'

As a refugee who carried war traumas to an unfamiliar country, my mother had to deal with people's fear of immigrants, their disdain for names and habits different to their own. She had to deal with students and teachers who ridiculed her, who stripped her of dignity. She had to deal with her parents endlessly comparing her to gifted cousins whom she admired and was desperate to please. But because of her delayed schooling, she could never match their scholarly and musical achievements. 'Why can't you bend your toes?' one would taunt her in ballet class.

How could my mother explain rickets disease and starvation to people who had never gone hungry? For years she spun dizzily on a 'merry-go-round of guilt and shame'. She had to deal with hate, rejection and her own trauma and fears, all the while deflecting Alicja's.

But Alicja was the one who found her that day, who stepped around scarlet pooling on the bathroom floor. Alicja swaddled Mum's arms tightly with bandages. Alicja bundled my mother into the car and wiped the blood off her leather seats. Alicja did.

Over time, my mother would find ways to vent the resentment and anger boiling inside her. She stole her classmates' lunches. She shoplifted. She smoked. She slept with boys, fell pregnant, had an abortion. She got drunk at parties. She became accustomed to the eerie sense of orphanhood and split identity.[302] She hoped life would be better. She learned to reshape the parts of her past that haunted her, the parts safest to remember. She created a fantasy world. One where she felt accepted.

'I didn't tell her about my nightmares,' my mother said of Alicja decades later. 'I didn't tell her a lot. What was the point?'

After she discovered forgiveness, my mother's night terrors faded away.

On Sunday, after a family lunch, Mum places all her jewellery boxes on the dining table. Royal-blue cardboard boxes. Black velvet bags. Jewellery box ring liners. She asks Jacqui and me to choose pieces we'd want to keep after she's gone. This mortifies us, but Mum has witnessed among her friends how death has a way of pitting siblings against each other. So, she pushes diamond earrings at us. She removes her engagement ring.

Slowly, my sister and I pick through Mum's pearls, sapphires, rolled gold bracelet, emerald earrings, a ruby heart on a miniature chain. Gifts my father brought back from trips overseas. Necklaces that belonged to Alicja. Jacqui and I twist rings on and off. We swap them across the table. My father logs the items we select into a spreadsheet. He closes his laptop. 'It's sorted,' he says.

Years later, when my mother's jewellery is locked away, when Uncle Tony is back in her life, sitting by her bed every week telling her funny stories, only her gold wedding band and diamond engagement ring sink heavy on her reedy finger. I will massage her seahorse-like hands with oils. Rose and lavender will help stop the swelling, but rubbing her rings dull will rouse compunction in me. I will avert my eyes. I know the day is coming. Like a thief, I will do as she wanted. I will knead her diamond ring off.

That ring will sit undisturbed in my bedside drawer for two years. One morning, I will try it on. A perfect fit. I will know then that I need to wear my mother's ring. I will find the courage to wear it. I will.

45

The 747 tears down the runway, four engines screaming. Just when I think the concrete will end, the plane tilts. Take-offs always split me: after years away, an immigrant in America, a stranger in Australia. When the plane soars into the clouds, I smile and think of 'home' in New England. But my family and closest friends live down there, I think, staring back at dust swirling in sand-coloured paddocks on Melbourne's outskirts. Dust my mother could never tolerate.

I float over the blue eucalypt Dandenong Ranges, over vineyards towards Sydney. I peer out at the silvery shadow of bush. Twice on this route I have stared down at smoke clouds. I have watched raging balls of fire skip across mountain ridges. Massive fires tear through bush every few years somewhere in Australia. They torch homes and wildlife and burn land to a char.

After hundreds died in the 2009 Black Saturday fires, I stood on a hillside in apocalyptic silence. Fire had melted fences and metal poles on roadsides and bent them like Alicja's pained, bowed back. The earth stood still. Not a single birdcall. No wind. Only black moonscape and ghostly ash. But when I returned a year later, green shoots sprouted from the stoutest blackened tree trunks. Parrots screeched along valleys, their mating calls echoing. It was as if the hillside was being rebirthed. Only thinner trees appeared dead. Soon, new leaves would ring them, too, like dancers jiggling feather boas.

In Sydney, I wait in the lounge for my delayed flight to Los Angeles. I think about my conversation in a café with Mum last week, when she informed me she's planning her bat mitzvah. She will read from the Torah with two other Holocaust survivors at a Jewish Messianic congregation in Caulfield, where she celebrates her Christian faith in context with her Jewish roots. My mother has come full circle. Roots and branches finally together. For Mum, this is closure.

For me, however, the circle will always be open. I see God when I walk in the woods and hike in the mountains. I see God stretched across the vast sky. Sometimes I mutter to God, asking for wisdom. Sometimes I whisper in the strange language I don't understand, echoes of the Pentecostal church I attended all those years ago. Although I don't pray often, it always happens under trees, or on the sand watching waves foam and crash. Just God and me.

I've learned to accept my mother's relationship with religion, the comfort and support the church provides her. Even if

I struggle to accept it for myself, I respect it. The church, and her relationship with God, saved my mother's life.

When I first set out for Poland, I thought if I could piece together what happened during the war, I'd understand the rift between Alicja and Mum. It was a silly assumption on my part. I have learned that stories we tell aren't always truthful. Truth, if we find it, can be ugly. The world isn't straightforward, good or evil. And the line between right or wrong, guilty or blameless, is not clear. Alicja said there's evil inside all of us, and when societal norms of respect and decency collapse, we're capable of treating each other like animals; when we dehumanise 'others', we can justify the denial of rights and all kinds of depravity and violence.

I've learned how Alicja hurt my mother. But given the murder and cruelty embedded in Alicja, she did the best she could raising a traumatised child. I think I know now why she always had poodles. They would wag their tails and adore her. They didn't need to know about her choices or her grief. They gave her the unconditional love and affection that I gave her, too.

I want so badly to take Alicja to her favourite patisserie. To sip tea with her. To tell her I have retraced her life, her big romance and the family who anchored her for a few fleeting years. To tell her I have pieced together the woman she needed me to see, but also the one she wanted hidden: a woman destroyed by war who, perhaps unconsciously, infused her anger into my mother. I want to tell her I understand why she kept Dick's secret silent, that she believed revealing it would hurt my mother even more. But when it came to her denying she mistreated my mother, I would tell her I believe my mother.

An announcement bellows over the PA system. People stand, gather bags and head to the gate. I linger, happy to stretch my legs before the fifteen-hour flight to LAX, a long layover, then six more hours to Boston.

Inside the jet bridge, twenty-somethings chatter excitedly about rides they've lined up for Disneyland. I edge closer to the aircraft door. The United Airlines flight attendant flashes a smile at me.

'Welcome aboard,' she says.

Epilogue

Recently, I travelled to Paris with my husband, Peter, to celebrate our wedding anniversary. One afternoon, I walked for hours on my own through one neighbourhood after another. I stopped to admire stacks of goat's cheese and piles of fruit at food stalls along footpaths. I wandered into patisseries where I marvelled at macarons sandwiched with strawberry ganache, delicate pistachio-green cakes iced a lemon yellow, glistening chocolate éclairs, all lined up like Christmas ornaments in a shop.

En route back to the hotel, I found myself outside the 1874 Grand Synagogue de la Victoire, its facade traversed with rose-petalled windows. I walked by galvanised security barricades through a steel gate to the portico. Two men sitting near the entrance stopped me. 'You can't go in,' one with a short black beard said.

'Oh,' I remarked. 'It's closed?'

'There's a wedding,' the man said apologetically.

'Shalom,' I said, surprising myself, uttering one of the few Hebrew words in my vocabulary.

The man tilted his head. He asked where I was from. Then he motioned me to follow him. He opened a door and led me to the last pew, up the back.

A man was singing a minor-key melody in a tenor voice that soared. It pierced me. The feeling was so strong, it filled me with a kind of longing. It rippled through me: my heart, the tips of my fingers, my toes. The song sounded sad and ancient. It had travelled centuries, through Russia, across Hungary, Lithuania. It carried me back to Poland.

As the notes climbed, I breathed with them. When they fell, I exhaled and let go. For a while, I didn't notice the towering stone arches lining both sides of the long nave, or the stained-glass windows at the front. I sank back into the song. I wiped my eyes with the back of my hand. I watched a bride and groom up ahead of me on a dais huddle under a red canopy.

I thought about Nana Alicja's mother, Dorota, in Warsaw's Grand Synagogue on Tłomeckie Street, the one the Nazis blew up. I was witnessing the traditional kind of wedding Dorota wanted for Alicja and Irena. This kind of synagogue. Filled with friends and relatives to witness her daughters marrying. A synagogue where, if I squinted, I could see Dorota holding my mother's hand, her granddaughter, both waving at me from the balcony above.

'Listen, Joasia,' I could hear Dorota whisper in my mother's ear. 'This is how love sounds. This is the song of your people.'

Acknowledgements

I am indebted to the dozens of historians, institutions, archivists and experts who illuminated this story, including but not limited to: Vincent Slatt and Jude Richter at the United States Holocaust Memorial Museum; Krzysztof Bielawski at POLIN Museum; Anna Przybyszewska Drozd at the Jewish Historical Institute in Warsaw; historians Dr Idit Gil, Dr Sebastian Piątkowski for his insight into Radom Prison, Dr Kamil Kijek for his fact-checking; and Dr Toby Haggith of the Imperial War Museum in London for his role in restoring the film *German Concentration Camps Factual Survey*, in which my grandfather, Dr Mieczysław Dortheimer, is interviewed.

Thanks to my teacher, mentor and friend, Christina Thompson, who, after I naively announced I'd finish this book in a year, predicted (correctly) it would take ten. I owe much to writing instructors Alex Marzano-Lesnevich and Kevin Birmingham for teaching me how to illuminate pasts and places I did not inhabit; to Kevin for shepherding 'Searching for the Nazi Who Saved My Mother's Life' into existence; and to Narratively editors Brendan Spiegel and Lilly Dancyger, who believed in my very first essay despite its unresolved ending.

This book exists thanks to the brilliant tutelage of Alysia

Abbott, head of Boston's GrubStreet Memoir Incubator program, who helped me unearth the heart of this complicated story, and fellow Incubees Rita Chang, Anne Crane, Virginia DeLuca, Linda Cutting, Ani Gjika, Theresa Okokon, Trần Vũ Thu-Hằng and Anri Wheeler, who propelled me through multiple drafts delving into our darkest secrets and boosted me during the worst of the pandemic on our Zoom cafés. Thanks also to the generosity of Incubator alumni Michelle Bowdler, Dolores Johnson, Molly Howes, Catherine Guthrie and Judy Bolton-Fasman; and authors Maya Shanbhag Lang, Elizabeth Graver and Jennifer S. Brown, who championed me from the beginning.

In Otwock, I am beholden to too many to list. Thanks to Świdermajer activists for lobbying to protect Otwock's architectural treasures; to Barbara Matysiak; to historian and community activist Sebastian Rakowski and his mother, Jadwiga, for their commitment to memory and their courage to overturn the more comfortable versions of their town's history. Thanks to Monika Czub of Forum Dialogu for always coming to my rescue, most importantly during my recent train trip to visit Treblinka; and also to Kasia Zakrzewska: thank you both for dropping everything whenever I'm in town to interpret and to indulge in my sernik and szarlotka addiction. To Kasia, Piotr, Jarek and other Otwock teachers, thank you for guiding your students into the minefield of memory. Most of all, I owe so much to my dear friend Zbigniew Nosowski for his warmth and kindness, for always saying 'yes' to anyone with roots in Otwock, for his tireless work fostering understanding between peoples and for standing against hatred and discrimination. He is a beacon to the world.

I am grateful for the long conversations with my dear, recently departed 'sister' Iwona, to Iza for our unforgettable moments with Sister Honorata and the Imienia Jezus sisters, and to Joanna Cutts, who from that first day we sipped tea in her salon-like home filled with books and music, introduced me to Zbyszek and others, translated photos and documents, and deepened my understanding of life in post-war Poland.

Thanks to my 'shitty-first-draft' readers, Joanna, Gina Aarons, Conceicao Andrade, Terry Perlmutter, Ilana Wind, Iris Muzila and Shirley Straface; to Ilana for deliberating our histories on long walks; to Jill Gibson and Vincent Martinelli; Patrik Muzila; to the Aussie expat community – particularly Toni Laracuente and Rebecca Chan; and to Iris Muzila for her voluminous love and kindness, for tolerating the ugliness of my tortuous journey and for her unfailing support. Above all, I want to thank my beloved Victoria Baxter and Wendy Miles for never losing faith in me, for carrying me through the months and years I doubted this book's possibility.

Irena's Gift includes memories family members have shared with me. Thank you to my siblings and Simone; to my Aunt Mary for photographs and letters; and in particular to my Uncle Tony and Auntie Jill for their love and visits to Mum in her last years. Thanks to my mother's legion of friends for loving 'Joasia' and, by extension, me and my siblings. I also want to express gratitude for the support of my husband's family in New Zealand and in Brisbane.

I am incredibly grateful to my unflappable agent, Chris Bucci, and to Amaryah Orenstein, who from that first light-bulb moment we met at an agent–pitch event realised our Warsaw families had likely crossed paths before and during the ghetto uprising, and welcomed me into the fold of her survivor family. She has always believed in the importance of this story and our shared history.

I wish to thank my publisher at Penguin Random House Australia, Sophie Ambrose, for championing this book with tender, wise and ever gracious guidance; my fastidious and kind editor Clive Hebard; Penguin's marketing team; and all those behind the scenes who were vital to this book's existence.

Most of all, I could never have written this book without the love and support of my husband and best friend, Peter Shaw, the smartest and wisest person I know, who along with my late schnoodle, listened to dozens of drafts but were the worst critics. They loved every word.

Notes

1   Epstein, Helen, *Children Of The Holocaust*, Penguin Books, 1979, p. 209.

2   Rutland, Suzanne D., 'Australian responses to Jewish refugee migration before and after World War II', *Australian Journal of Politics & History*, vol. 31, no. 1, pp. 29–41.

3   quickstats.censusdata.abs.gov.au/census_services/getproduct/census/2016/quickstat/208021177?opendocument

4   australianjewishnews.com/record-number-of-jews/

5   brandeis.edu/cmjs/community-studies/boston-report.html#:~:text=Greater%20Boston%20is%20home%20to,of%20approximately%204.6%25%20since%202005

6   Adlington, Lucy, *The Dressmakers of Auschwitz*, Harper, 2021, pp. 146–7.

7   Fetting, Ed, 'Dachau Court Closes', *Stars and Stripes*, 29 December 1947.

8   1938 Polish Public Companies, Industry, and Trade 11392. E. Mizne, {1905}. Wr. A. Warsawa, Orla 11. Tlf: 11-30-36. PKO: 4.278. Bk: B.H. w Warsz., B. Zachodni. Rejester: Warsawa A/XXIII 28. B. Eliasz Mizne. E. Dora Mizne {prok.}.F.Przedstraw: Bydgoszcz, Katowice, Lwow, Lodz, Poznan, Wilno. H.Centrala Zw., Kupcow, Wr. N. * Fabryka rekawiczek skorkowych {3350}.Import skor {1295, 3626}.Eksport rekawiczek skorkowch do Anglii Ameryki, Szwecji, Holandii, Rumunii. (Export of leather gloves to England of America, Sweden, the Netherlands and Romania.)

9   Unilowski 1938, 43. Mark, Bernard, 1960, pp. 223–8.

10 Singer, I. B., *Every Jewish Street in Warsaw Was an Independent Town*, 2 July 1944, pp. 21–6.

11 oddurbanthings.com/music-of-interwar-warsaw

12 Mietek's application for assistance from the Preparatory Commission for the International Refugee Organization (PCIRO), 10 July 1948.

13 Mick, Christopher, *Lemberg, Lwów, and L'viv 1914–1947: Violence and Ethnicity in a Contested City*, Purdue University Press, 2016, p. 244.

14 Fremont, Helen, *After Long Silence: A Memoir*, Delta, 2000; Rabinowicz, H. 'The Battle of the Ghetto Benches', *Jewish Quarterly Review*, vol. 55, no. 2 (1964), pp. 151–9, doi:10.2307/1453795

15 onr.czyz.org/artykul-3-t-ideologia-i-program-obozu-narodowo-radykalnego.html and falangeoriental.blogspot.com/2012/08/wojciech-jerzy-muszynski-ideologia-i.html

16 Brzezinski, Mathew, *Isaac's Army*, Random House, 2012, p. 75.

17 encyclopedia.ushmm.org/content/en/article/the-nuremberg-race-laws

18 Michlic, Joanna, *Poland's Threatening Other: The Image of the Jew from 1880 to the Present*, University of Nebraska Press, 2006, pp. 69–108.

19 kpbc.ukw.edu.pl/dlibra/publication/188160/edition/190274/content

20 tabletmag.com/sections/arts-letters/articles/polish-anti-semitism-zionism

21 In 1935.

22 worldfuturefund.org/wffmaster/Reading/Total/Polish%20Antisemitism. htm#[9] 'Raport Dyr. Mieczyslaw Lepeckiego z Podrozy na Madagaskar' (Warszawa, 1937). A version of this report from 1938 is available at the Library of Congress in Washington, DC. Call number D285.8.B4 L4.

23 sztetl.org.pl/en/node/779/99-history/138313-history-of-community

24 Marcus, Joseph, 'Social and Political History of the Jews in Poland 1919–1939', De Gruyter Mouton, 1983.

25 worldradiohistory.com/UK/World-Radio/World-Radio-1935-05-03-S-OCR. pdf

26 Soddu, Marco, 'Anti-Semitism in Inter-war Europe: the Cases of Poland & Hungary', *Foreign Policy Journal*, 26 November 2012.

27 Mahler, Raphael, 'Jews in Public Service and the Liberal Professions in Poland, 1918–39', *Jewish Social Studies*, vol. 6, no. 4, 1944, p. 298; youtube.com/ watch?v=Eqf1zz-KnB4 (Aleksiun, Natalia; 16:45) and yivoencyclopedia. org/article.aspx/poland/poland_from_1795_to_1939

28 28 per cent of boys circumcised in Victorian hospitals: cirp.org/library/ statistics/CandNon-C/

29 Epstein, p. 209.

30 zydziotwoccy-history.pl/historia-spolecznosci/; 19,206 Otwock residents, including 10,689 Polish citizens of the Mosaic faith; there were 37,713 vacationers.

31 Hamerow, Theodore S., *Remembering a Vanished World*, Berghahn Books, 2001, p. 91.

32 culture.pl/en/article/a-guide-to-the-wooden-villas-of-otwock

33 Hamerow, p. 109.

34 Ibid., p. 98.

35 Przygoda, Zdzisław, *The Way to Freedom*, Lugus, p. 199.

36 Known also as Danzig, Gdansk was a semi-autonomous city/state, officially separated from Germany and Poland, but under the protection of the League of Nations.

37 yadvashem.org/holocaust/about/combat-resistance/jewish-soldiers. html#narrative_info

38 Lieutenant Stefan Hirszberg.

39 gedenkstaette-vaihingen.de/geschichte-des-lagers

40 kz-gedenkstaette-dachau.de/en/historical-site/virtual-tour/crematorium-area/

41 tri-r-ministries.com/product/focusing-on-christian-womanhood-fcw/

42 news.bbc.co.uk/2/hi/health/564540.stm

43 holocaustresearchproject.org/ghettos/otwock.html

44 britannica.com/topic/education/Froebel-and-the-kindergarten-movement

45 en.wikipedia.org/wiki/Froebel_gifts

46 Tuszynska, Agata, *Family History of Fear: A Memoir*, Anchor Books, 2017, p. 311.

47 Perechodnik, Calel, *Am I a Murderer? Testament of a Jewish Ghetto Policeman*, Westview Press, 1996.

48 wiez.pl/2019/04/06/swastyki-na-kamieniu-pamieci-otwockich-zydow-blyskawicznie-usuniete-przez-proboszcza/

49 lato39.pl/summer39.html

50 *Gazeta Polska* daily, after 'Almanach 1939', 12 July.

51 *Dobry Wieczór! Kurjer Czerwony* afternoon daily, after: 'Almanach 1939', Warsaw, 5 July 2008, accessed via: lato39.pl/summer39.html

52 Albert Forster in *LIFE* magazine, 21 August 1939, p. 18, accessed via books.google.co.nz/books?id=9EEEAAAAMBAJ&q=Albert+Forster& redir_esc=y#v=snippet&q=Albert%20Forster&f=false

53 krakowpost.com/1472/2009/08

54 Ibid.

55 Ibid.

56 krakowpost.com/1531/2009/09

57 sztetl.org.pl/en/towns/o/590-otwock/99-history/137815-history-of-community

58 Brzezinski, p 4.

59 Ibid., p. 15.

60 Ibid., p. 23.

61 Ibid., p. 19 and also in Przygoda.

62 Brzezinski, p. 21.

63 criticalpast.com/video/65675043611_Adolf-Hitler_German-troops_conquer-Polish-territories_Poles-will-fight-for-Danzig

64 Some 1,200 aircraft. Zaloga, Steven J., *Poland 1939: The Birth of Blitzkrieg*, Osprey Publishing Ltd., 2002.

65   Brzezinski, p. 30.

66   Berger, Joseph, *Displaced Persons: Growing up American after the Holocaust*, Scribener, 2001, p. 132.

67   military-history.fandom.com/wiki/Siege_of_Warsaw_(1939)

68   Brzezinski, p. 21

69   Ibid.

70   Ibid., p. 33.

71   Engelking, Barbara and Jacek Leociak, *The Warsaw Ghetto: A Guide to the Perished City*, Yale University Press, 2009, p. 33.

72   krakowpost.com/1531/2009/09

73   dziennikpolski24.pl/niemcy-w-krakowie/ar/3270968

74   panzerworld.com/german-armor-balkenkreuz-tactical-numbers

75   Benisch, Pearl, *To Vanquish the Dragon*, Feldheim Publishers, 1991, p. 12 and krakowpost.com/1531/2009/09

76   Ibid., p. 12.

77   www.krakowpost.com/1531/2009/09

78   en.wikipedia.org/wiki/Battle_of_Lw%C3%B3w_(1939)

79   upload.wikimedia.org/wikipedia/en/f/fa/Lviv_1939_Soviet_Cavalry.jpg

80   wrap.warwick.ac.uk/35661/1/0170657-lb-250711-wrap_mick_aufsatz3_2.pdf pp. 5–6.

81   en.wikipedia.org/wiki/NKVD

82   Fremont, p. 11

83   yadvashem.org/odot_pdf/Microsoft%20Word%20-%206217.pdf

84   sprawiedliwi.org.pl/en/news/guardian-memory-jakub-muller-has-passed-away

85   sztetl.org.pl/en/towns/n/538-nowy-sacz/114-cemeteries/24348-jewish-cemetery-nowy-sacz-rybacka-street

86   encyclopedia.ushmm.org/content/en/article/hans-frank

87   ushmm.org/outreach/en/article.php?ModuleId=10007732

88   Brzezinski, p. 46.

89   Przygoda, chapter 5.

90   Engelking and Leociak, p. 33.

91   lexikon-der-wehrmacht.de/Personenregister/N/NeumannNeurodeKarlUlrich.htm

92   eilatgordinlevitan.com/warsaw/w_pix/front/071206_110a_b.gif

93   vqronline.org/essay/what-became-prussian-army

94   Only 250 zloty withdrawal per week allowed. Engelking and Leociak, p. 37.

95   Brzezinski, p. 104.

96   Ibid. In a prewar census, only 5 per cent of Warsaw's Jews classified themselves as Polish speakers.

97 Ziolkowska-Bohem, Aleksandra, *The Roots are Polish*, Canadian-Polish Research Institute, 2000, p. 150.
98 Engelking and Leociak, p. 53.
99 Ibid.
100 Ibid.
101 Brzezinski, p. 120.
102 Engelking and Leociak, p. 53.
103 Ibid., p. 54.
104 new.getto.pl/pl/Kalendarium and Engelking and Leociak, p. 37.
105 Brzezinski, p. 48.
106 Ibid., p. 37. 1 December 1939.
107 Ibid., pp. 48–9.
108 Engelking and Leociak, p. 54.
109 Brzezinski, p. 82.
110 Ibid., p. 48.
111 Rubach, Leon, *The Autobiography of Leon Ruback: The First Twenty Years*, AuthorHouse, 2010.
112 encyclopedia.ushmm.org/content/en/article/german-soviet-pact
113 Fremont, p. 120.
114 brill.com/downloadpdf/journals/lhs/7/1/article-p95_5.xml
115 trove.nla.gov.au/newspaper/article/17672245
116 In the village of Dolishnye.
117 wrap.warwick.ac.uk/35661/1/0170657-lb-250711-wrap_mick_aufsatz3_2.pdf, p. 6.
118 PCIRO Application for Assistance, 1947.
119 Rutland, Suzanne, 'Australian responses to Jewish refugee migration before and after World War II', *Australian Journal of Politics and History*, 1985, vol. 31, issue 1, p. 42.
120 wykop.pl/cdn/c3201142/comment_oEbtOlikCXOfV2lmFKv3qDWDOQ6FHkej.jpg
121 riowang.blogspot.com/2010/09/autumn-in-lwow.html
122 lvivcenter.org/en/umd/mapdetails/lemberg-c1939/
123 Yones, Eliyahu, *Smoke in the Sand: The Jews of Lvov in the War Years 1939–1944*, Gefen Publishing House Ltd, 2004, p. 75.
124 Fremont, p. 137.
125 Eliyahu, p. 80.
126 Fremont, p. 134.
127 autoevolution.com/news/war-machines-maybach-powered-panzer-tanks-126225.html#agal_3
128 Eliyahu, p. 79.

129 encyclopedia.ushmm.org/content/en/film/pogrom-in-lvov

130 Walker, Shaun, *The Long Hangover: Putin's New Russia and the Ghosts of the Past*, Oxford University Press, 2017, p. iv.

131 encyclopedia.ushmm.org/content/en/film/pogrom-in-lvov

132 encyclopedia.ushmm.org/content/en/article/lvov

133 upload.wikimedia.org/wikipedia/commons/4/4d/Kennkarte_-_A._Melnyk_-_inside.jpg

134 Goldberg, Amos, 'Rumor Culture Among Warsaw Jews Under Nazi Occupation: A World of Catastrophe Reenchanted', *Jewish Social Studies: History, Culture, Society*, vol. 21, no. 3 (2016), pp. 91–125, doi:10.2979/jewisocistud.21.3.04

135 Engelking and Leociak.

136 Ibid.

137 Brzezinski, p. 111.

138 yadvashem.org/holocaust/about/ghettos/warsaw.html

139 United States Holocaust Memorial Museum, 'Warsaw Map': ushmm.org/wlc/en/media_nm.php?MediaId=3375&ModuleId=10005069

140 Ibid.

141 Engelking and Leociak, p. 98.

142 Gutman, Israel, '*The Jews of Warsaw 1939–43: Ghetto, Underground and Revolt*', Branch Line, 1982, p. 66; Brzezinski, p. 111.

143 Engelking and Leociak, p. 387 and p. 488.

144 Brzezinski, p. 124.

145 Ibid. p. 112.

146 Ibid. p. 140; Engelking and Leociak, p. 86; echoesandreflections.org/wp-content/uploads/2021/07/08-01-05_Student-Handout_Those-Who-Dared-Rescue and Brzezinski, p. 113.

147 Engelking and Leociak, p. 473.

148 jewishvirtuallibrary.org/lvov-ukraine-jewish-history-tour

149 holocaustresearchproject.org/ghettos/lvov.html

150 jewishgen.org/yizkor/lviv/lvi593.html

151 en.wikipedia.org/wiki/Kennkarte

152 in2013dollars.com/1941-dollars-in-2017?amount=500

153 jwa.org/encyclopedia/article/womens-health-in-ghettos-of-eastern-europe and ima.org.il/filesupload/imaj/0/45/22849.pdf

154 Engelking and Leociak, p. xiv.

155 Ibid., p. 42.

156 Brzezinski, p. 142.

157 Engelking and Leociak, p. 454.

158 Ibid., p. 743.

159 Perechodnik, p. 101.

160 ushmm.org/m/pdfs/20170502-Grabowski_OP.pdf and Perechodnik, p. 57.

161 Engelking and Leociak, p. 93.

162 April. Ibid., p. 43.

163 holocaustresearchproject.org/ghettos/chaimkaplan.html

164 Engelking and Leociak, p. 43.

165 Gutman.

166 Engelking and Leociak, p. 704.

167 Ibid., p 93.

168 Brzezinski, p. 176.

169 Engelking and Leociak, p. 699.

170 Brzezinski, p. 178.

171 Battalion, Judy, *The Light of Days*, HarperCollins, 2020, p. 88; Meed, Vladka, *On Both Sides of the Wall*, (trns. Steven Meed), United States Holocaust Library, 1993, p. 65.

172 yadvashem.org/education/educational-videos/video-toolbox/hevt-lewin.html

173 Engelking and Leociak, p. 133.

174 Brzezinski, p. 180.

175 Engelking and Leociak, p. 703.

176 jhi.pl/en/articles/warsaw-ghetto-one-week-after-start-of-great-deportation, 5147

177 Brzezinski, p. 178.

178 Engelking and Leociak, p. 711.

179 Ibid., p. 702.

180 holocausthistoricalsociety.org.uk/contents/treblinkadeathcamp/treblinka eyewitnessstatements.html and jewishvirtuallibrary.org/operation-reinhard-the-camps-of-belzec-sobibor-and-treblinka

181 Brzezinski, p. 227.

182 Tamaszewski, Irena and Tecia Webowski, *Zegota: The Rescue of Jews in Wartime Poland*, Price-Patterson, 1995, p. 136.

183 Engelking and Leociak, p. 741.

184 Brzezinski, p. 248.

185 Engelking and Leociak, p. 775.

186 amopod.org/uprising/WarsawPerspective.htm

187 Przygoda.

188 Engelking and Leociak, p. 769.

189 Dorembus, Helena Elbaum, 'Through Helpless Eyes: A Survivor's Diary of the Warsaw Ghetto Uprising', *Moment*, April 1993, p. 60.

190 new.getto.pl/en/Sources/Relacja-301-5223-w-Archiwum-ZIH-Apolonia-Gosciej-Lola-Szpigelman-Matylda-Kozlowska-Helena-Przygoda.

191 jhi.pl/en/articles/the-last-breath-about-the-demolition-of-the-great-synagogue,111

192 Wilkerson, Isabel, *Caste: The Origin of Our Discontents*, Random House, 2020, pp. 5, 64–5.

193 Ibid., p. 49.

194 Wilkerson, p. 65 and sitn.hms.harvard.edu/flash/2017/science-genetics-reshaping-race-debate-21st-century/

195 timesofisrael.com/ashkenazi-jews-descend-from-350-people-study-finds/

196 worldjewishcongress.org/en/about/communities/PL

197 theguardian.com/commentisfree/2019/sep/17/populist-rewriting-polish-history-museum-poland-gdansk

198 time.com/5128341/poland-holocaust-law/

199 nytimes.com/2019/07/27/world/europe/gay-pride-march-poland-violence.html

200 en.wikipedia.org/wiki/Polish_Army_oaths and Zimmerman, Joshua D., *The Polish Underground and the Jews, 1939–1945*, Cambridge University Press, 2015, p. 332.

201 auschwitz.org/en/press/basic-information-on-auschwitz/

202 Bartosz, Adam, *In the Footsteps of the Jews of Tarnów*, Tarnowskie Regionalne Centrum Koordynacji i Obsługi Turystyki, 2000, p. 12.

203 holocaustresearchproject.org/nazioccupation/tarnowdeport.html

204 Brandt, Karl and Otto Schiller, 'Management of Agriculture and Food in the German-occupied and other areas of Fortress Europe: a Study in Military Government', quoted in *The Journal of Economic History*, vol. 15, no. 2, pp. 30–1.

205 Przygoda, chapter 8.

206 cozadzien.pl/radom/ponura-historia-pieknej-kamienicy/32438

207 Przygoda, Zdzisław, 'Slide Rule Column Brings Back Memories', *Canadian Consulting Engineer*, July 1983.

208 Piątowski, Dr Sebastian, *Więzienie niemieckie w Radomiu 1939–1945*, Instytucie Pamięci Narodowej Oddział Lublin, 2009.

209 Ibid., p. 34.

210 ushmm.org/m/pdfs/20170502-Grabowski_OP.pdf

211 Tamaszewski and Webowski, p. 137.

212 Döblin, Alfred, *Journey to Poland*, Paragon House, 1991, p. 42.

213 culture.pl/en/article/the-hussies-and-gentlemen-of-prewar-poland

214 Piątowski, p. 54.

215 ushmm.org/m/pdfs/20170502-Grabowski_OP.pdf, p. 4.

216 Ibid., p. 2.

217 cozadzien.pl/radom/ponura-historia-pieknej-kamienicy/32438

218 righteous.yadvashem.org/?searchType=righteous_only&language=en&ite
mId=10493486&ind=0

219 Goda, Norman J. W., 'Black Marks: Hitler's Bribery of His Senior Officers
during World War II', *Journal of Modern History*, vol. 72, no. 2, p. 444,
doi:10.1086/315994

220 ushmm.org/m/pdfs/2000926-Poles.pdf, p. 11.

221 Krasuski, Josef. 'Education as Resistance: The Polish Experience of
Schooling During the War', *Education and the Second World War: Studies in
Schooling and Social Change*, Routledge, 1992, p. 132.

222 Ibid., p. 130.

223 Bogner, N., 'The Convent Children: The Rescue of Jewish Children in
Polish Convents During the Holocaust', *Journal of Polish-Jewish Studies*,
vol. 3, p. 3.

224 Ibid.

225 cozadzien.pl/radom/ponura-historia-pieknej-kamienicy/32438

226 polskatimes.pl/paul-fuchs-zwany-lisem-z-radomia-gestapowiec-
ktory-szachowal-podziemie/ar/10012656

227 deathcamps.org/occupation/radom%20ghetto.html

228 Ibid. and holocaustresearchproject.org/ghettos/radom.html

229 Interview with Izzy Rosenblat, 27 February 1992, Rockville, Maryland.
collections.ushmm.org/oh_findingaids/RG-50.233.0113_trs_en.pdf

230 auschwitz.org/en/history/life-in-the-camp/nutrition

231 Adlington, pp.23, 174, 176.

232 boell.de/en/2020/05/18/sexual-violence-holocaust-perspectives-ghettos-
and-camps-ukraine

233 Helm, Sarah. *If This Is a Woman: Inside Ravensbrück: Hitler's Concentration
Camp for Women*, Little, Brown, 2015, p. 409.

234 Ibid., testimony from Halina Wasilewska.

235 Ibid., p. 463.

236 Ibid., p. 26.

237 Adlington, p. 268 and uczycsiezhistorii.pl/projekt/kop-tam-gdzie-
stoisz-malachow-oboz-przylegly-ravensbruck-grabe-wo-du-stehst-
malachow-ein-aussenlager-von-ravensbruck/

238 bunker-und-mehr.de/b_malchow_t.html and collections.ushmm.
org/search/catalog/irn504659, testimony Ruth Meyerowitz, and
geschichtsspuren.de/artikel/ruestungsproduktion-logistik/104-munition-
swerk-malchow.html and bunker-und-mehr.de/b_malchow_t.html

239 bunker-und-mehr.de/b_malchow_t.html and ortschroniken-mv.de/
images/a/a2/MAL_Munitionswerk.pdf

240 Verified by: Ruth Meyerowitz via ushmm.org/outreach/en/media_
oi.php?MediaId=7025

241 Helm, p. 441.

242 Adlington, p. 157.

243 Helm, p. 489.

244 Ibid., pp. 494, 495.

245 ravensbrueck-sbg.de/en/visitor-service/site-plan/

246 Helm, p.501.

247 Ibid., p. 501.

248 Ibid., p. 510.

249 Ibid., p. 554. testimony from Karolina Lanckoronska.

250 Ibid., p. 513.

251 Ibid., p. 503.

252 Adlington, p. 268.

253 Helm, p. 435. Late 1944.

254 Ibid., p. 540. 16 Feb.

255 Ibid., p. 588.

256 Ibid., p. 589.

257 Ibid., p. 591.

258 collections.ushmm.org/search/catalog/irn1000758

259 criticalpast.com/video/65675068323_Jewish-religious-services_David-M-
     Eichhorn-speaks_people-gathered_people-hold-flags

260 Harold Porter's letter in slate.com/blogs/the_vault/2014/05/02/holocaust_
     liberation_letter_from_american_soldier_at_dachau.html

261 Helm, p. 633 and europe.newsweek.com/swedish-schindler-how-count-
     bernadotte-saved-thousands-jews-death-327234

262 Mankowitz, Zeev W., *Life Between Memory and Hope: The Survivors of the
     Holocaust in Occupied Germany*, Cambridge University Press, 2002, p. 39.

263 encyclopedia.ushmm.org/content/en/article/the-kielce-pogrom-a-blood-
     libel-massacre-of-holocaust-survivors

264 Brzezinski, p. 385.

265 search.archives.jdc.org/multimedia/Documents/NY_AR_45-54/NY_
     AR45-54_Count/NY_AR45-54_00013/NY_AR45-54_00013_01167.
     pdf#search='dortheimer'

266 search.archives.jdc.org/multimedia/Documents/NY_AR_45-54/NY_
     AR45-54_Count/NY_AR45-54_00032/NY_AR45-54_00032_00419.
     pdf#search='przygoda.

267 https://encyclopedia.ushmm.org/content/en/article/polish-victims and
     Judt, Tony, *Postwar: A History of Europe Since 1945*, Penguin, 2006, p. 18.

268 Testro, Ron, 'Hitler Prescribed Poison for Rommel', *The Argus*, 9 July 1949,
     trove.nla.gov.au/newspaper/article/99058954

269 Wardi, Dina, *Memorial Candles: Children of the Holocaust*, Routledge, 1992, p. 115; Shoham, G. S., *Valhalla, Golgotha and Auschwitz*, Bowman & Cody, 1995, pp. 5, 174.

270 Brzezinski, p. 369.

271 Michlic, Joanna B., *Jewish Children in Nazi-occupied Poland: Survival and Polish-Jewish Relations During the Holocaust as Reflected in Early Postwar Recollections*, Yad Vashem Publications, 2008, p. 66.

272 Ibid, p 70.

273 Michlic, Joanna B., 'Who Am I? Jewish Children's Search for Identity in Post-War Poland 1945–1949', in Gabriel N. Finder, Natalia Aleksiun and Antony Polonsky (eds), *Polin: Studies in Polish Jewry Volume 20: Making Holocaust Memory*, Liverpool University Press, 2007, doi:10.3828/liverpool/9781904113058.003.0004

274 Williams, Marleen S. 'Bringing to remembrance: The trauma memory debate', *Issues in Religion and Psychotherapy*, vol. 23. no. 1, pp. 97–109; Bauer, Patricia J. 'What do infants recall of their lives? Memory for specific events by one- to two-year-olds', *American Psychologist*, vol. 51, no. 1, p. 29; news.cornell.edu/stories/2014/04/psychologists-ask-what-your-earliest-memory

275 Datner, Helena, 'Dziecko Żydowskie (1944–1950)', [in] Feliks Tych, Monika Adamczyk-Garbowska (eds), *Następstwa zagłady Żydów. Polska 1944–2000*, Lublin, 2012, p. 256.

276 Brzezinski, p. 397.

277 encyclopedia.ushmm.org/content/en/article/warsaw

278 Brzezinski, p. 84.

279 Ibid., p. 383.

280 Ibid., pp. 383, 384.

281 kz-gedenkstaette-dachau.de/en/biografien-en/biografie-arthur-haulot-id-11/

282 Michlic, Joanna, 'The War Began for Me After the War: Jewish Children in Poland, 1945–49', in Friedman, Jonathan C. (ed.), *The Routledge History of the Holocaust*, Routledge, 2010, p. 487.

283 ncbi.nlm.nih.gov/pmc/articles/PMC1523417/

284 Michlic, Joanna, 'The War Began for Me', p. 487.

285 Trent, James T., *Mission on the Rhine: Reeducation and Denazification of American-Occupied Germany*, University of Chicago Press, 1982, pp. 45, 64, 70 and 201.

286 Michlic, Joanna, 'The War Began for Me', p. 494.

287 Gross, Jan T., 'Polish-Jewish relations during the war: An interpretation', *European Journal of Sociology*, vol. 27, no. 02, p. 202.

288 M.R. Jarvelin, I. Moilanen, L. Vikevainen-Tervonen, N.P. Huttunen, 'Life changes and protective capacities in enuretic and non-enuretic children', *Journal of Child Psychology & Psychiatry*, vol. 31, pp. 763–77, ncbi.nlm.nih. gov/pmc/articles/PMC2139977/

289 Frankl, Viktor E., *Man's Search for Meaning: An Introduction to Logotherapy*, Simon & Schuster, 1984.

290 McAdam, Alison, 'Finding Faith From Life's Darkest Days', *Warrnambool Standard*, 28 March 2001.

291 Gross, Jan T., 'Polish-Jewish relations during the war: An interpretation', *European Journal of Sociology*, vol. 27, no. 2, pp. 199–214.

292 wikipedia.org/wiki/Trial_of_the_Sixteen

293 Brzezinski, p. 383.

294 wikipedia.org/wiki/Cursed_soldiers

295 bbc.com/news/world-europe-43330963

296 Tamaszewski, Irena and Webowski, Tecia, *Zegota: The Rescue of Jews in Wartime Poland*, Price-Patterson, 1994, p. 136.

297 Feeny, Norah C., Lori A. Zoellner, Lee A. Fitzgibbons and Edna B. Foa, 'Exploring the roles of emotional numbing, depression, and dissociation in PTSD', *Journal of Traumatic Stress*, vol. 13, no. 3, pp. 489–98.

298 focusonthefamily.com/marriage/communication-and-conflict/learn-to-speak-your-spouses-love-language/understanding-the-five-love-languages

299 Wardi, p. 88.

300 apa.org/monitor/2019/02/legacy-trauma

301 Epstein, pp. 204–7.

302 Michlic, Joanna B., 'A Young Person's War: The Disrupted Lives of Children and Youth', in Gigliotti, Simone and Hilary Earl (eds), *A Companion to the Holocaust*, Wiley, 2020, p. 304.